LITERARY LANGUAGE FROM CHAUCER TO JOHNSON

LITERARY LANGUAGE FROM CHAUCER TO JOHNSON

A. J. Gilbert

BOOKS
10 East 53d St., New York 10022
(a division of Harper & Row Publishers, Inc.)

© A. J. Gilbert 1979

All rights reserved. No part of this publication may be reproduced or transmitted, in any form or by any means, without permission

First published 1979 in the U.K. by
THE MACMILLAN PRESS LTD
London and Basingstoke

First Published in the U.S.A. 1979 by
HARPER & ROW PUBLISHERS, INC.
BARNES & NOBLE IMPORT DIVISION

British Library Cataloguing in Publication Data

Gilbert, A. J.
    Literary language from Chaucer to Johnson
      1. English literature–History and criticism
      2. English language–History
    I. Title
    820'.9   PR83

MACMILLAN ISBN 0–333–21704–7

BARNES & NOBLE ISBN 0–06–492403–3
LCN 79–53434
                    Printed in Great Britain

For Susannah

Contents

Preface ix
Introduction 1

Part I: Poetry 27

1. Chaucer and Skelton 29
2. Spenser and Shakespeare 63
3. Donne and Dryden 89
4. Milton and Pope 111

Part II: Prose 133

5. Sidney and Bacon 135
6. Andrewes and Donne 155
7. Dekker and Dryden 174
8. Browne and Johnson 193

Conclusion 212
Notes 217
Index 221

Preface

I owe a debt of thanks to Professor S. S. Hussey of the Department of English Language and Medieval Literature, the University of Lancaster, and to Professor M. L. Samuels of the Department of English Language, the University of Glasgow. I am grateful for their advice at an early stage, when this book was in its first draft; I hope I have benefited from their comments. Any errors or confusion that remain must be my own responsibility.

A. J. Gilbert
Lancaster, 1979

Introduction

The purpose of this book is to provide the modern reader with a guide to literary language between Geoffrey Chaucer (1343–1400) and Samuel Johnson (1709–84). Is it possible to explain the range of choices available to a writer in this period, with all its diversity and variation of language, and from that explanation come to a closer understanding of the uniqueness of individual style? The traditional approach to literary style in this period is first to identify the meaning of archaic or difficult words in a text, then perhaps to note the rhetorical figures that the writer uses, and finally to trace typical patterns of imagery or thought in the text. Since this method requires work and close scrutiny of the text a great deal can be found out about a writer's techniques and use of language. But there are a number of fatal objections to this approach. It assumes that a piece of writing is the same in style throughout; a writer's language is like a yard of cloth. If it is a long work, he uses more of it. There is absolutely no explicit attention to context or to the effect of language use on the reader or hearer. The value of the same rhetorical figure may vary from one occurrence to another; yet it will be treated as the same. The writer's motives are assumed to be unknown, and unimportant, as though he had no particular reason for writing anything in the first place. The motive is assumed to be found in the thought or argument of the text, and no further inquiry is needed. However well a glossary supplies contextual meanings of words, it cannot identify contextual variations in syntax (and rhetorical schemes are not sensitive to context in the way they are treated). Yet, of course, the syntax significantly conditions the contextual sense of the words used. The traditional approach assumes that the reader is entirely dependent on his own sensitivity, when it comes to stylistic analysis. If this is so, then the task of analysing style can be safely left to him, without any assistance from the editor of the text, who has more solid jobs to get on with. Anyway, isn't good literary criticism more important than stylistic analysis? So the argument goes. The mistake here is to suppose that attention to style is a substitute for literary criticism; the present writer's contention is that criticism can be conducted more adequately by using the findings of stylistics. But only if stylistics shows the same concern for the reality of the text which the philologist demonstrated. For inadequate as his methods were, he was concerned with data open to discussion by other students of the subject, and his traditional interest in literary language is of crucial importance. There is an indefensible but qualitative difference between the language of literature and that of the popular press. But let us return to the philologist's narrow view of style. He did not believe it was a matter of data but a matter of response in the educated reader. But he went no further, since theory had no interest for him. Now he is partly right. Style is not a linguistic feature of the text like a grammatical aspect of the language. It is a relationship between form and meaning, and we have to understand the meaning of a text before we can begin to get at the style. In the period covered by this book it is not a difficult matter to understand the general meaning. But how do we relate meaning to form? Surely, the whole text, in raw grammatical analysis, could be said in some sense to be its form? The student of style has to find a way of identifying the expressive areas of a text, those that are motivated stylistically, and select on this principle from the raw data. But isn't this going back to the intuitive approach dismissed by traditionalists? How do we decide what is significant variation in a text and what isn't? If we rely on certain formal features of a text (such as a rhetorical scheme, for example), we are no better off than the traditionalists. This is where we have to widen the discussion, before we can answer this objection. The present writer believes stylistics is not an intuitive area of study, but if it has any claims to a methodology, they must be based on some general characteristics of language use. Literary language is a selection from natural language use and all rhetorical figures are originally 'natural' rhetoric.

The tacit assumption behind the traditional view of style is that all language acts, because of their necessary occurrence in a particular time and place, are unique in a more general way. But a reader is no more isolated than a listener from the way we experience language in normal use. A reader is an active interpreter of language in a non-casual form; but he cannot intervene like the listener to modify or extend what the writer 'says'. The reader is not dynamically involved in a communication act that can develop and change by interaction of the participants. Nevertheless, his understanding of language use is not, as the traditional viewpoint implies, fragmentary and anecdotal. A native speaker or listener (and hence a native reader) generalises his experience of particular instances of language use into principles of use in similar contexts. Language has as a result a systematic structure in its grammar (to mention only one level of ordering), and is also far from random in its use. In all language acts there is some determination that carries over from one similar context to another. This in no way prevents a speaker's choice of language being his own – but it will be his own selection from an appropriate (or deliberately inappropriate) form of the language developed for that particular context of use. Every context will be made up of a number of aspects that have developed their normative patterns in the language. While the speaker's language is 'idiolectal' (a unique selection from the dialect of his community), he has to choose from a number of established 'registers' in the language if he is to be easily understood. In a similar way, every work of literature is certainly unique, but if it is to be understood, it must be capable of analysis in terms of recognisable 'registers' or 'styles' of language. These may be typical of the genre of the work, or closely related to some common variants in natural language use. Alternatively, the writer may choose to create a style that indicates his scepticism about normal usage; he may actively resent the assumption of established contexts of use. He may wish to construct contexts of such complexity and uniqueness that very few indicators of common usage will be found in his writing. This does not mean that we will not understand something of his language; it may, however, be so rich in private metaphor and personal perception that its sources in common usage will be disguised. The vocabulary will be intelligible, but the syntax and thematic relations may well be enigmatic. These intensely idiolectal styles verge on private language, yet they are public performances. Such writers assert a uniqueness that is peculiarly common in modern literature. But it is a question of critical judgement rather than stylistic analysis to evaluate their success. Normal meaning may well be under attack in modern poetry of a certain kind, or in some modern novels. This may require an attack on natural language use which assumes norms of meaning. The literature discussed in this book is not so deeply affected by the sickness of the language as more recent works. Many of the writers dealt with have evidently some scepticism about the inherited traditions of literary language they found; but they were able to develop other styles within the traditional categories, and avoided a complete break with the past. Society still held shared values and there was common ground between writer and reader. So we can arrive for the moment at a simple conclusion: if we take into account the historical condition of society, and the way language is related to contexts in normal usage, we can escape from a completely subjective view of stylistic analysis. We still have to consider what was normal literary usage in the period of this book.

Before we turn to a statement of historical literary register in linguistic terms, we should reflect on the general problem of understanding archaic registers of literary English. How can we claim to have a knowledge of such registers? How can we be sure that they are not quite different from our modern use of language? The answer must be that if we can understand the literature of this period, we are fairly sure of understanding its registerial variations, because meaning in context depends on some registerial norm. This doesn't mean that we will not have to work at the meaning of a particular passage; it will not emerge without effort. But our task is to make the process of understanding as clear as possible. If others agree with our reading of a passage, this supports the idea of some determining factor in language use. And this means agreement with our view of syntax as well as vocabulary; it is not enough to accept merely the glossary meaning of words. This is a matter of careful textual analysis; the evaluation of any passage in the context of the whole literary work is another entirely separate operation. Disagreement at this level is often more complex and difficult to resolve. Our first priority should be to arrive at an adequate textual analysis that recognises what is there in the literary work. If there was wide and contradictory disagreement, we would have to accept an intuitive view of stylistic analysis. Now we have already discarded this approach. It is because evaluation is so often confused with analysis that people imagine stylistics is a subjective discipline. Evaluation can decide on the relative importance of the data; but a good stylistic analysis should bring out the primary features of style in a passage, whatever their relative importance in the act of criticism. Even the philologist readily accepts that we can understand literature from this period (with his assistance). But in so doing he is also agreeing to a much more interesting view of language which he leaves unexplored. Since Chaucer the expressive aspects of language have in fact modified more in vocabulary than in syntax. People experienced the same responses to the commonplaces of life as we do today; the human condition is not so variable as it is often made out to be. We are, after all, talking about the continuity of one area of western culture; the picture would be entirely different if we wanted to compare the work of writers in two remote societies that had never been in historical communication with each other. Within the historical continuity of one society there may be changes in language, social conventions and political structure; this is inevitable. But language changes more slowly (hence the modernist discontent with language). Much of Chaucer's syntax is almost modern. The modern reader then is not reduced to relying on a purely random knowledge of historical style. As a native speaker of modern English he has already acquired a range of insights into expressive form in natural language use. The foreign speaker of English is in a more difficult position; this book is partly designed to provide him with a way in to the intelligent reading of earlier literature. Some will say that the argument presented here is only a way of introducing the experienced reader into the discussion – a reader who is somehow (by wide reading, perhaps) already aware of what we want him to know. But we are concerned with the latent knowledge of expressive form in a native speaker's mind, which he derives from his own experience of natural rhetoric. We make no claims about his knowledge of literary language as such. An experienced reader is someone who has read widely, but he may not have applied his own experience of language to his reading. He may well, as often happens, gain an exact knowledge of genre and literary convention. But this is only half the experience he could have. He has moved immediately to the stage of evaluation before textual analysis. This is a step in the appreciation of literature that is so often omitted, although its value is evident. How does a student understand the first piece of Chaucer he reads? Certainly, there are limits to his insight into the meaning of the text, and he will make the usual crop of howlers. But the sheer accessibility of Chaucer is obvious to any teacher from secondary school onwards. Frequently the novice has a better understanding of the tone of the passage than his mistakes in lexical meaning would suggest. He can grasp the expressive emphasis of the syntax without noticing he has done so. It is part of his experience of modern English. What the student needs is an explicit method of relating the vocabulary to the syntax, which will give him an insight into the stylistic features of the context.

Then we shall find fewer mistakes of meaning, because the whole context will condition his translation, instead of lexical items alone. This might well seem a very ambitious undertaking, because contexts are so various and almost any feature of one context can appear somewhere in another. What are the significant features that the student needs to know about? This issue will occupy the rest of the chapter.

There are some crucial stylistic differences between historical literary language and the enormous variety of literary styles in more recent work. Natural rhetoric – the emphases, redundancies and repetitions of speech – are only one area of influence on earlier writers; a writer in the period covered by this book was conscious of a rhetorical tradition of style that began in classical times, and had survived in the work of medieval writers. If we are to read anything written between Chaucer in the late medieval period and Johnson in the eighteenth century, we have to be prepared to set aside some of the stylistic assumptions we have acquired from modern literature. Writers in the earlier period did not turn immediately to the range and variety of speech as the central influence on their style. Nor did they choose to exploit extensively the range of specialised registers from all walks of life available to any writer at almost any time in the past as now. Literary language, it was agreed, must be distinct from natural registers in ordinary contexts of use. But the principles of the restricted literary registers that found favour were, of course, based on common usage. If they had not been, no one could have easily understood the writer. Communication was also his first duty; a work of literature was not expected to resist the reader's intelligence, but to engage it in a dialectic process. But is this saying anything more than the obvious – that earlier literature is more rhetorical? The present writer believes that the argument can be taken a lot further than this. A knowledge of historical literary registers enables us to understand more clearly a writer's techniques, and the way he translates his own insights into acceptable literary language.

Classical rhetoricians advised that three styles of speech were appropriate for the orator in the law court. These styles provided him with a range of devices suited to particular functions of speech, and in time became a principle of selection in literary language throughout western Europe. In the Renaissance they took on a new lease of life when the original rhetorical doctrines came once again into public view. But they had always been widely recognised by the more literary writers in the medieval period. Chaucer, for example, shows his familiarity with such doctrines from his remarks on appropriate language in *The Prologue* to *The Canterbury Tales*. The effect of this tradition was two-fold: it restricted the range of variation a writer was willing to use in his work, compared with the wider range available to him in speech, and it gave a useful clarification of the problem of style. Writers need a set of conventions against which to develop their originality; complete freedom of choice in literary language often leads to a lack of clarity, incoherence and weakness of effect. On the other hand, a mechanical imitation of the doctrines of classical style produces an empty formalism. There is inevitably a great deal of writing of this kind. But it is not proof of the worthlessness of the original theory. What then were these three styles, and what was their function as a pattern of stylistic choice?

Each of the three styles originally reflected a different function of the orator's language – the low or plain style serving for proof, the middle style for persuasion and delight, the high or vigorous style for swaying the hearers. Cicero adds a number of details to these broad distinctions showing how function affects the character of each style. The low or plain style is 'low key and unpretentious, giving an appearance of using ordinary language, but in reality differing from the inexpert more than is commonly supposed'; it is 'freed from the shackles of rhythm', but 'even short and cut-up sentences are not to be organised negligently'; 'all obvious pearls of ornament to be removed'; 'only elegance and neatness will remain'; 'clear and unambiguous'; 'our slender orator . . . will perhaps use comparatively frequently the type of metaphor most commonly found in all conversation, of town and country folk alike – for it's countrymen who say "the vines are gemming", "the fields are thirsty", "the crops are cheerful", "the corn is luxuriant". Each of these is bold enough, but in every case the comparison is very close, or, if a thing lacks a name of its own, it is obvious that the metaphor is used to get the meaning across, not for fun.'[1] The low or plain style has an expository function in its learned form; it is an elegant selection from speech designed to convey information and argument. There was also another form of the low style which was more popular and used in the classical theatre for comic subjects, the satirical, the realistic, and the obscene.[2] Here the original functions of exposition and argument have been transferred into a visual context; the writer thinks up arguments against certain topics and creates characters that reflect the argument in a schematic way. This variant tradition of the plain style can be seen in Chaucer's comic tales in the French *fabliaux* genre. Both the learned and the popular traditions survive to influence later writers. The middle style Cicero defines as 'fuller than the concise type, more restrained than the ornate and copious style . . . all stylistic ornaments are appropriate . . . decorative, flowery . . . wide ranging and learned disputations will be deployed, and commonplaces recited without heat'.[3] The high style is marked by 'emotional appeal' and 'force', it has 'splendour', 'vast flow and sound', and is 'full, copious, and ornate'.[4] To sum up, the three styles represent distinct areas of meaning and expressive form in literary language. We may define them as realisations of three separate semantic fields: the low or plain style involves the semantic components 'imitation, realistic denigration, exposition or narration', the middle style 'idealisation, analysis, polite praise or blame', the high style 'emphatic assertion, generalisation for emotive effect'. Not all these elements in the three styles are necessarily active in any particular example. They may be further distinguished from each other by the varying level of detail implicit in the distinctions between each style: the low style has clear isolated detail which will not impede exposition or narration, the middle style limits the complexity of detail in its idealisation of experience, while the high style implies very little detail, which would distract attention from the writer's attitude to his subject. None of these styles is part of a tradition of fully representational realism. The systematic variation of the three styles in semantic field and hierarchy of detail gives good grounds for supposing they are more than tendencies in a writer's language; on the contrary, they are three distinct styles or 'registers' with their own characteristic contexts. But it may seem rash to interpret these anecdotal remarks of a classical rhetorician as the basis for an explicit modern theory of register. After all, Cicero had never heard of the idea. But he did know about literary language in his own time, and he was an accurate and sensitive observer of language. Again, his views are familiar commonplaces to any classicist; they represent a consensus of opinion in the ancient world which became an agreed model for literary language in later centuries. Different styles or 'registers' of language exist naturally, outside of any literary function. These types of style are in fact natural variations in language which have been exploited by writers in all Indo-European languages. There may be different conventions outside western Europe. However, an introduction to what may seem to Europeans an obvious aspect of literature may well be useful to those from a very different background.

An explicit modern theory of literary registers can be comprehensive but not exhaustive. No complete item inventory of each register can be given, for there are many different ways in which a writer may interpret the classical doctrine. But there are some necessary constraints on his choice. The essential point is that the three styles are mutually exclusive, for the semantic components of each cannot be brought together without setting up a contradiction in the reader's mind. The writer cannot express admiration for a topic in the high style, and denigrate the same topic in the *same* registerial context. There are however ways of avoiding contradiction, while bringing two distinct contexts into close proximity. In the classical tradition of the legal address, the register varied according to the speaker's purpose and subject at that point in his remarks; a sequence of single contexts would be appropriate in such a tradition. We find such sequences in writers with a strict sense of classical decorum like Milton or Skelton. Out of this tradition there developed another more complex usage, where contexts concerning the same subject varied because several contexts were seen as complementary to the writer's viewpoint. Neither the high style, nor the middle or plain style were seen as entirely adequate to explore the writer's meaning. In place of a sequence of registerial contexts, we find instead a constant reference back and forth to several contexts where each provides some essential aspect of meaning for the complex subject matter, and the writer's attitude to it. Distinctive contexts could be brought into close contact as long as they did not imply a contradiction. A writer must have some coherent view of his subject, even if it is ironic and ambiguous. These types of work we may describe as *multiple* contexts, and we should distinguish them from the traditional sequence of single contexts in the pure classical tradition. In satire and parody, some elements of one register (its syntax or vocabulary) can be borrowed to be used in *contrastive* contexts for the same subject. But this is not an example of contradiction; the reader resolves the discrepancy between variant styles by treating *one* variant as the writer's implicit comment on the subject matter in *both* contexts. We have to know how the writer regards his material, and which is the genuine standpoint, or we miss the whole purpose of the satire. The contrast between the ideal and the real is usually the centre of satirical writing, so that high or middle style language contrasts with plain style realities.

If a writer has a wide freedom of choice within these limits, can we be sure to identify the style level he happens to be using at any moment in the text? If we try to distinguish intuitively between various intermediate levels within the three styles, we shall reduce our method to a loose description. Instead, we should consider whether the passage under scrutiny has any 'indexical markers' of one style or another. An 'indexical marker' is an index of style level. In each instance necessarily the density or frequency of indexical markers will vary; some forms of register will be gross, emphatic realisations, others delicate, allusive versions of a particular register. The forms of the indexical marker will also vary – in one case it may be a question of certain items of vocabulary, in another a piece of syntax that the writer has used for particular effects. There may be, as linguists claim, a neutral register of English which has no literary value. But within a literary work all language has literary value; certainly, the plain or low style would in one of its forms be used for exposition and narration. But that in itself is a rhetorical act; the reader is bound to be affected by the way the narrative unfolds. We have to remember that although literary registers are based on general principles of language use, literary language is non-casual, a conscious and contrived activity, while natural uses of language are often unselfconscious, and certainly always casual compared with written forms. This shows in the much greater complexity and variation of speech, even quite formal conversation, beside the relative orderliness and clarity of written English. This is not very plausible to users of English until they record casual speech and see how varied it in fact is. Often, as has been said, we find all three registers in one work, for example a long narrative such as *Paradise Lost* or Sidney's new *Arcadia*.

In modern theories of register it is normal to identify language use across five 'parameters' or areas of variation: (i) the subject matter of the text, (ii) the situation or immediate purpose for which the language is being used in the text, (iii) the participant roles of writer and reader (although the reader is not a participant in a speech act, he undergoes a similar kind of conditioning as a listener, and he has to interpret the language), (iv) mode of discourse – is the text written with certain dominant mood choices in the clause types? (v) medium of discourse: sermons are written works designed to be heard not read; Chaucer presented his work through public readings and it was copied later. We need to apply these distinctions to each traditional style in order to see more explicitly their registerial characteristics.[5]

The primary subject matter of a text controls its vocabulary. Within each register there are a number of sub-registers marked out by their vocabulary; these are topics that are familiar to the literary critic. For example, the generalised description of arms and armour in the high style, the analytical complexity of courtly love in the middle style, or the social observations of the low style. The subject matter is not, of course, primarily classical. The tradition Cicero reports is only a system of categories, it makes no exact statement about what subject matter should be included where. The refined analysis of love in medieval poetry would have been quite inappropriate to classical forms of the middle style; the relations between the sexes were not important enough in literary tradition of the period. Such a topic would have been relegated to the low style satire of the theatre. Imagery may seem a more random area of style with a subject matter that bears no systematic relation to the primary subject. In fact, the evidence shows that there was a decorum in the style level that conditioned the range and choice of imagery for that style. Imagery may therefore be treated as a special area of the subject matter. Where imagery contrasts with the primary subject, or that subject is ambiguous (for example, in Shakespeare's sonnets), this indicates an important shift of attitude in the writer which any contemporary reader would have noticed. Here we can only outline what the examples in the rest of the book will clarify. In general, we can classify the range of subject matter as follows. The high style describes the public life of public figures, and their public appearance. Man is regarded as a spectacle, not an individual with normal social relations and a private life. The high style describes the drama of the will exerted in its most obvious form. Other themes also occur: universal topics such as the seasons of the year, the order of the natural world (expressing God's will), the pagan gods, fate, and great national events – battles and high diplomacy. These topics are not treated in a realistic way; they become instead opportunities for the display of the writer's virtuosity in giving emphasis to the subject matter. Milton uses the high style to describe the horrors of Hell, Satan's weapons, the fall of the rebellious angels from Heaven, and so on. But he often changes the context, and his style is full of variety; this is in part because one topic is seldom sustained at great length. The moral and the epic aspects of the subject matter are intertwined, and this accounts for the variation. The rhythms of Miltonic verse are infinitely flexible and responsive to the particular context. The epic high style is reserved for the spectacular and the supernatural, while the middle style analyses the moral significance of each moment in the narrative. And there are many passages of plain style–for Milton is always concerned to inform the reader of the exact historical reference for every episode. Chaucer's *Knight's Tale* has many examples of the spectacular set-piece, such as the tournament, or the funeral of Arcite. These are consciously modelled on Virgilian epic. In sacred discourse, the high style is also used for dramatic emphasis; the preacher represents the condition of suffering humanity in his own person, or he brings out the dramatic revelation of some aspect of biblical history. The sermon is a genre of literature without any classical antecedents, and its vocabulary is based on the low style simplicities of the Bible. In high style passages, a preacher may use more complex vocabulary derived from theology or the Fathers of the early church, but on the whole the careful avoidance of hard words is typical of the genre. This is one sub-register of the high style that remains separate from other genres. The middle style presents an ideal view of the social aspects of man; idealised topics such as love and refined feeling are treated in the light of reason. Man is regarded as the master of his fate (unlike the assumptions of the high style) and aware of his own nature (in contrast to the low style where he is the victim of his own temperament). Art and intellectual activity generally are proper subjects of the middle style; but these topics are not treated technically. For example, Theseus's philosophical speech at the end of *The Knight's Tale* is an intellectual gloss on the epic narrative; it at once explains the nature of tragedy, and consoles the listeners for the loss of Arcite. It is a learned but elegant explanation that involves few technical details, while getting at the essential points of Boethian philosophy. It assumes an intelligent audience capable of following a rather abstract argument and applying it to the particular experience they all share. The speech stands in strong contrast to the colloquial, exasperated low style of Theseus's earlier remarks, when he comes across the rivals fighting in the grove. The topic there is the God of Love and his 'miracles', not the Boethian chain of love and its First Mover. The 'miracles' Theseus refers to are the traditional folly and rashness of lovers, and the absurd situations they get into. The comic world of circumstance is an implicit comment on the ideals of courtly love. In the middle style, these ideals are felt to have some reality. Often the middle style flatters the reader by bland reference to an assumed knowledge. Dryden's critical essays have this effect; his version of the middle style is persuasive because it has strong moral assumptions behind it. But the actual content is very slight, and the register lacks conceptual clarity. Dekker, however, is able to adapt the traditional middle style to a new satirical accuracy. In Shakespeare's sonnets, the middle style has more refinement of an analytical kind; the last traces of a Petrarchan tradition of love poetry are still alive in his work. Imagery in the middle style is always formal, literary and consciously poetic; this is necessary to supply the analytical function of the style. Realistic imagery would not have the same value; it would show vividly the perception of the writer, but imply too unsophisticated a view of the world. Immediate impressions are to be classified and submitted to analysis before they are acceptable as art. But in the low style common expressions and proverbial wisdom can be used, since the topics proper to the style are mundane and artless. The low or plain style has two versions: one, the classical version of the style used for argument and exposition, and another formulation of the style where caricature is primary. In sermons, the low style has a powerful moralising focus, for unlike the legal address, the sermon is arguing a moral position. The commonplace experience becomes, in the Augustinian tradition of the sermon, a matter of ultimate moral significance. A cup of water may seem trivial and unimportant, but it may be the difference between eternal misery and eternal happiness.[6] In the secular low style almost any subject can be dealt with, if it falls outside the areas described by the high or middle styles. Art and philosophy, love and indeed any kind of aesthetic idealism are not fit subjects for the low style. Man is seen in the secular form of this register as a social being without a philosophy of life. His primary interest is in survival and the satisfaction of the crudest social and physical appetites. He has no leisure to attend to higher things. In Bacon's *Essays* the crude social appetites of ambition and political success are examined without caricature, while in Dekker's *Gull's Horn-book* the same topics are handled in a far more popular manner. The complete absence of any idealism in both writers in these contexts is typical of the style, and not a cynical trait in their temperament. Bacon follows the advice of Machiavelli that a writer should describe what men do, not what they ought to do. But he also uses the high style for emphasis in his work. His aphoristic low style is far more penetrating and persuasive than these high-style passages. Again, Milton presents the cynical arguments of the serpent in a plain style of classical elegance and effortless tenacity of purpose. This register is close to the forensic plain style of classical tradition. In Chaucer we find a contrast of styles between the caricature of some *fabliaux* works, such as *The Reeve's Tale* and *The Miller's Tale* (with their incipient realism), the sacred low style in pious fables such as *The Clerk's Tale* or *The Man of Law's Tale*, and the low style of argument in parts of *The Knight's Tale*. Chaucer can also use the moralised low style of the sermon for comic purposes, as in *The Wife of Bath's Prologue*, where a sacred low style clashes with a profane variant. The Wife's earnest claims to piety are set off by her strong natural appetites. Elsewhere, in Skelton, we find the element of caricature in the low style very much more obvious than in the comic tales of Chaucer. But it is associated with a political concern absent from the social comedy of the *fabliaux*. Skelton has returned to the earlier classical tradition of the low style with its legal and political arguments. Enough has been said to give some idea of the range and scope of the subject matters proper to each register.

The situation or immediate purpose of the register varies for each style. The high style is designed to induce in the reader quite uncritical admiration in keeping with the apparent state of mind of the writer. It is difficult for the writer to maintain the reader's interest in this unreflecting condition for long. A reader cannot be held passive and inert, for in the very act of reading he is interpreting and comparing the language with other contexts in order to understand it. The high style is perhaps the most unnatural of literary registers. The activity of decoding the message to find its meaning forces the reader to recognise the purely aesthetic and assertive value of the language, since its general meaning is so thin. The discrepancy between elaborate form and minimal content has, at length, a very tiring effect. The absolute simplicity of the high style in its immediate purpose is disguised by the extravagance and variety of its form. But as we see the reader must become aware of this deception very quickly. On the whole the high style is not sustained over long passages at a time; it is a means of emphasis, an intense moment of truth. In the other styles there is less redundancy of form beside content, and the reader is correspondingly more engaged in the response to the text, and so less inclined to grow weary. The middle style is designed for analysis; its idealisation is a persuasive self-scrutiny that the reader shares in. The intention is to please or to divert with urbane irony. The didacticism of the classical low style, or the vulgarity of its popular variant are quite foreign to this register. In the middle style the writer assumes a deferential pose towards the reader; in the high style the writer asserts his ascendancy over him. There the full fury of poetic inspiration can be felt, while here in the middle style world the reader is encouraged to reflect and use his reason. He discovers a refined version of his own experience which is pleasing to his self-esteem. The scrupulous analysis of motive and attitude is also flattering to the reader's intelligence. He is encouraged to believe he too might have faced up to that particular problem in that way; his belief in his own importance is renewed. He too, he can believe, is sophisticated enough to observe, assess and discriminate like the writer. Now we see why the setting of the middle style is always idealised, because too realistic an analysis might be painful or embarrassing, and alienate the reader from the subject matter, and from the writer. For the writer is part of the social structure in this style; he is a conformist trying to sustain the traditional values of a leisured class. The low style portrays, in its popular form, the opinion of this class about the rest of society; a satire on the lower classes or tradesmen, as in *The Miller's* or *The Reeve's Tales*, is in part a sophisticated satire on oafishness, gullibility, and cunning. These were not thought to be the attributes of courtly persons. Skelton uses a more popular version of this low style in his *Tunning of Elinour Rumming*, while in *Colin Clout* and *Speak, Parrot* the serious classical variant of the low style also appears. These works are full of argument and cunning innuendo which are part of the forensic tradition. We may also contrast the political concerns of Skelton with the social purposes of Chaucer. For him, the secular low style of the *fabliaux* tradition was designed to entertain by portraying a gross satire on the lower classes, for their betters. But Chaucer's intuitions about character and his social observation turn his comic tales into art of another kind. They entertain by the truth of their descriptions of temperament and motive. Yet the plots remain conventional and non-realistic. They are very well told jokes. In the sermon, the moralised plain style is the only variant used. In writers like Spenser and Milton a moral purpose contrasts with the overt functions of traditional levels of style in epic. As a result, the high and middle styles are frequently used to show the corruption of moral values in contrast to a low style that exposes the moral truth. Plain language and plain truth become synonymous in their styles. The visual detail of the low style in Spenser is often grotesque and unnatural, but affirms a strong moral direction in the writing. Context is more complex in Milton; Satan, disguised as a serpent, can produce spurious reasons for eating from the Tree of Knowledge, in a classical form of the low style. But here the clarity of the arguments shows their falseness, if the reader pays attention. This is perhaps a crucial case, for Milton is trying to show the persuasiveness of Satan, and his corruption of innocent reason in Eve. For innocence cannot anticipate fraud, but may be led into it by deceit. God always speaks in a logical low style, the epitome of reason. Bacon and Sidney had certain beliefs about the way reason could convince the reader of the truth, if only he could understand and grasp the arguments presented to him. Their low styles are therefore expository and lucid.

In the writer's fictional world, the reader has an imagined role as the observer or confidant. This privileged position is analogous to that of the listener in natural uses of language. The reader cannot intervene and respond by asking questions as in the natural context; but the writer may give the impression that he is responding to the probable reactions of his audience, even when he does not address them directly. The three registers recognise the reader's presence in different ways. The high style, with its emphatic assertion and grandiose manner, is implicitly directed at the reader, even when it takes the form of ornate address to kings and princes; the reader is supposed to sense the high formality of the occasion and imagine the majestic presence of superior persons. In narrative accounts of battles (insofar as the high style can narrate by a sequence of incidents), the reader is a spectator of epic encounters, and surveys in his imagination the fortunes of the whole battlefield. The high style gives the reader a god's-eye view of public spectacle. But the relative lack of detail in the description of episode and scene means we have only a broad general impression of conflict. The middle style is more explicitly attentive to the reader, and engages his interest by addressing him directly (sometimes even in the familiar form of address borrowed from the low style). The writer displays polite informality, and adopts an ease of manner that is neither grand nor intimate. There is an assumption of inner artifice even in the apparent confidences of the writer. The social values of the middle style are especially noticeable in this suppression of the spontaneous in the writer's voice. This does not mean the middle style is insincere; it is very conventional, and these conventions are useful to a writer as a protective stance. He may wish to remain detached, enigmatic and remote from the reader. His purpose may be to create an ironic disparity between what the reader thinks he stands for, and what he actually believes. This is a form of the middle style that Shakespeare uses in the sonnets. Where the middle style is ironic, it can appear with a plain style that reveals the true attitude of the writer. But the middle style can also trap the reader into assenting to something with implications he has not quite grasped. The portrait of the Prioress in *The General Prologue* of *The Canterbury Tales* is an eloquent and pleasing example of the middle style; but its charm cannot disguise the discrepancy between the nun's calling and her worldly character. On the contrary, the aesthetic, secular values of the middle style in that portrait are a vivid reminder of what has been lost in moral terms. The portrait is an ironic appraisal of a woman who happens to be a religious, but whose values are entirely secular. There is no need in that instance for any explicit comment. The subject matter is religious and moral, the treatment secular and aesthetic. The low style insists on familiarity, but it may be no more sincere than the middle style. The idea of sincerity is a recent one in literature, and arises when literary language is more realistic and closer to colloquial expression than it is in the period of this book. In the low style the writer claims a common experience with the reader, and an equality of view. The writer is no longer the poet possessed by a divine frenzy as in the high style, or the witty and enigmatic analyst of the middle style; if his purpose is to instruct and explain, he must assume equality with the reader and treat him as an equal too. Sometimes this relationship becomes a conspiracy in which the writer encourages the reader to laugh at another group socially inferior (so the writer implies) to that shared by the reader and himself. This is the tradition of secular low style in Chaucer's *General Prologue*, and Dekker's version of the style in his satire on the country-bumpkin. Occasionally the low style can be used with an insolent frankness that reflects the lover's attitude to his mistress, as in some of Donne's poetry, and a few of Shakespeare's sonnets. In parts of Bacon's *Essays*, or in the low-style passages of Donne's sermons, we find a more serious expository role that has no explicit social implications. The essayist and the priest are dealing with serious topics of common experience, and in these contexts speak to the understanding, not to the social consciousness.

Registers may also vary according to the mode of discourse. This refers to the dominant orientation of the writing. From the classical rhetoricians we know the high style is vehemently assertive. What does this imply about its syntax? The high style is most commonly found in the epic genre; it freezes episodes within a larger narrative into a series of portentous moments. In this register, the amplification of phrase structure is primary, to give emphasis to statement. The register involves heavy subordination, relatively few clauses in any particular sentence, beside a large number of complex noun phrases and prepositional phrases. The rhythmical shape of the sentence is powerfully developed by careful parallelism and variation of phrase length. Verb mood in this register will be indicative, either the simple past for narration (although the high style is not primarily a narrative style), or the historic present or the simple future (often in direct speech, announcing intentions or debating future actions); non-finite forms of the verb will occur in the extensive subordination of clauses. But there are more delicate versions of the style where the rhythmical sentences are more loosely co-ordinated (as in Milton, for example), or where parallelism of an exact kind replaces the sequence of subordinate clauses (as in Donne's high style emphases). In Pope's *Rape of the Lock*, the high style is almost entirely realised as lexical source; the heroic couplet provides no opportunities for the extended sentence pattern. In the high style mode, in general, clauses and phrases are linked by listing or correlating devices – the writer scans each moment of an event, or each aspect of a scene or topic, and elaborates freely from that specific point. The connection between points of amplification is the main theme of the sentence. This can be abandoned and taken up again after some extended parenthesis; the delayed completion of sense can increase attention while making the sentence more difficult to read. This does not occur frequently in sermons where the audience has to listen, and cannot retain complex information easily. In the high style, the will is the centre of attention, and the amplification centres on the power and strength of its assertion. In *Paradise Lost*, the descriptions of Hell in Book I are an image of God's judgement on the fallen angels; they are constantly reminded at every moment of his anger and punishment. In the middle style we have an aesthetic view of the world designed to give a sense of order and harmony. The subject and situation parameters imply that the mode will be supplicatory and deferential; but this will take many forms. The language will have a tentativeness which is part of the elegant persuasion of the style. But clauses will be causally linked: the writer appeals implicitly to the refined reasonableness in the reader. He does not expect to overwhelm the reader with spectacle as in the high style. To insist so openly in the middle style would be a breach of decorum. Yet examples and opinions are examined and assessed; it is an analytical style in spite of its idealism. There is the greatest interest in the human predicament, and a belief that it can be understood by reason. The tradition of 'wit' is a natural development from the analytical aspects of the middle style. The reader is assumed to have a lively and active intelligence capable of responding to the most delicate variations of meaning. The middle style contrasts with the low style involvement in the immediate, tangible and unconceptualised experience of daily life; middle style commonplaces are abstract statements, often presented in consciously analytical metaphor. In the low style, proverbial truths from speech are similar in function; they lack the refinement of the middle style mode. The low style is a verbal style, that is to say, it relies on clause variation, rather than phrase variation as in the high style. There is far more use of simple addition and exemplification to supply argument. The complex verb phrase forms often found in the middle style are replaced, in the low style, by simple narrative past or present tense forms of verb. The clauses often have an implicit connection, close to the way people use language in its natural setting. Yet it is more carefully ordered and clearer than the randomness and redundancies of speech. Syntax may be more varied and unpredictable than the middle style, with its leisurely rhythms and selfconscious poise. The reader or listener may, occasionally, get the impression of those spontaneous variations in pace and rhythm that are natural in common speech. This effect is carefully avoided by the writer in high and middle style. The low style can create a dramatic literary personality, as in Bacon's *Essays* or Donne's sermons; this can become a covert form of persuasion, as in these examples. Familiarity can be as calculated as formality.

 A literary work may be written to be heard, or to be read. Certain differences of style follow from the choice of medium. Written works can have a complexity that would make them quite unintelligible when read aloud. Sidney's new *Arcadia* (1593) is an extreme example; it may have been read aloud, but it is obviously designed to be read, not heard. Not only is the syntax complex and elaborate, but the variety of ideas in any sentence is also difficult to follow. In low style passages of course the difficulty is reduced, but there are relatively few contexts of this kind. Sidney has amplified equally the two opposed dimensions of language, syntax and vocabulary. Each sentence is a paragraph, and contains perhaps half a dozen sentences in a hierarchy of subordination. And each of these sentences contains new ideas, and there is little overlap of meaning. Clearly the style is not designed for oral delivery. Only the most acute mind could follow and retain the amount of information given in each sentence at one go; the modern reader is bound to re-read even with the text in front of him. There is simply a limit, and quite a low limit, to the amount of information anyone can take in from a spoken discourse. Milton's *Paradise Lost* is an entirely different case. Here the listener can follow and take in the ideas of the poem; it is perhaps a consequence of its oral composition that the poem is so accessible to an audience. The text shows distinct differences from the *Arcadia*: Milton avoids heavy subordination of a clausal type, his sentences being made up of some subordination and a great deal of looser sequences. Co-ordination is common between clauses and phrases, and he relies on the pauses and rhythms of speech to distinguish relevant patterns of meaning and relationship, even in the most complex sentences. The compositional method shows through in this aspect of style. His vocabulary, too, is not as varied and complex in meaning as is often supposed. Sidney becomes the victim of his belief in the importance of meaning at any price; he ignores, or delights in, the unnatural complexity of clause structures in his sentences. The more meaning he can cram into a sentence, the happier he is with it. Given that his view of style was perhaps inadequate, we have to recognise the visual and literate assumptions behind his method of writing. In the sermon, Andrewes and Donne provide a contrast of selection from spoken usage. While Andrewes uses conciseness as the general principle of his style, Donne explores the possibilities of elaboration for sermon writing. Both principles of style are derived from common techniques of emphasis in speech. Andrewes uses the syntax of phrase for emphasis and exposition; he maintains a close control over the argument of his sermons by this deliberate reduction of language to a narrow range. Donne works in another direction, and his sermons are fluent rhythmical structures with extraordinary coherence. He achieves this by heavy repetition and reformulation of his arguments, constantly returning to the general points that mark the structure of his work. His syntax is linear without subordination, while his vocabulary is very varied and wide in range. Both the method, and the general principles of these sermon writers depend stylistically on oral delivery. When we read such writers, we have a very limited view of their full stylistic range, for so much is necessarily lost to us without the performance of the text. The medium of expression then is a major influence on writers. But can it affect the form of particular registers? From what has been said, we can see that, in the high style, a syntactic structure will have greater complexity and variation in a written form, than in a form designed to be heard. The same applies to middle and low styles. They are also affected by the medium of expression. Compare the complex syntax of a middle style Shakespearean sonnet (for example, sonnet 1), its precise and intricate vocabulary, subtle metaphor, and delicate shifts of sense, with a middle style passage from Chaucer. *The Franklin's Tale* (ll. 1311–38) is a typical and eloquent example. Chaucer's formulation of the style is much more diffuse and periphrastic because of the medium of expression. He has to repeat and rephrase important parts of the speech; he rarely uses any unusual metaphor, and the syntax is elegant but very easy. Both examples are petitions on different subjects to a social superior; but one is conceptually far more complex than the other. It is important not to tax Chaucer with incompetence in writing what was designed to be heard, by treating it as though it was written to be read.

We have been discussing the various aspects of the local context across the three styles. But surely the study of style ought to be the study of a writer's unique choice of language? The modern reader wants to know in what ways a particular author's style differs from another, and hence the actual characteristics of each writer's style. Now it may be true that there are features of a writer's style which occur to some extent in all contexts, and may be called stylistic features of the general context. A writer uses different local contexts in different ways; the general context is his general linguistic ability, which is the raw material of all the local contexts. There seems no reason why we should be able to make gross generalisations about a writer's usage irrespective of the local context of his work. Indeed, some readers will already regard the idea of registers and local contexts as gross enough assertions. They might say that registers are, in their view, stereotyped areas of vocabulary and syntax, with clear-cut functions and precise subject matter. Registers can only be learnt automatically because they are restricted in scope. Now these literary registers are variable in subject matter and syntax. All this is true; but registers need not be treated as a stereotype. Some may be;

for example, a formal letter from a firm appointing a person with standard conditions of service. But these are not the only areas of language use, and where language is used, there must be some registerial variation at work. Why is this? Because meaningful language must in some way be related to normative contexts. Otherwise there would be no point in using it. There may be some who argue that registers are merely the rhetoric of the text, but this is a matter of terminology. There seems to be no real difference between 'rhetoric of the text' and 'register' in the sense given it here. Naturally all uses of language involve rhetoric in its broadest sense; the point is, what kind of rhetoric, and how can we define it more adequately? Let us return to the question of a writer's general context. It sounds plausible that if we can identify the writer's work as a whole, we ought to be able to say something about his general style. But is it worth saying? What sort of statement can we expect to find at that level of generality? A comparison between writers can become a very laborious process if they are close to each other in style (as often happens in the eighteenth century, for example), and if we insist on an inventory of all differences in their language. This is no doubt a useful method for identifying authorship; but it frequently comes down to such refined distinctions as the use of the definite article or adverbs. This is not the kind of information the modern reader wants to know. What we need is a way of getting at the chief characteristics of a writer's style, without denying the possibility of a more refined analysis in some areas of the text. We cannot make worthwhile generalisations about individual usage; we can, however, take up some of the local context features and find common patterns from one local context to another. These characteristic patterns are at a lower level of description than the more ambitious generalisation. On the other hand, we should be able to point out how the lower level description relates to more general statements, if we find a way to make them. At the broadest possible level we can distinguish between moral and political writers, and those whose interests are mainly social and philosophical. This is not a stylistic judgement, but a loose categorisation of dominant tendencies in a writer. General statements are necessarily abstract and indefinite; their value lies in how we interpret them. Again, this general contrast of tendencies in a writer's view of the world is quite arbitrary; it just happens to fit in with the range of authors in this book. It has an empirical basis and no theoretical status. But it provides us with a starting point. How do such tendencies manifest themselves in a writer's style, in the three contexts?

A writer concerned with morality has some kind of ideology to advance; he is anxious to interpret what he records in the direction of certain strongly-held beliefs. He is not much involved with any general truths of natural observation except insofar as they support his opinions. From his viewpoint, there are no objective general truths, but only certain right and wrong ways of looking at the world. A moral stance can lead the writer to a more comprehensive view of morality that adds up to a political judgement; certain groups in society are then regarded as opposing his beliefs. But even if he remains a moralist without political motivation, he will always advance his own special arguments behind the apparent freedom of choice in the local context. The reader will have to take into account the moral perspective and alignment of the three styles. Such writers will have relatively little complexity in their work; the success of their cause depends on the clarity and fluency of their argument. They quickly descend to caricature and satire; they have a strong sense of order that is easily aroused, and little tolerance for neutral positions that do not support their own. Their language therefore will tend towards a categorising and schematic manner; they will make explicit propositions and arguments about reality instead of rendering a description of experience in a direct form. There will always be the feeling of a debate or argument being pursued with relentless energy. Life has a moral meaning, and it can be found by direct inquiry. A writer who takes a social or philosophical interest in the world will also interpret his experience. But the degree of emphasis will be different. He is closer to the truth of natural observation (conditioned of course by what is conventionally accepted in his society); he has no explicit purpose that can be reduced to a conceptual argument. He is open to the contradictory impressions that all experience offers the writer in all societies. He may sense discrepancies and paradox in the values of the world around him; this only leads him to an ironic detachment, it does not set him in pursuit of a higher truth to which all else must be reduced. He spins out the process of description and is less conceptual and argumentative than the other kind of writer. His observations can be complex and ambiguous, with an unresolved richness of meaning. The detachment of philosophy is also an appealing refuge for the social interpreter; insights into the human condition lead naturally to a consideration of the common ground of all human experience. The social interpreter will also seize on the typical and commonplace and show its uniqueness; the moralist will translate the same thing into evidence for his argument. Both the general truth and the particular fact are important to the social interpreter; he wants to know more about the human condition. He wants to understand what kinds of motivation and attitude exist; he does not wish to direct the reader to particular conclusions or ideas about life. The moralist will tend to simplify and codify experience into a covert or explicit allegory. He is usually a writer with certain obsessive traits in style, such as the use of a very restricted range of vocabulary and a formulaic choice of syntax. His chief quality is strength of assertion and intellectual energy; the reader or hearer senses he is being offered a performance not an experience in the way the social interpreter would offer it. The moral writer is interventionist in his tactics; he does not allow the reader to become absorbed in the fictional world of the text. The writer sees it as his duty to explain and gloss the experience contained in his work. He may do this by a structural alignment of local contexts, so that the low style represents moral truth, the middle style the world of art and deception, and the high style the world of heroic virtue. So Spenser has imposed a moral perspective on his epic universe. Milton's solution to this problem of directing the reader to the right view is different. He will intervene explicitly in the text to gloss each episode; but his use of the three styles is ultimately indebted to the Spenserian moral alignment. Keats's famous idea of a 'negative capability' in the artist is a reference to the social or philosophical writer's approach to the problem of style. He does not reduce experience to pleasing, intelligible but limited patterns. Instead he is willing to record the complexity which is uninteresting to the moralist. These two contrasting general contexts are in effect 'group styles'; they give us a way of talking about individual style without being trapped into referring to every local context separately. They are the primary material out of which the writer builds his expressive form; they give us a sense of coherence and consistency in a writer's style whatever the context locally in his work, and they are all we can expect to know of a writer's style. We may still want to say that this expression, or that grammatical choice, is typical of a certain writer; but on its own this information is trivial and uninteresting. It tells us nothing about the writer's art. It would be possible to record exhaustively the distinctive features of a writer's style, if we had a closed system of finite variations in the three styles.

But literary registers are no more mechanical and restricted than most natural registers. A writer's style then is a principle of coherence between one local context and another; it is also the linguistic foundation of that range of contexts. There are many different forms of style within these two broad groupings – as many forms as there are writers. Each chapter examines two unique interpretations of literary language, one moral and political and the other social and philosophical. The book is designed to give us a range of contrasts across local and general contexts in each chapter as well as a thematic unity throughout.

Finally, some general linguistic principles which support the arrangement of this book should be explained. There are two ways of looking at language. The first is to examine some aspect of its structure as it is realised in many different texts at one particular period in time. Since the rate of linguistic change is fairly slow, a limited period of time can be regarded as negligible in the analysis of the data. This synchronic study of language ignores the fact that language changes, although it implicitly recognises that different texts show variant developments of earlier changes. The second way is to examine how particular patterns of language change as they develop in the course of time; this diachronic study of language involves comparison and contrast between texts in a chronological order. The theory of language use outlined above is primarily a synchronic statement about language, although in the course of explanation examples have been given from writers who lived at different times. This was necessary to give a general introduction to the whole book, but it also reminds us that registers, since they are part of language use, have a diachronic aspect as well. The language system and its registerial ordering, even in literary language, change in the course of time. At any given moment, literary language contains new forms and tendencies that will eventually become generalised into new patterns, while apparently established forms and tendencies will atrophy and disappear. In the case of literary registers in English, we suggested that the primary semantic contrasts between the three styles have persisted for some considerable time, although their evolution and variation is distinctive at any given moment. Throughout the book we shall have to notice the variation of subject matter and vocabulary in all three local contexts. Again, in some examples of style we shall have to consider the influence of theories of art such as mannerism or the baroque, which modify the writer's approach to his task. The important shift in techniques of literary composition from rhetorical invention to logical invention, which took place in the late sixteenth century, cannot be ignored as an influence on the tradition. The idea of Pierre de la Ramée that there was such a thing as 'natural logic' which operated in all literary language, and which provided the perfect method of ordering a discourse, is the source of this development. From a survey of the local contexts in each writer, the general influences on style, and the variation between moral and social assumptions in a writer's art, we shall get a clear idea of the unity as well as the diversity of literary language from Chaucer to Johnson.

Part I: Poetry

1 Chaucer and Skelton

The variety of style in *The Knight's Tale* makes a useful starting point for our inquiry. The poem shows Chaucer's skill in handling all three traditional styles. First, we can begin with an example of high style:

> To ransake in the taas of bodyes dede,
> Hem for to strepe of harneys and of wede,
> The pilours diden bisynesse and cure
> After the bataille and disconfiture.
> And so bifel that in the taas they founde,
> Thurgh-girt with many a grevous blody wounde,
> Two yonge knyghtes liggynge by and by,
> Bothe in oon armes, wroght ful richely,
> Of whiche two Arcita highte that oon,
> And that oother knyght highte Palamon.
> Nat fully quyke, ne fully dede they were,
> But by hir cote-armures and by hir gere
> The heraudes knewe hem best in special
> As they that weren of the blood roial
> Of Thebes, and of sustren two yborn.[1]

The passage is a delicate version of the high style, but it has all the markers of that register. The syntax is reminiscent of the periodic sentence with its measured rhythmical development. The inversion of clauses in the first sentence, the amplification of the object in the second, and the periphrasis of the third all contribute to this impression. There is significant use of parallelism in phrase and clause and the three sentences vary the pace of development. The second sentence has greater density and focus because clause and line boundaries coincide, while the first and last sentences use parallelism and run-over lines to create an impression of sustained energy. The high style has a wide variety of forms in syntax. In diction, the classical lack of detail in the high style can be seen everywhere: 'harneys', 'wede', 'bisynesse', 'cure', 'many a grevous blody wounde', 'in oon armes, wroght full richely'. We get no sense of an immediate impression such as an observer of the scene would have. The nominal tendencies of amplification in the high style can be found throughout the passage: 'bataille and disconfiture', 'bisynesse and cure', 'by hir cote-armures and by hir gere'. There is emphatic modification of nouns: 'many a grevous blody wounde', 'armes, wroght ful richely'. But once again this emphasis is generalising. The formality of high style diction is also carefully sustained. Periphrasis in the last sentence gives an eloquent form to simple statement. The passage as a whole introduces the reader, or listener, to the main characters of the tale; the two fated lovers are placed in a context of splendour and tragedy which sombrely anticipates their future. The high style may be informative, as it is here, but the names of the two knights are less important than their symbolic status in the poem – tragic heroes, whose friendship and knighthood clash disastrously with their ideals of love. If there is an element of diffuseness in this passage, it may be identified as part of the oral tradition of medieval verse. Even the most literary of writers had to take into account the medium in which he published his work, and an audience would find these lines quite informative and full. The reader may have found them very easy to take in without pause.

If we read on from that passage, we find a distinct shift of tone into the low style where narrative is primary:

> Out of the taas the pilours han hem torn,
> And han hem caried softe unto the tente
> Of Theseus; and he ful soone hem sente
> To Atthenes, to dwellen in prisoun
> Perpetuelly, – he nolde no raunsoun.
> And whan this worthy duc hath thus ydon,
> He took his hoost, and hoom he rit anon
> With laurer crowned as a conquerour;
> And ther he lyveth in joye and in honour
> Terme of his lyf; what nedeth wordes mo?
> And in a tour, in angwissh and in wo,
> This Palamon and his felawe Arcite
> For everemoore; ther may no gold hem quite.   1020–32

The formality of diction in the high style contrasts with the plainness here. The heroic emphasis of 'this worthy duc' (imitating a Latin construction) is the only high style feature of the passage. There are hardly any modified nouns; 'the pilours' (a low-style term, as in the previous lines), 'his hoost', 'his lyf', 'a tour' have grammatically necessary determiners. They unfold the narrative but do not elaborate. An isolated detail describes the triumphal return of Theseus, in unpoetic and factual diction: 'With laurer crowned as a conquerour'. Even 'to ransake' and 'to strepe' from the first passage have a general sense beside 'Out of the taas the pilours han hem *torn*', suggesting the struggle to part the heap of bodies, and the line 'han hem carried *softe* unto the tente' uses an unheroic adverb of manner, implying their painful wounds. The verb phrase is far more frequent and usually finite: 'han hem torn', 'han hem carried softe', 'ful soone hem sente', 'he took his hoost', 'hoom he rit anon', 'ther he lyveth'. The references to '*This* Palamon and his *felawe* Arcite' are uncourtly, colloquial and unpoetic, unlike the description of them on the battle-field. The two knights are guilty of helping the tyrant Creon, and so deserve no mercy or chivalric courtesies such as ransom. They have to suffer because they fought on the wrong side and justice requires their punishment. Unlike Theseus, they are not 'worthy' ('valiant'). But the issue of guilt is not Chaucer's main purpose and he presses on, leaving a contrasting image of suffering and rejoicing. The parallel phrases 'in joye and in honour' and 'in angwissh and in wo' are a feature of oral style in the text, reminding us of the medium of delivery. They are commonplace plain style phrases. The writer's direct appeal to the audience is another feature of plain style: 'what nedeth wordes mo?'. Finally, the casual metaphor borrowed from speech at the end – 'ther may no gold hem quite' – is dismissive and perfunctory. This does not mean that in another context Arcite and Palamon will not have the respect and courtesy they deserve. But at this moment in the narrative their fate is to be treated as common criminals, and Chaucer's language reflects this. What follows immediately is our first view of Emily, presented in the middle style lyricism of courtly love:

> This passeth yeer by yeer and day by day,
> Till it fil ones, in a morwe of May,
> That Emelye, that fairer was to sene
> Than is the lylie upon his stalke grene,
> And fressher than the May with floures newe-

> For with the rose colour stroof hire hewe,
> I noot which was the fyner of hem two-
> Er it were day, as was hir wone to do,
> She was arisen and al redy dight;
> For May wole have no slogardie a-nyght.
> The sesoun priketh every gentil herte,
> And maketh hym out of his slep to sterte . . .   1033-44

At once we notice the analytical mode of the register; its explanatory and descriptive manner argues a degree of sophistication absent from the low style. The writer becomes involved in a series of explanations of a poetic kind, and each explanation is another poetic image. It is an idealised view of reality, which adds an ever increasing richness of reference to the primary image of Emily in the garden. This device of style is distinct from the plain style verbal and narrative mode, with its sequence of clauses; it also contrasts with the high style amplification of an emphatic kind. But it is essentially a nominal style, like the high style. Its aestheticism marks it out as a separate level of courtly style. Elegant invention of arguments suitable to the main topic replace the emphatic gloss of the high style. The artifice of these poetic explanations is distinct from the realism of the low style. If we were to read this passage as a literal statement, it would lose all its traditional meaning. The writer expresses a conventional uncertainty about which was finer to look at, the rose or Emily's complexion. We are not supposed to think he is really uncertain, for Emily is the epitome of grace and beauty. The diction can be colloquial, as in 'For May wole have no *slogardie* a-nyght' (although this is a traditional personification), 'al redy dight' (a colloquial adverb) and 'maketh hym out of his slep to *sterte*'. These casual forms of language lend a gossipy tone to the passage, encouraging intimacy between the audience and the speaker. The writer may be capable of formality, but he is also aware of the audience's sophistication. He flatters their self-esteem by such ease of manner. But the passage is light on information; we are told little about what Emily did in the garden where she was walking, or what she saw or thought. The writer is rendering a traditional topic of courtly poems; the idea of the May morning and the lover are inseparable throughout medieval literature. In the second passage above, there is no traditional topic for the writer; he refers directly to the sentence of Theseus – 'he ful soone hem sente/ To Atthenes, to dwellen in prisoun/Perpetuelly . . . '. Here, the language is realistic and blunt; 'perpetuelly' may be a legal technical term in the low style, borrowed to give realism. Perhaps the writer is reporting the Duke's actual words. Such language would be quite unsuitable for the refined idealism of the middle style. In this brief sequence of three passages from *The Knight's Tale* we can observe a narrative function in the low style, a descriptive function in the middle style, and the pathos and tragic splendour of the high style. The tone of the poem as a whole is built up from such variety of style, and character is seen in the light of the varying local context. There is no one, simple view of Arcite, Palamon, Emily and Duke Theseus.

There are also a number of passages in the poem where these traditional styles are realised more densely. There is an intensification of stylistic effect within the particular register. In the high style, the portraits of Lycurgus (ll. 2128–52) and Emetreus (ll. 2155–86) epitomise the heroic warrior. Detail in each of the portraits is generalised to impress the listener with the energy and vitality of the figure, and the triumphant assertion of the will behind the appearance. There are no ambiguities of the middle style in these portraits. In the opening lines of the second portrait, Chaucer imitates the periodic sentence structure with its delayed main clause:

>   With Arcita, in stories as men fynde,
>   The grete Emetreus, the kyng of Inde,
>   Upon a steede bay trapped in steel,
>   Covered in clooth of gold, dyapred weel,
>   Cam ridynge lyk the god of armes, Mars.   2155–9

The syntax makes the listener take more note of the detail, added phrase by phrase to the subject; it is a dramatic way of presenting a complex image. The writer reminds us of the heroic analogies: 'in stories as men fynde' is a high style formula, proper to epic. Emetreus is compared to a god, and introduced with a laudatory epithet. Martial valour is suggested in his horse trappings, and splendour in the intricate cloth-of-gold covering. But the detail is schematic; yet it is not fanciful and inventive as the analogies in the middle style. Nor does it involve conceptual argument; these details symbolise heroic virtue. The same categorising tendency can be seen in the diction of the following lines:

His cote-armure was of clooth of Tars
Couched with perles white and rounde and grete;
His sadel was of brend gold newe ybete;
A mantelet upon his shulder hangynge,
Bret-ful of rubyes rede as fyr sparklynge;
His crispe heer lyk rynges was yronne,
And that was yelow, and glytered as the sonne.
His nose was heigh, his eyen bright citryn,
His lippes rounde, his colour was sangwyn;
A few frakenes in his face yspreynd,
Betwixen yelow and somdel blak ymeynd;
And as a leon he his lookyng caste.   2160—71

The details associate the figure with natural energy and an ideal perfection, but none of them convey a precise impression of his appearance. Instead of describing his silk coat-armour in visual terms, the writer identifies it with a famous name for Chinese silk. The epithets are consistently general: 'yelow', 'heigh', 'bright citryn', 'rounde', 'white', 'blak' and 'grete'. The portrait is far from naturalistic, for the yellow eyes ('citryn') and freckles are iconographic details which relate the figure to medieval ideas of the Martian type of man.[2] For Arcite has accepted the protection of Mars, and the god's assistance in the tournament is shown by his earthly supporters, among them Emetreus. Most of the clauses are simple equative structures, without conjunctions. This gives impact and emphasis to the catalogue of details. The audience gets the impression of a rich profusion of detail and an exuberant energy. The passage reads easily, but the listener would be overwhelmed with a more complex syntax. Why, then, is it not an example of low style in syntax at least? The answer is that we have to take it as axiomatic that the diction and the syntax of a passage are related where there is no clear evidence of a transferred context (as in irony or parody). Certainly the syntax is elementary (but the loose ordering contains quite a number of non-finite clauses–e.g. 'Couched . . .', 'hangynge . . . sparklynge', 'yspreynd . . . ymeynd'). There is just sufficient weight in these subordinate structures to give adequate complexity to the sense, while preserving the essential clarity of style for the audience. Given the medium in which Chaucer was working, this is quite a dense form of the high style. The focus of stylistic ordering is not, however, in either syntax or diction alone. Both aspects of language interact to create the context. Chaucer's evocative use of high-style syntax in the opening lines of the portrait gives the syntactic cue for what follows. A mental comparison with the colloquial language in *The General Prologue* to *The Canterbury Tales* reminds us at once of the rather careful archaic diction of this passage. Colloquialisms seem to be kept out on purpose. There is formality in the syntactic inversion of 'Bret-ful of rubyes rede as fyr sparklynge', and 'sparklynge' is formal and proper to the sense; rubies sparkle as they catch the light. Again, 'glytered as the sonne' has a formal tone. A more banal rendering, such as 'shone like the sun', at once shows up the artifice. 'And as a leon he his lookyng caste' also has a formal inversion, and the diction is similar. Even today we distinguish between 'he looked about him' and 'he cast a glance around him'; most people would find the first less formal than the second. Both the portrait of Emetreus and that of Lycurgus retard the narrative and make the audience admire the chivalric ideal symbolised in these warriors. They are not seen as individuals but as emblems of heroic purpose.

In the middle style, the description of the temple of Venus is a typical intricately worked example of the register; in this formulation of the style, its abstractions have become allegorical figures, and the detail is analytic and conceptual:

> First in the temple of Venus maystow se
> Wroght on the wal, ful pitous to biholde,
> The broken slepes, and the sikes colde,
> The sacred teeris, and the waymentynge,
> The firy strokes of the desirynge
> That loves servantz in this lyf enduren;
> The othes that hir covenantz assuren;
> Plesaunce and Hope, Desir, Foolhardynesse,
> Beautee and Youthe, Bauderie, Richesse,
> Charmes and Force, Lesynges, Flaterye,
> Despense, Bisynesse, and Jalousye,
> That wered of yelewe gooldes a gerland,
> And a cokkow sittynge on hir hand;
> Festes, instrumentz, caroles, daunces,
> Lust and array, and alle the circumstances
> Of love, which that I rekned and rekne shal . . .   1918–33

Jealousy has marigolds ('gooldes') in a garland because they symbolise her anxieties; the French 'souci' is the name of the flower and also means 'care'. The cuckoo is a symbol of infidelity familiar to the Elizabethans as well as Chaucer. These details identify one aspect of the 'circumstances of love', but only to the initiated. The list of allegorical figures is rapidly sketched in; few details, if any, distinguish them. To the audience, they are well-known aspects of the courtly tradition of refined love; they imply a self-knowledge and introspection we cannot expect to meet in *The Miller's Tale*, for example, or other forms of the popular *fabliaux* tradition. There love is a matter of physical satisfaction only. Here it is a social code, implicit with the self-esteem and sophistication of a leisured class. Who else would take the idea of love so seriously, except an audience that had time to spare on its hands? Chaucer gives an epitome of the experience abstracted from its particulars. To the modern reader, this is a very odd way of describing such a unique and essentially personal experience. Behind the catalogue of ideas there is an assumption that reason can analyse all expressions of feeling, and the successful lover must find his way through the labyrinth of his own emotions. All social occasions were a test of the lover's scrupulous self-regard; his job was to turn them into suitable opportunities to advance his cause. The diction is formal and serious, and there is no Chaucerian irony in the passage. The opening lines present a sequence of striking images (where the attributes of suffering are substituted for the lover who suffers); the shift of sense is violent and emphatic, implying the irrationality and tyranny of love, in its first onset. What follows is an analytic reading of the progress of lovers in their pursuit of the loved one, and the diction becomes abstract and full of social nuance. The topics are traditional and require only the slightest reference to remind the audience. Chaucer becomes quite explicit about his literary technique in the closing lines, where he tells the audience that he has used the argument from circumstances to develop his theme, and intends to go on doing so. Only an audience with a keen literary interest could stand this kind of reference; in the *fabliaux* tales, such remarks are never found. The Franklin, whose *Tale* is an elegant middle style romance, is also inclined to enter into discussions of literary techniques, even if it means deploring (quite disingenuously) his own lack of them. Literature was expected to show complexity and artifice in accord with the skill of the writer, and he was allowed to show his hand occasionally, and point out to the learned audience a particular felicity. But this was not something that could be proper to the high or low style contexts; in the first, direct intervention by the writer is not allowed, and in the second, the art is in concealing art, and giving the impression of a spontaneous (if subtly contrived) performance. Only in the middle style can art be consciously presented from a technical point of view, so that a connoisseur can share directly in the skill of the writer, and be flattered by the writer taking him into his confidence. After all, the writer's patron ought to know something about what he is paying for. In this passage, we have given little attention to syntax, because of the medium of the work. The catalogue of noun phrases, in a loose accumulation, is suited to oral delivery; the topic is familiar to the audience, and the covert ordering of the lines (mentioned above) provides sufficient shape and focus. The analytic imagery of the earlier middle style passage is replaced here by a dense nominal style; the pursuit of reason in all human experience is the centre of this register.

In the temple of Mars, we find a contrasting portrait of malice, murder and anarchic destruction. These are not ideas or states of mind as much as events – for even malice can only show in actions. The artist rightly chooses the low style for such topics; they are part of the real world, not a social ideal such as courtly love. The discordant imagery in these lines is far more familiar and realistic than the middle style; the disorder and random effect is quite alien to the high style. Here is no integrated assertion of the will towards an heroic end:

> Ther saugh I first the derke imaginyng
> Of Felonye, and al the compassyng;
> The crueel Ire, reed as any gleede;
> The pykepurs, and eek the pale Drede;
> The smylere with the knyf under the cloke;
> The shepne brennynge with the blake smoke;
> The tresoun of the mordrynge in the bedde;
> The open werre, with woundes al bibledde;
> Contek, with blody knyf and sharp manace.
> Al ful of chirkyng was that sory place.
> The sleere of hymself yet saugh I ther,–
> His herte-blood hath bathed al his heer.
> The nayl ydryven in the shode a-nyght;
> The colde deeth, with mouth gapyng upright.   1995–2008

There are poetic figures of speech in these lines, but they have a distinctive effect. The catalogue of personifications is active and threatening, unlike the abstract ideas of the middle style. In the low style, personification is actual description of an example; the isolated detail of the register gives the idea a solid presence. The diction is unpoetic and limited to the most simple range of vocabulary. Again, however, some words seem more formal than in the *fabliaux* version of the low style. 'Contek' ('Strife'), 'Felonye' ('Treachery'), and 'Drede' may represent common aspects of the malevolent god of war, but 'contek' and 'felonye' have a French formality of tone, while 'drede' is a native word. The style is verbal rather than nominal: verbal nouns are common, for example 'the derke imaginyng' ('the sinister plotting of . . .'), 'the compassyng', ('the stratagem') 'the smylere', 'chirkyng' ('creaking, grating noises'; a word used for its closeness of sound and sense), 'mordrynge', 'the sleere of hymself'. None of these are in any way poetic; they dominate the passage, along with other common diction – 'pykepurs' ('pick-purse'), 'shepne' ('stable'), 'knyf', 'cloke', 'bedde', 'smoke'. These are mostly monosyllabic and native words. Critics have noted the unheroic images of domestic crisis amongst the sinister: 'The sowe freten the child right in the cradel; The cook yscalded, for al his longe ladel' (ll. 2019–20). These are typical low style proverbial images, using the commonplace as part of the argument. The low style can give a sense of immediacy and exact detail which horrifies, as in the line, 'His herte-blood hath bathed al his heer' (notice the figurative sense of the verb, borrowed from speech). It can also use the common experience of daily life. 'The cartere overryden with his carte' (l. 2022); this, too, is a proverbial image for a mishap. But the point that critics have ignored is that this is not a tragic context; the low style is suitable for Mars, the bringer of misfortune, even if Mars, as god of war, merits a high style portrait. This is another aspect of the topic, and as a bringer of misfortune, Mars is central to the narrative. For it is his malevolent interpretation of Arcite's petition – 'Yif me victorie, I aske thee namoore' (l. 2420), which brings about Arcite's death. Mars himself, with his collaborator Saturn, whose attributes are similar, causes Arcite's horse to stumble and throw him, when he has taken his helmet off. As Saturnus says, when Arcite rides in triumph down the lists, 'Mars hath his wille, his knyght hath al his boone'. Those fatal words of Arcite, 'I aske thee namoore', return to destroy him. Mars is far too malicious to miss the chance of this cruel trickery. And his temple should have told Arcite what to expect. The audience would at least have read the signs aright. The tragic romance narrative is a structural artefact, shaped and designed for them. Arcite, unlike the audience, is blind to the full pattern of Fate.

The temples of Mars and Venus show two sides of the feudal world, as Chaucer understood it. There is always the threat of disorder, conflict and fierce self-assertion, which can be seen in the most ordinary circumstances of life as well as in open war. There is also the irrational power of profane love in its many forms:

> Thus may ye seen that wysdom ne richesse,
> Beautee ne sleighte, strengthe ne hardynesse,
> Ne may with Venus holde champartie,
> For as hir list the world than may she gye.   1947-50

This paranoid vision of incipient anarchy and the rule of unreason is part of the Boethian philosophy of the poem. Chaucer deliberately glosses the whole narrative in these Christian terms, and so translates the poem into a much darker tone than in its original. Again, in spite of the middle style idealisation of courtly love, the topic is frequently described in comic or tragic terms. Chaucer suggests the complexity of experience by such variations. We move constantly from the inner reality (in the middle style) to the comic observation of the lovers' sufferings (in the low style), and the heroic valour of armed combat for love (in the high style). In the temple of Venus, the sufferings of those in love are also described in tragic terms, in the middle style. Why does Chaucer introduce this implicitly Christian gloss? Such a question ought to be answered, because the complexity of the whole work depends on the Boethian elements in it. Partly, it is his attempt to give an explanation of the plot in conceptual terms, proper to the middle style; hence Theseus's speech at the end of the poem. But Chaucer also faced the problem that the feudal traditions of courtly love and service to the beloved, like the ideals of knighthood in warfare, were already archaic and eroded. They could no longer have the validity of their earlier form in the high middle ages. They could be better understood as a secular attempt to give meaning to the human condition, and they are shown to fail in the light of Boethian philosophy, as all humanist philosophies can be said to fail. 'What is this world? what asketh men to have?' Arcite cries out on his deathbed; these questions are Boethian, and the Christian answer is given in the poem. The peculiar force of some other lines in the poem arises from the fusion of the physical and spiritual in the chivalric ideal:

> The fresshe beautee sleeth me sodeynly
> Of hire that rometh in the yonder place,
> And but I have hir mercy and hir grace,
> That I may seen hire atte leeste weye,
> I nam but deed; ther nis namoore to seye.   1118–22

For a moment, the idea of brutal death in battle, and the idea of profane love are brought together in a middle style conceit. In the Boethian context of the whole work, this is an inevitable and prophetic association of ideas.

Chaucer also uses the forensic version of the low style in *The Knight's Tale*. The context implies exposition and argument:

> 'Thow shalt,' quod he, 'be rather fals than I;
> And thou art fals, I telle thee outrely,
> For paramour I loved hire first er thow.
> What wiltow seyen? Thou woost nat yet now
> Wheither she be a womman or goddesse!
> Thyn is affeccioun of hoolynesse,
> And myn is love, as to a creature;
> For which I tolde thee myn aventure
> As to my cosyn and my brother sworn.
> I pose that thow lovedest hire biforn;
> Wostow nat wel the olde clerkes sawe,
> That "who shal yeve a lovere any lawe?"'   1153–64

But we can also see the underlying similarity with other examples of the low style. The lines are concise and linear in syntax (there is a preference for addition at phrase and clause level), and the diction is generally familiar and emphatic. The scholastic middle style phrase 'affeccioun of hoolynesse' ('devotion to the holy') is a calculated shift into learned language, making a distinction that assists the argument. The phrase stands out in the context as weighty and authoritative, as it was meant to do; it contrasts with the simple authenticity of the next line. Chaucer also exploits the rhythms of natural emphasis and imposes them on the metrical pattern of the verse. This creates the exasperated tone of the passage. The variation between 'Thow *shalt*. . . be rather fals than I' (with its normal main stress) and the stronger contrastive emphasis of 'And thou *art* fals . . .'; the annoyance behind the rapid questioning – 'What wiltow seyen?', and the sarcasm of 'Thou woost nat yet now/ Wheither she be a womman or goddesse!'; the recovery of reasonableness (or its appearance) in 'I pose that thow lovedest hire biforn'; all these features are close to the rhetoric of speech. They are no part of the high or middle style manner. These devices of style give spontaneity and energy to the language. However, we must not underestimate the elegant reasoning at work in these lines; it is easy to misread the appropriateness of Arcite's final remark:

> We stryve as dide the houndes for the boon;
> They foughte al day, and yet hir part was noon.
> Ther cam a kyte, whil that they were so wrothe,
> And baar awey the boon bitwixe hem bothe.
> And therfore, at the kynges court, my brother,
> Ech man for hymself, ther is noon oother.   1177–82

The image is meant to clarify and bring home his arguments in a typical low style usage borrowed from proverbial speech. Arcite does not mean to suggest that the issue between them is trivial or absurd. The kite is a familiar image of fickle fortune, and the only way to deal with such uncertainty is to defy fortune and rely on one's own resources; this accounts for the individualism of the last lines. But Arcite has forgotten that Fate governs fortune, and behind Fate is God, making sense of the whole apparently random sequence of events. Or so Boethius would have us believe. Chaucer appears to accept this view in the poem, for Arcite sounds very much like the blind worldly person who does not understand the higher good, and thinks only in material terms. Arcite's view of love is debased and limited, as we see here, and in his petition to Mars (himself an uncourtly figure).

There are other passages of dense stylistic variation in *The Knight's Tale*: in the high style, the introductory formula of each prayer to the gods (ll. 2221–6; 2297–303; 2373–8); the fight in the wood (ll. 1637–60); the tournament (ll. 2599–635); the funeral (ll. 2882–962); in the middle style, the petitions of Palamon, Arcite and Emily to the gods (ll. 2227–60, 2379–420, 2304–30); Theseus's closing speech (ll. 2987–3089); the account of the banquet before the tournament (ll. 2190–2206); the funeral arrangements (ll. 2853–81); in the low style, the preparations for the tournament (ll. 2491–520); Theseus's witty speech defending the folly of lovers (ll. 1785–825), the medical account of Arcite's death (ll. 2743–61), and the events following the tournament (ll. 2700–42). Such variation from one local context to another, as the subject requires, conceals the literary tradition of the three styles. It requires close scrutiny to notice how the style changes, yet it is crucial to do so, for the tone of the poem is built up from these shifts of local context. Chaucer's purpose is to re-write his romance narrative source in a way that shows this philosophical interests, and also finds new meaning in the original work. The naturalism of late medieval art disguises his techniques, and makes them appear spontaneous. When we turn from Geoffrey Chaucer (1343–1400) to John Skelton (1460–1529) we notice an immediate contrast in the writer's approach to his task. While Chaucer conceals his command of rhetorical devices and style levels behind a fluent naturalism of expression (assisted by the tradition of oral delivery), Skelton wishes, like all Renaissance writers, to make his work as distinct as possible from natural uses of language. This does not mean he adopts a private language full of subjective metaphor and unusual usages (such as an English poet of the 1940s might). But his work is published in written or printed form to be read, not heard. The tradition of oral delivery has given way to the more private tradition of reading books. Literature becomes more selfconsciously artificial because it is found in an artificial context, the printed book. For the early Renaissance writer, literature is a matter of formal invention of arguments which give an ordered structure to his work. The complex arguments of *The Knight's Tale* (apart from the final explication by Theseus) are not explicit enough for the Renaissance. The search for formal beauties in literature is stimulated by a renewed interest in classical rhetoric. Form means argument and explicit order in the structure of a work; these arguments are founded on traditional topics proper to the subject matter of the poem, which in turn decides the style level in which it is written. A writer must demonstrate his fluency, his command of language aptly ordered and deployed, and there is less importance attached to originality of observation or complexity of attitude in the writer's view of the subject. Indeed, complexity is a sign of inadequate preparation for the resolving processes of art; clarity, order, vitality, an unmistakeable command of formal rhetorical devices (in all style levels, for all literary rhetoric is formal compared to natural rhetoric) – these are the ideals of the Renaissance writer.

How, then, did such a changed view of the artist's role affect his use of the three styles?

All three styles became more distinct from each other and very different from forms of speech. Skelton is not a narrative poet; he does not need the illusion of naturalism which the narrator cannot afford to sacrifice. Chaucer, of course, also wrote a number of lyrics and other short poems, but these are not typical of his work, and narrative is his normal choice of genre. Skelton's poems are also set in contemporary contexts, and they raise immediate issues of a political, moral and intellectual kind. Again, this distinguishes his work from Chaucer's more traditional and literary subject matter. But this does not prevent us making a comparison of the two writers. So diverse is the subject matter of literature that we cannot expect a close correspondence of topic in any two works. We can nevertheless compare the treatment of similar contexts within the three styles we have identified. In keeping with the renewed interest in formal argument and pattern in literary language, Skelton's style is generally more abstract than Chaucer's. The social and philosophical interests of the medieval poet have also been replaced by a moral and political context. This second factor intensifies the differences between the two writers. Skelton is less complex and observant than Chaucer because he has a further purpose in all his writing, while Chaucer has a strong sense of the real value of experience as an end in itself.

The high style language of spectacle in *The Knight's Tale* is not to be found in Skelton. The high style of public address, which occurs briefly in the lovers' petitions to their gods, also appears in a number of Skelton's poems. It is far less archaic than those earlier formulations in the *The Knight's Tale*, where the epic use of titles has a Virgilian quality. In Skelton, the high style is an abstract language of ritual public respect:

> I wail, I weep, I sob, I sigh full sore
>   The deadly fate, the doleful destiny
> Of him that is gone, alas, without restore,
>   Of the blood royall descending nobelly;
>   Whose lordship doubtless was slain lamentably
> Thorough treason again him compassed and wrought,
> True to his prince in word, in deed, and thought.[3]

The sustained amplification of syntax and vocabulary, the clarity of sentence ordering, and the formality of the diction are all markers of the high style. Measured and formal emphasis, the ritual of public respect translated into appropriate language, makes the poem dignified and sententious in the best Renaissance traditions. The vocabulary is closely organised around certain topics, and synonymy is the primary means of development. The Renaissance valued the 'copious' writer, who could demonstrate his fluency and command of the widest lexical resources in the language. Conciseness and density of thought were unacceptable, even in the low or plain style. Skelton's view of Chaucer was that he lacked 'copiousness' and was perhaps a little unsophisticated because of this deficiency:

> His English well allowed,
> So as it is enprowed,
> For as it is employed,
> There is no English void,
> At those days much commended . . .
> Chaucer, that famous clerk,
> His termes were not dark,
> But pleasant, easy and plain;
> Ne word he wrote in vain. 30/82–6/83

Skelton praises Chaucer's economy of language, his richness of meaning and refusal to waste words (unlike his follower, Lydgate); he also makes clear his sense of the different standards of style held then as opposed to the Renaissance. Then, the problem was to avoid diffuseness and prolixity without argument ('English void'); in the Renaissance, Skelton imagines that improvements can be made in the diction and in the quality of argument. To the modern reader this may well seem an astonishing assumption, and many readers of Skelton find his poetry uninteresting because they look for the same effects as in Chaucer's work. But the whole idea of literary standards had changed, although the classical tradition of the three styles survives and gains importance. Learning and scholarship were back in fashion as an overt accomplishment of the writer; for Skelton, the test of a writer's skill was his ability to avoid uninteresting plainness (an unfashionable plain style) and his capacity to demonstrate his erudition. In the high style language of petition, Skelton's style becomes even more selfconscious than in the first example:

> Princess most puissant, of high pre-eminence,
>   Renowned lady above the starry heaven,
> All other transcending, of every congruence
>   Madam regent of the sciences seven,
> To whose estate all nobleness must leanen,
> My supplication to you I arect,
> Whereof I beseech you to tender the effect.   1–7/349

The difficult language is a sign of scholarly knowledge and not an example of stilted affectation.

In the middle style, we find the same concern for diction and formal pattern of structure. Again, Skelton assumes a learned reader aware of the conceptual refinement in the tradition of courtly manners:

> Knowledge, acquaintance, resort, favour with grace;
>   Delight, desire, respite with liberty;
> Corage with lust, convenient time and space;
>   Disdains, distress, exiled cruelty;
>   Wordes well set with good hability;
> Demure demeanour, womanly of port;
> Transcending pleasure, surmounting all disport;   1–7/30

This nominal style is more concise than the high style, more complex in meaning, and very allusive. Unlike Chaucer's middle style, it is not visual or iconographic; Skelton does not intend to describe any process of experience directly. He reminds the reader of a familiar courtly tradition. Chaucer's portrait of the Duchess Blanche from *The Book of the Duchess* gives an example of the narrator's techniques with the same middle style tradition:

>   I sawgh hyr daunce so comlily,
> Carole and synge so swetely,
> Laughe and pleye so womanly,
> And loke so debonairly,
> So goodly speke and so frendly,
> That, certes, y trowe that evermor
> Nas seyn so blysful a tresor.
> For every heer on hir ned,
> Soth to seyne, hyt was not red,
> Ne nouther yelowe, ne broun hyt nas,

> Me thoghte most lyk gold hyt was.
> And whiche eyen my lady hadde!
> Debonaire, goode, glade, and sadde,
> Symple, of good mochel, noght to wide.   848–61

The illusion of an observer gives this hieratic figure some life. The emphasis in this passage is on courtly grace and art, the manner in which the lady's accomplishments impress the observer. The activity is a means of focusing on the ideals the lady embodies. This is not a narrative verbal style. There is a density of adverbial phrases describing manner and gesture, the writer pretends once again to find his powers of description inadequate for the experience, and the passage ends with a careful moral affirmation couched in aesthetic terms. The moral and the aesthetic are more overt in Skelton because he has to make a formal structure out of his material. Chaucer can rely on the dream-vision reminiscence as a natural pattern for the anecdote.

Skelton, however, developed the middle style by bringing into serious literature subjects which had been regarded as too popular and satirical for polite audiences. Chaucer carefully avoids all direct discussion of court politics, but Skelton found in the intrigues of court a fertile subject for invention. The conflict between the urbanity of courtly language and the rapacity of will beneath it is a fit subject for his imagination. His vivid satire *The Bouge of Court* is written in a range of middle and plain styles. It depends for its success on accurate observation and witty application of ideas to apparently natural uses of language. Yet it is far from naturalistic; Skelton's strength as a writer is his ability to translate ideas and moral experience into dramatic form. He does not attempt the illusion of naturalism, preferring to keep the reader aware of the formal conventions of literature, and therefore aware of the artifice and skill of the writer. Experience and observation in his work is reduced to essential logical patterns; his clarity of meaning can seem simple-minded beside the allusiveness and associative reference in Chaucer. That does not mean that he lacks Chaucer's knowledge of the human condition; he presents it in a rationalised form. The middle style of political and moral satire in Skelton is a new subject in the traditional register; Skelton returns to the earlier classical tradition that regarded love as unimportant beside affairs of state and the court. There was nothing in Chaucer for Skelton to imitate; he had to rely on his own sense of local context. Each middle style passage is organised around a central moral or political idea. For example, Favell ('Flattery') addresses the dreamer in this manner:

> No thing earthly that I wonder so sore
>   As of your conning, that is so excellent;
> Deyntee to have with us such one in store,
>   So virtuously that hath his dayes spent;
>   Fortune to you gifts of grace hath lent:
> Lo, what it is a man to have conning!
> All earthly treasure it is surmounting.   22–8/41

The idealism of the middle style is translated into a fatuous social compliment which neatly defines the speaker's deception; while Favell pretends to admire 'conning' in the sense of 'learning, scholarship' (middle style), he actually admires it more (as his name tells us) in its other sense of 'deception, worldly wisdom' (plain style). He speaks in vapid commonplaces that fail to disguise his real motives, which are self-advancement. In this way Skelton can give some renewed credibility to the middle style, atrophied though it may have been; he accepts its limitations and uses it because of them. The formality of 'excellent', 'Deyntee', 'virtuously', 'gifts of grace', 'surmounting' contrasts with the self-seeking motive of the speaker. The language pretends to an idealism which the central pun and the whole context denies. The situation, or immediate purpose of the utterance, is to ingratiate the speaker with the listener, whose name ('Dread') implies his fear. Favell is both a moral and a political idea in which the political observation gives authenticity to the moral platitude. It is however a very schematic and abstract statement, compared for example with the plain style figures in *The Prologue* to *The Canterbury Tales*. But we should be careful to notice the general distinction between middle style concepts and plain style description. Suspect ('Suspicion'), another allegorical figure in the poem, is quite right to warn the narrator:

> Ye remember the gentleman right now
>   That communed with you, methought a pretty space?
> Beware of him, for, I make God avow,
>   He will beguile you and speak fair to your face.
>   Ye never dwelt in such another place,
> For here is none that dare well other trust-
> But I would tell you a thing, an I durst!   13–19/43

This is no naturalistic imitation of courtly speech, but a carefully organised argument about the nature of political intrigue. It appears to be courtly speech, and has the markers of middle style formality: 'gentleman', 'communed', 'beguile' are not colloquial in tone. There are also the easier grace notes of familiarity (allowed in courtly speech) 'right now', 'methought a pretty space', 'I make God avow', 'an I durst'. But the conceptual focus of the passage is such that even these markers of style are transformed into devices of meaning. Suspect is always afraid of threats to his survival from unexpected quarters; his paranoia is implicit in the insinuating tone of his first words – 'That communed with you, methought a *pretty space?*' His fears are immediate and continually require attention – 'Ye remember the gentleman *right now* . . .'. If no one dare trust another person with the truth, it follows that his own avowals are equally suspect. The last lines of this verse, like the rest of his speech, turn on the paradox of the need for trust and confidence in a situation where these things are by definition absent.

Elsewhere Skelton demonstrates his fluency in the courtly lyric. Parts of *Philip Sparrow* are in this tradition of the middle style, although it is also a work with plain style. *The Commendations* in praise of Jane Scrope are in the middle style, while the plain style is used for the mock elegy, *The Office for the Dead*. In both distinctive styles we can observe the 'copiousness' of variation which was so much admired in Renaissance poetry; the tendency is always to catalogue and amplify every topic, as here, in the middle style:

> Her eyen grey and steep
> Causeth mine heart to leap;
> With her browes bent
> She may well represent
> Fair Lucres, as I ween,
> Or else fair Polixene,
> Or else Calliope,
> Or else Penelope;
> For this most goodly floure,
> This blossom of fresh colour,
> So Jupiter me succour,
> She flourisheth new and new
> In beauty and virtue . . .   13–25/89

Skelton is casual with his classical references, using them to make up the rhyme in a generous, light-hearted manner. The moral and the aesthetic aspects of the middle style give poise to his invention, but the formal aspects of language are primary. Skelton uses the conventional imagery proper to the middle style for rhyme words, devaluing the seriousness of the convention. The poem is a mock elegy, and so the praises of Jane Scrope are equally light-hearted. There is less argument and assertion than in the more serious forms of middle style, such as the satire of *The Bouge of Court*.

In the lyrics of *The Garland of Laurel*, Skelton shows his formal skill as a court poet, using the traditional imagery of the middle style with wit and grace:

> With majoram gentle,
>   The flower of goodlihead,
> Embroidered the mantle
>   Is of your maidenhead.
> Plainly I cannot glose;
>   Ye be, as I devine,
> The pretty primrose,
>   The goodly columbine.
> With marjoram gentle,
>   The flower of goodlihead,
> Embroidered the mantle
>   Is of your maidenhead.   6–17/377

The detail is entirely emblematic, a tribute to social virtues. The lyric relies on the device of a conceit that requires expansion and interpretation. 'Plainly I cannot glose' means both that the writer's art is exhausted by the strenuous demands of the topic (a modesty formula), and that he knows he should not flatter (a more common sense of 'glose') in a plain style manner. He has to explain and expand the conceit ('glose' in the middle style sense of 'gloss') in a proper middle style. The decorum of the lyric is sustained when it might break down ('maidenhead' can have a plain style sense). Skelton returns to a direct identification of the subject with moral and social virtues, abandoning the conceit of the first lines; then he repeats the image in a new context. The reader sees that decorum has been upheld, when it might have been lost. The resolving power of art triumphs over the apparent faultiness of the writer's technique. The compliment is enriched and made to seem more sincere by such calculated hesitation.

In one version of the low or plain style, Skelton returns to the classical tradition of argument and invective. But his form of the register is less elegant than Chaucer's version in *The Knight's Tale*. Skelton depends more on the figurative language of speech than Chaucer does with his carefully selected proverbial images. But the total effect of Skelton's plain style is quite remote from speech, because, unlike Chaucer, he does not use the emphases and natural rhetorical devices of spoken usage. On the contrary, he develops the low style contexts by formal repetitive devices such as parallelism of clause and phrase; his fluency and eloquence make these passages quite unlike speech. The register is also more conceptual than it was in Chaucer; Skelton relies heavily on the ideas behind proverbial expressions, although these ideas are only vague and ill-defined. There is less forensic analysis and direct argument, more statement and repetition; in this passage from *Magnificence*, Fancy describes his nature in a sequence of proverbs:

> That was before, I set behind:
> Now too courteous, forthwith unkind,
> Sometime too sober, sometime too sad,
> Sometime too merry, sometime too mad;
> Sometime I sit as I were solemn proud,
> Sometime I laugh over-loud,
> Sometime I weep for a gee-gaw,
> Sometime I laugh at wagging of a straw;
> With a pear my love you may win,
> And ye may lose it for a pin.   1–10/197

The plain style in this context presents arguments in terms of physical action, which Skelton amplifies by his Renaissance interest in 'copious' or varied language. He is inventive and fertile in choice of proverbs, but the overall effect is to blur meaning. Skelton may have deliberately amplified his tendency to elaborate because this interlude was designed for performance. *Colin Clout*, however, shows the same technique in the plain style, and it was designed to be read. While the plain style in this form has energy and variety it is by definition unable to analyse or advance complex argument. The traditional functions of this style are exposition and narration, and Skelton joins these to the moral invective of the sacred plain style found in sermons and, in secular form, in classical satire. Skelton is nothing if not eclectic in his use of stylistic resources. At his best, in

Speak, Parrot, the contemporary allusions add point and wit to the attack on Cardinal Wolsey, but again, much of the complaint in this poem is traditional and a general denunciation of the times. We see how a writer with a strong sense of indignation and great moral fervour can reduce the complexity of experience to a number of isolated and separate details. This is no substitute for a coherent attack based on argument. The plain style in Skelton's handling of it lacks the wit and sting of later more accurate forms (although his ironic middle style lyrics are far more penetrating). An example from *Speak, Parrot* will show the scope of his method:

> So little discretion, and so much reasoning;
>   So much hardy-dardy, and so little manliness;
> So prodigal expense, and so shameful reckoning;
>   So gorgeous garments, and so much wretchedness;
>   So much portly pride, with purses penniless;
> So much spent before, and so much unpaid behind—
> Since Deucalion's flood there can no clerkes find.   10–16/305

The additive syntax of the plain style is amplified by parallelism and repetition; the occasional alliterative phrase reminds us of Skelton's exploitation of common proverbs. But the attack remains conventional criticism of extravagance and wastefulness. It is still a serious form of of the plain style with less caricature than the more popular version we shall now turn to.

Both Chaucer and Skelton use this popular tradition of plain style. It is quite unsuitable for *The Knight's Tale*, which is a serious romance narrative. Chaucer uses the register in *The Miller's Tale* and *The Reeve's Tale*. In Skelton, characters like Harvey Hafter and Riot, in *The Bouge of Court*, are typical low style creations, and the whole of *The Tunning of Elinour Rumming* is composed in the register. In the mock-elegy *Philip Sparrow*, *The Office for the Dead* is a parody of sacred low style in a secular form. Once again, the contrast between the two writers turns out to be a difference of organisation in the language. Chaucer uses isolated detail to build up a view of character, but there is an inner logic behind his description. Skelton exploits fluent repetition of the same idea in a number of different forms; his portraits give the reader an idea of the topics associated with the main subject. They are too schematic to give an impression of actual drawing from the life. The eloquence of Renaissance literary styles contrasts with the complexity and irony of late medieval usage. For the medieval writer saw it as his duty to give a new aspect to traditional material by adding his own original commentary (concealed in his treatment of the subject, as in the variety of styles in *The Knight's Tale*). The Renaissance writer demonstrates his easy technical skill in handling any subject that comes up as part of the argued structure of the work. He does not intend to make needless complexities (in his view), but to conceal the intellectual vigour of his art beneath the clarity of presentation. In Chaucer's *General Prologue*, multiple contexts, in which middle and plain style define the observer's scepticism, are frequently to be found. Multiple contexts are rarely found in Skelton, who usually works within one style level at any moment in his work. His sense of order and principle will not allow him a more equivocal view. He always tends towards caricature, and the reduction of experience to simplified patterns.

Chaucer's portrait of the Miller in *The General Prologue* is the simplest example of the popular low style in his work. The portrait comes alive because of his acute observation and lively wit:

> The Millere was a stout carl for the nones;
> Ful byg he was of brawn, and eek of bones.
> That proved wel, for over al ther he cam,
> At wrastlynge he wolde have alwey the ram.
> He was short-sholdred, brood, a thikke knarre;
> Ther was no dore that he nolde heve of harre,
> Or breke it at a rennyng of his heed.
> His berd as any sowe or foxe was reed,
> And thereto brood, as though it were a spade.
> Upon the cop right of his nose he hade
> A werte, and theron stood a toft of herys,
> Reed as the brustles of a sowes erys;
> His nosethirles blake were and wyde.   545-57

This is a study of brute strength and cunning (the fox-red beard suggests the idea). The isolated physical details are repulsive and uncourtly, and his sporting activities are comically similar. Lack of self-knowledge is implicit in the naivety of his boastings; this, too, is typical of the low style character. The diction is common usage, concrete in sense, and unpoetic. There are a number of low style features from speech in the phrasing of the passage: 'for the nones' ('extremely'), 'That proved wel' ('that was lucky for him'), 'And thereto' ('And moreover'). Such words as 'carl', 'a thikke knarre', 'cop', 'spade' and 'brawn' are common colloquial English. Character is defined through appearance and activity, but without the constant reference to abstract ideals we find in the middle style. There is nothing aesthetic or complex about the description; it is unambiguous and concentrates on the ideas of intimidating physical presence and self-assertion. The syntax has the rhythms of concise speech without the eloquence of middle style persuasion; the additive, linear syntax gives the impression of an observer noting down the Miller's appearance and conversation as it seems at first meeting. The passage has an incipient realism which goes beyond conventional low style characters in Skelton. A figure in the same register in his work is more mechanical:

> With that came Riot, rushing all at once,
>   A rusty gallant, to-ragged and to-rent;
> And on the board he whirled a pair of bones,
>   *Quater trey dèws* he clattered as he went.
> 'Now have at all, by Saint Thomas of Kent!'
> And ever he threw and cast I wote ne'ere what:
> His hair was growen thorough out his hat.
>
> Then I beheld how he disguised was:
>   His head was heavy for watching over night,
> His eyen bleered, his face shone like a glass;
>   His gown so short that it ne cover might
> His rump, he went so all for summer light.
> His hose was garded with a list of green,
> Yet at the knee they were broken, I ween.   1–14/48

Chaucer has a much finer ear for language than Skelton; he uses sound to match sense in the powerful emphasis of 'Ful byg he was of brawn, and eek of bones', or 'He was short-sholdred, brood, a thikke knarre'. This richness of spoken English is perhaps a feature of the medium in which Chaucer worked; he wrote to be heard not read silently. Skelton writes for that silent audience of readers, and his language loses the essential vitality of spoken English. He works instead in terms of the ideas his figure represents; Riot means wanton and wasteful living, extravagance of all kinds, and Skelton duly associates the figure with these attributes. Riot's clothes and appearance betray his penniless state, and his actions explain why he has no money. He wastes it all on gambling. Nevertheless, the portrait lacks authenticity; it is too general and schematic. The reader, and the fictitious observer, see the portrait from a distance, and the isolated detail is random and superficial. Chaucer's description of the miller suggests the immediate reaction of a close observer; the physical presence is a coherent impression on a particular mind. The anecdotes the writer remembers about the miller also contribute to this effect of coherence; they are the kind of odd detail about a person someone might remember casually. The whole passage is organised around the idea of memory fashioning an organic unity out of random and multiple impressions. The immediacy of those impressions survives, but they become more meaningful than a casual reporting or catalogue of every possible detail. But this is unfortunately what Skelton decides to do here, because he has to show the fluency and variety of Renaissance fashion. The clarity of his style requires that there can be no covert suggestions of meaning in the satire, so the figure appears mechanical, acting out his nature like the Mad Hatter. The detail is grotesque and unnatural, an'd the allegory too explicit. The portrait is far less successful than Skelton's middle style ironies in the same poem. None of Riot's actions have that specific value that would make them part of a real person's behaviour. Skelton is not capable of creating a truthful version of the conventional villain; he can assemble all the materials associated with the topic, and present them fluently. But he shows the limits of conventional realism when we compare him with a writer of Chaucer's ability who can achieve effects close to fully representational realism out of similar materials. Chaucer's exploratory approach to description is finer and more sensitive to experiential reality; the additive syntax of the low style takes on an artistic function in this usage.

In *The Tunning of Elinour Rumming*, Skelton's language is more colloquial, and he uses dialectal words for rhythm and alliterative phrasing:

>Her eyen gowndy   [full of 'gownd' or matter]
>Are full unsowndy,
>For they are bleared;
>And she gray-haired,
>Jawed like a jetty;
>A man would have pity
>To see how she is gummed,

Fingered and thumbed,
Gently jointed,
Greased and anointed
Up to the knuckles;
The bones of her huckles   [haunches]
Like as they were with buckles
Together made fast.
Her youth is far past;
Footed like a plane,
Legged like a crane,
And yet she will jet
Like a jolly fet   [fat woman? or elegantly attired lady]
In her furred flocket,
And gray russet rocket,
With simper-the-cocket. 2–23/113 [an affected simpering manner]

The disapproval is more explicit than in Chaucer's portraits of women (even the vulgarity of Alison, in *The Miller's Tale*, is treated more enthusiastically). The sarcasm of middle style terms such as 'pity' and 'gently' is obvious in context, and rather a rare example of such variation in Skelton. But the target is safe and easy, for Elinour is a grotesque and revolting drunkard. The writer is not under any pressure to define an experience, observed and re-created for the reader. Here the parody of middle style description is an exercise in ribald inventiveness. The literary problem of amplification takes over from the accuracy of observed detail.

Skelton's description of Philip Sparrow is more realistic, reminding us of the early Renaissance interest in the exact imitation of the natural world:

Sometimes he would gasp
When he saw a wasp;
A fly or a gnat,
He would fly at that;
And prettily he would pant
When he saw an ant.
Lord, how he would pry
After the butterfly!
Lord, how he would hop
After the gressop!

And when I said, 'Phip, Phip!'
Then he would leap and skip,
And take me by the lip.
Alas, it will me slo
That Philip is gone me fro!   30/63–11/64

The amplification of the topic is still overtly rhetorical, but the accuracy of the detail sustains the style. There are also, in this low style realistic context, some features from middle style courtly language: 'prettily' is aesthetic, and idealised, if unpoetic in a formal sense, while 'take me by the lip' and the lament in the last couplet are traditional love-lyric formulas. The rest of the passage is low style without the caricature of most contexts in Skelton. Chaucer rarely describes animals, but the same realism can be seen in his description of the whelp in *The Book of the Duchess* (ll. 387–415).

Chaucer's use of multiple contexts, where the plain style gives ironic sense to middle style insertions, is particularly clear in *The General Prologue*. The middle style becomes in these contexts a means of exposing cunning and hypocrisy, or self-delusion of various kinds. For the appropriateness of the plain style in this introduction is made certain by Chaucer's remark that he will tell us 'al the condicioun/Of ech of hem'. Where moral principles are a genuine part of professional practice, Chaucer uses the sacred plain style, as in the portraits of the Parson and Ploughman, but no courtiers are present in the company, and many of the pilgrims are disreputable. Naturally, the poem begins in the high style proper to opening lines of major works, but this register only extends to the first eighteen lines. The sequence of portraits is carefully ordered so that those with most status come first and the least respectable last. This has important consequences for the style of the poem. The Knight is described in a serious plain style (with some sacred low style insertions), and there is no need for us to think his exploits are meant to expose his false pretences. It is significant that Chaucer uses no form of the middle style in his portrait, and, as we shall see, he relates the Knight's idealism to that of the Parson and Ploughman. The Squire is presented in a whimsical version of the middle style, suggesting his youthful enthusiasm and energy. No one can accuse Chaucer of cynicism in such delightful lines as these:

Embrouded was he, as it were a meede
Al ful of fresshe floures, whyte and reede.

> Syngynge he was, or floytynge, al the day;
> He was as fressh as is the month of May. 89–92

The rest of the portrait describes a model character and a genuine idealist. The local context is entirely middle style, and there is no alternative view of this figure. But since it follows the portrait of his father, we may believe that Chaucer meant to suggest something of the earnest literary ideal of chivalry that the Squire has absorbed from books. He has yet to know the sterner side of knighthood in its dedication to duty. The Squire is living a literary fiction, even if he is too young to be responsible for all his actions. His servant, the Yeoman, is a contrasting plain style portrait, with occasional middle-style details that are made acceptable in the heraldic context. He is after all the Squire's servant, and has to dress reasonably well. His equipment is not fancy and ornamental either, as Chaucer reminds us:

> A sheef of pecok arwes, bright and kene,
> Under his belt he bar ful thriftily,
> (Wel koude he dresse his takel yemanly:
> His arwes drouped noght with fetheres lowe). 104–107

Now 'bright and kene' are conventional terms from the middle style, but Chaucer goes on to reinforce the dominant plain style with such adverbs as 'ful thriftily' and 'yemanly', emphasising the usefulness of the equipment rather than its decorative quality. The terms 'dresse', 'takel' and 'drouped . . . lowe' are also plain style realistic language, setting off the poeticism of the middle style.

The Prioress is an attractive portrait in the middle style, but there is an implicit clash between the secular and aesthetic ideals of the middle style and her religious calling. This becomes more striking when we consider the sacred plain style descriptions of the Parson and Ploughman; but a serious and moral portrait of a nun would have been far less interesting than this one. The Prioress, like the Squire, has modelled her behaviour and social manner on literature, and she has unconsciously absorbed all the characteristics of the romance heroine, in the same way as the Squire has adopted the mannerisms and appearance of the romance hero. The details of the Prioress's portrait have been examined by many critics, and there is little new to add now. But we cannot escape the fact that Chaucer uses terms of an ambiguous religious and secular kind in the account he gives, thereby driving the reader to notice that the Prioress may be a woman first, but she is also a nun. In their secular sense, 'charitable', 'pitous' and 'conscience' mean 'generous', 'compassionate', and 'fine feeling'; but these middle style terms have their sacred low style senses too, 'generous in giving alms to the poor', 'showing Christian mercy towards human suffering', and 'the moral faculty that distinguishes between right and wrong'. Both areas of meaning are present in the contexts. The same technique is exploited in the Monk's portrait. Chaucer uses terms with an ecclesiastical and sacred association in contexts where they become literal and secular, without losing their original sense. But again, the worldly nature of the Monk is a subject for amusement rather than criticism. He is a country squire in outlook, with a settled dislike of the religious life. His portrait is generally plain style, and contrasts with the sacred plain style used to describe the Parson and Ploughman. The portrait opens with a colloquial phrase quite inappropriate for his calling: 'A monk ther was, a fair for the maistrie' – 'an extremely fine example'. This idea of a specimen under the narrator's scrutiny at once puts us on our guard, for Chaucer must be aware of the ironic perspective such language opens up. The monk is 'An outridere that lovede venerie': his job is to ride round supervising monastic property, and Chaucer adds quite inconsequentially that he loves hunting. The additive syntax of the low style is exploited to good effect here; whether this is the Monk's interpretation of his duties we are not told, Chaucer simply allows the secular interest to speak for itself. The plain style is concerned with the man, not the profession or the moral principle. The conflict of terms remains, and is supported by the next line, 'A manly man, to been an abbot able'. Virility and religious zeal are not normally associated with each other. The contrast continues into the famous simile with its low style decorum:

> And whan he rood, men myghte his brydel heere
> Gynglen in a whistlynge wynd als cleere,
> And eek as loude as dooth the chapel belle.   169–71

The comparison is commonplace and proverbial, no doubt; it also has another kind of ironic propriety in context. The religious calling of his profession is exactly what the Monk cannot understand or respond to. This device of style becomes a systematic ambiguity in the following lines. The dismissive culinary proverbs are both proper to low style argument, and suitable to the Monk as a man whose gluttony is established by his appearance. When we hear him cry out, in the direct speech of the plain style, 'How shall the world be served?' we should remember the Christian call to service, as well as the Monk's justification of his own good living. Again, 'He was nat pale as a forpyned goost' sounds like an echo of some sacred plain style register, although it is also a common proverb. The closing remark, 'Now certeinly he was a fair prelaat' is a startling middle style politeness, similar to the line, 'And I seyde his opinion was good'. Both lines represent the formality of an enigmatic observer, the narrator who happens to have engaged the Monk in conversation, and can scarcely admit to insulting him without offending the audience's good taste. But the low style description of the Monk shows he is possessed by gluttony (ll. 198–202), even if the narrator says nothing explicit. In this way, Chaucer, adds another specimen to his extraordinary collection.

In the Friar's portrait, we find a sharp implicit contrast between middle style idealism, and low style cynicism. The Friar is an expert at collecting money from everyone, and he uses his vocation to bring in the cash. He is also cynically aware of his materialism, and justifies it with spurious reasoning. Chaucer's technique in this portrait is to devalue brutally the middle style terms, focusing on the dishonesty by placing one middle style line against another low style exposure of the real motive:

> He was an esy man to yeve penaunce,
> Ther as he wiste to have a good pitaunce.   223–4
>
> It is nat honest, it may nat avaunce,
> For to deelen with no swich poraille,
> But al with riche and selleres of vitaille.
> And over al, ther as profit sholde arise,
> Curteis he was and lowely of servyse.   246–50.

The narrator admires the sheer competence of the man: 'Ther nas no man nowher so vertuous'. But by using 'vertuous' in the sense of 'capable' (its colloquial low style sense), Chaucer raises the discrepancy of the middle style meaning, 'virtuous', in such a context. Clearly, the low style meaning is the primary sense, but who could really admire such competence? Chaucer shows that admiration can be divorced from moral principles, as indeed the low style implies. This is very different from forgetting what principles have been abandoned by such accomplished villains.

Enough has been said to suggest how an analysis of the other low style characters could be undertaken. The Reeve, Summoner and Pardoner are carefully presented as corrupt figures whose claims to middle style ideals are quite false. The Reeve is a clever swindler of his master's estates – 'His lord wel koude he plesen subtilly' says Chaucer, with ironic grace; the Summoner is 'a gentil harlot and a kynde' – 'a pleasant fellow and a kind person', but he is hardly 'well-bred', the other middle style sense of 'gentil'; as for the Pardoner, he too is 'gentil' in the sense of 'effeminate', but 'in chirche a noble ecclesiaste'. The professional skill, however irrelevant to the moral status, is always the primary interest in the plain style. For a professional skill reflects on the man who has it, and can be admired as a human accomplishment on its own. Chaucer exploits this limitation in the plain style for his own purpose, and in withholding judgement he makes an urbane assessment of his fellow pilgrims. The formality and abstraction of middle style vocabulary can be used as a counterpoint to the visual and technical precision of the low style. The syntax of the middle style is more elusive in these multiple contexts, but the variation of mode is often very sharp:

> In al the parisshe wif ne was ther noon
> That to the offrynge bifore hire sholde goon;
> And if ther dide, certeyn so wrooth was she,
> That she was out of alle charitee.   449–52

Conciseness and plainness of diction in the low style is replaced in the last line by a periphrastic form of the middle style. In these lines, too, we see the contrast of syntax and vocabulary:

> For thogh a wydwe hadde noght a sho,
> So plesaunt was his '*In principio*',
> Yet wolde he have a farthing, er he wente.   253–5

The Friar's courteous greeting, borrowed from the first chapter of St John's Gospel, is a traditional formula. The sudden shift from this agreeable social observation to the rapacity of motive behind it is also a shift of style. 'So plesaunt was his "*In principio*" ' is a middle-style line; it has an easy rhythmical grace, and appears to be a spontaneous response from the narrator. But it is inserted between two halves of a plain style antithesis – 'thogh . . . Yet', and the line becomes, in context, causative and mercenary in sense. The cynical calculation of the Friar is contained in that antithesis, and in the determination of 'er he wente.'

There was also a sacred version of the low style which combined a degree of conventional realism with a strong sense of the moral imperative. The Parson and the Ploughman are described in this archaic register. It survives in sermon writing much longer, but it seems crude in its effects beside secular literary language. In this form of the low style, reality is turned into a moral fable, and the relation between motive and action is emphatically simplified:

> This noble ensample to his sheep he yaf,
> That first he wroghte, and afterward he taughte.
> Out of the gospel he tho wordes caughte,
> And this figure he added eek therto,
> That if gold ruste, what shal iren do?   496–500

Such simple ideas have great strength and force, whether they are true or not. The moral abstract is made into a tangible course of action, or an observable physical process. Even if gold cannot rust, the idea is a familiar one; we transfer the observed facts of the natural world into a paradoxical moral perspective. But the paradox leads to a truth about human conduct that justifies the allusion. People learn by example, and the behaviour of the other servants of the church is a corrupted pattern of the Christian life. The Parson is not the only Christian symbol in *The Prologue*; the Ploughman represents the type of the good Samaritan, and the Knight consistently follows out the same Christian principles in action. We need only compare two passages from the portraits of the Parson and the Knight:

> And though he hooly were and vertuous,
> He was to synful men nat despitous,
> Ne of his speche daungerous ne digne,
> But in his techyng discreet and benygne.
> To drawen folk to hevene by fairnesse,
> By good ensample, this was his bisynesse.   515–20

> And everemoore he hadde a sovereyn prys;
> And though that he were worthy, he was wys,

> And of his port as meeke as is a mayde.
> He nevere yet no vileynye ne sayde
> In al his lyf unto no maner wight,
> He was a verray, parfit gentil knyght.   67–72

Ambiguity and irony are carefully kept out, by reinforcement of words that could have a low style or ironic middle style sense: 'And though he *hooly* were and *vertuous*' (where 'hooly' is necessary to mark the serious moral sense of 'vertuous'); 'He was a verray, parfit gentil knyght' ('gentil' here has the sacred plain-style sense of 'noble', not the middle-style sense 'well-bred'); 'To drawen folk to hevene by *fairnesse,*/By *good ensample* . . .' ('fair' is, as we have seen, a loose and ambiguous term). Each figure is an example of charity in its traditional sense; the Knight, as a secular figure, is also an example of prudence ('he was wys'). The simile in this portrait sounds inappropriate to the modern reader; after all, can such a successful mercenary be 'as meeke as is a mayde'? In the sacred low style, this is a traditional formula; we are meant to see the moral idea, and not the person. For the Knight is sustained by genuine moral principles, however unacceptable they may seem to us. Christ himself is often described as a symbol of gentleness in sacred literature. Further, 'vileynye' has a moral as well as a social meaning; both 'moral reproach' (sacred plain style) and 'discourtesy' (middle style) are implied. This rather unworldly figure (in spite of his military prowess) is, as we might expect, shabbily dressed (ll. 74–8). His dedication to his calling is far more ascetic than the commitment of the Prioress, the Monk or the Friar. Chaucer allows the contrast to emerge by this grouping of the Parson, Ploughman and Knight in the sacred low style. In *The Bouge of Court*, Skelton is right to remember 'poets old, which ful craftily,/Under as covert terms as could be,/Can touch a truth and cloak it subtilly . . .' (9–11/37).

2 Spenser and Shakespeare

Edmund Spenser (1552-99) develops the visual aspect of the three styles. He introduces a new range of aesthetic refinement in his interpretation of the classical and medieval registers; his work is dedicated to the later Renaissance ideals of grace, variety, difficulty and conscious artifice. These features of his style are typical of the mannerist phase of European, and especially Italian, art in the sixteenth century.[1] Now mannerism is a nineteenth-century term for this period of later Renaissance art, and there is some controversy over the appropriateness of its use for the period. The Renaissance Italian term *maniera* means 'style', but it has been extended by art historians to define the characteristics of the fashionable style which dominated the arts from about 1520 to 1600.[2] There is no doubt, however, that this period has a distinctive approach to the traditional motifs of the high Renaissance, and it is useful to identify the new emphasis by a separate term. The origins of this development are to be found in that earlier period, and mannerism is no longer regarded as a reaction against the ideals of the high Renaissance.[3] There is good reason, then, to consider how Spenser has absorbed and interpreted these mannerist ideals within the traditional range of literary styles. There can be no simple relationship between the visual and the written, but if we examine how Spenser varies his local contexts in response to the general values of mannerist theory, we shall find an equivalent in literature for the painter's effects. There are also a number of important comments in his published work which indicate his interest in mannerism, as we know it today; these remarks, however cursory, should direct our response to the main concerns of the period in matters of style.

In the introductory *Epistle* to *The Shepheardes Calender* (1579), Spenser's friend, Edward Kirke, justifies the archaic plain style in the poems by an arresting visual analogy:

For, if my memory faile not, Tullie, in that booke wherein he endevoureth to set forth the paterne of a perfect Oratour, sayth that ofttimes an aunciént worde maketh the style seeme grave, and as it were reverend, no otherwise then we honour and reverence gray heares, for a certein religious regard, which we have of old age. Yet nether every where must old words be stuffed in, nor the common Dialecte and maner of speaking so corrupted therby, that, as in old buildings, it seme disorderly and ruinous. But all as in most exquisite pictures they use to blaze and portraict not only the daintie lineaments of beautye, but also rounde about it to shadowe the rude thickets and craggy clifts, that, by the basenesse of such parts, more excellency may accrew to the principall; for oftimes we fynde ourselves, I knowe not how, singularly delighted with the shewe of such naturall rudenesse, and take great pleasure in that disorderly order. Even so doe those rough and harsh termes enlumine, and make more clearly to appeare, the brightnesse of brave and glorious words. So oftentimes a dischorde in Musick maketh a comely concordaunce: so great delight tooke the worthy Poete Alceus to behold a blemish in the joynt of a wel shaped body.[4]

Kirke first refers to the original argument in Cicero, the veneration due to age, but since it is rather implausible as a stylistic argument, he adds a new point from contemporary tradition. The idea of *concordia discors* or *discordia concors* is a commonplace of the Renaissance, and derives ultimately from classical Greek philosophy. But Kirke translates it into a visual effect, although it originally referred to the harmony of musical composition or a theory of beauty itself.[5] He stresses the idea of contrast, and its associated idea of variety, and he quotes an example from the visual arts. The Chaucerian diction of Spenser's pastoral poetry is a deliberate imitation of classical ideas of pastoral; the archaic element in the classical tradition was thought to be a convincing touch of naturalism, close to the speech of shepherds. This argument is also used in the *Epistle*, but it is important to see how an old-established idea of genre is analysed in a new way to make it seem relevant to contemporary taste. The implications of the new aesthetic view of the pastoral can be seen by reference to one of the eclogues. The 'rough and harsh termes' of Chaucerian diction are pleasing because they contrast with the sophisticated ideas in the poem, and Kirke must intend these beautiful thoughts when he mentions 'the brightnesse of brave and glorious words'. Thought is the product of art, while Chaucer's diction, to the late Renaissance writer, is the innocent natural language of the common man. We can see the effect of such ideas in this passage:

But eft, when ye count you freed from feare,
Comes the breme Winter with chamfred browes,
Full of wrinckles and frostie furrowes,
Drerily shooting his stormy darte,
Which cruddles the blood and pricks the harte:
Then is your careless corage accoied,
Your carefull heards with cold bene annoied . . .

Februarie, 42–8

Kirke notes in the *Glosse* 'a verye excellent and lively description of Winter, so as may be indifferently taken, eyther for old Age, or for Winter season.' The emblem of Winter and Old Age is a grotesque, decorative element in the poem; 'chamfred' (glossed as 'chapped') and 'breme' (glossed as 'chill, bitter') are archaic terms used inaccurately for their sounds. It is a vivid plain style image, and its generality allows the ambiguity of reference. The theme of this eclogue, the eternal debate between youth and age, is the artist's main purpose in using the pastoral genre; the archaic diction is an ornament for that theme, and has in fact little to do with any ideas of naturalism. In this way, the mannerist virtues of variety and contrast make all aspects of the genre ornamental; the artist is, in his choice of theme and diction, entirely conventional. His task is to re-create a contemporary version of the classical tradition, and he does this by making a more refined and sophisticated pattern out of it. The artistic challenge is to combine delightful commonplaces with an artful imitation of the classical genre. This is not the poetry of experience, nor does the poet wish it to be.

In his *Letter to Raleigh*, explaining his intentions in writing *The Faerie Queene* (1589–96), Spenser again takes up the idea of variety and other mannerist ideals. He describes his poem as 'a continued Allegory, or darke conceit', 'clowdily enwrapped in Allegoricall devises'. These apparent difficulties to understanding he defends as a source of delight: 'To some, I know, this Methode will seeme displeasaunt, which had rather have good discipline delivered plainly in way of precepts, or sermoned at large . . . But such, me seeme, should be satisfide with the use of these dayes, seeing all things accounted by their showes, and nothing esteemed of, that is not delightful and pleasing to commune sence.' This consensus of opinion was not what we know as 'common sense', but the common view of men of taste and discrimination. The age of criticism had already begun, and art was expected to challenge the intelligence and to require effort. Delight came from such a testing of the reader's responses, and the 'stylish style' of mannerism insisted on technical accomplishment. So difficulty and grace in its presentation were additional virtues in a writer. Again, Spenser, arranges his work in a sequence of separate tales to make a 'pleasing Analysis of all'; he decides on an unusual order for the sequence and conceals the full explanation until the end. The fact that he did not finish the work in no way alters the importance of his formal intentions which articulate a mannerist view of literature. He also chooses 'an historicall fiction, the which the most part of men delight to read, rather for variety of matter then for profite of the ensample'. These ideas may be general and rather imprecise from our point of view, but they stand for formal properties of literature and art in the sixteenth century. Spenser did not need to define his position more exactly, since he was writing for an educated and informed audience who understood the terms he used. We must now apply these ideas to the concepts of the three styles, and see how they affect local contexts in *The Faerie Queene*.

The epic genre allows all forms of style variation, while the pastoral is restricted to the archaic plain style. At the same time, the range of diction in *The Faerie Queene* is carefully restricted to give the impression of a coherent pattern in the language. This gives the poet the opportunity to make very precise variations between the three local contexts of style. In Spenser's epic we find more clearly than elsewhere the discrimination of syntax and vocabulary according to register, and the determination of choice that this implies. We can also see that there is some degree of overlap in the range of vocabulary, where the same things are being described. Spenser has a number of repeated images in the poem, and one of the most useful for our purposes is the image of hair. In the portrait of Belphoebe (II. iii. 22–31), her hair epitomises her martial valour and her maidenly virtue:

> Her yellow lockes, crisped like golden wyre,
> About her shoulders weren loosely shed,
> And, when the winde emongst them did inspyre,
> They waved like a penon wyde dispred,

> And low behinde her backe were scattered:
> And, whether art it were or heedlesse hap,
> As through the flouring forrest rash she fled,
> In her rude heares sweet flowres themselves did lap,
> And flourishing fresh leaves and blossomes did enwrap.
>
> II. iii. 30

Spenser creates a distinct shift of tone in the two halves of this stanza. The first image suggests energy and martial valour. Her hair waves like a military standard carried by an approaching force. The diction is formal and difficult: 'crisped' is used for 'curled'; 'inspyre', for 'breathe'; 'dispred', for 'spread wide'. There is a degree of abstraction and generality in this language; the natural observation has been transformed by an intellectual preconception. Belphoebe is a warrior, and her hair must be an emblem of this quality. But in the second half of the verse, this high style manner is abandoned. We find ourselves in the ornamental world of art imitating nature. This middle style implies more leisure for analysis of effect and appearance; the writer equivocates about the cause of his impressions – 'whether art it were or heedlesse hap'. He knows that it is his art that transforms the warrior into the maiden. For Belphoebe is both, and so a living example of the mannerist idea of variety and contrast. Inevitably her portrait reflects this variation. The epithets become aesthetic, not elemental: we find 'the flouring forrest', 'her rude heares' (for in the middle style world, the warrior is a ruffian, not an object of admiration), 'sweet flowres', 'flourishing fresh leaves'. In the high style passage, *'golden* wyre' and *'yellow* lockes' (formal beside 'heares') are the only epithets. The hair waving in the breeze is described in the periphrastic syntax of the high style; a moment is amplified by a non-finite clause ('crisped like golden wyre'), and co-ordinate clauses that vary the form but not the facts. In the middle style, the syntax is more evasive, because there are more qualifications and analytical connections ('whether art it were . . . ', 'As through the flouring forrest'), the noun phrases are more important, conveying more complex information. The verb phrases are more static and imply artful arrangement: 'lap' and 'enwrap' contrast strongly with 'inspyre', 'dispred', 'scattered', which are far more dynamic in their sense. Again, 'rash' implies loss of poise, instead of the unwavering purpose of the heroic will, while 'wyde' and 'low' suggest the speed and power of her movement, but nothing about her appearance in detail. The two halves of the stanza provide just that sense of delight and technical skill which the informed reader would appreciate. The patterns of language are carefully restricted to specific variations within the decorum of the subject, for it would be inappropriate to shift from high to plain style in such a topic. In the portrait of Florimell, we find a similar variation between middle and high style:

Still as she fledd her eye she backward threw,
As fearing evill that poursewd her fast;
And her faire yellow locks behind her flew,
Loosely disperst with puff of every blast:
All as a blazing starre doth farre outcast
His hearie beames, and flaming lockes dispredd,
At sight whereof the people stand aghast;
But the sage wisard telles, as he has redd,
That it importunes death and dolefull dreryhedd.   III. i. 16

The first lines are middle style; they analyse action in terms of the emotional and the moral. The atrophied metaphor, 'her eye she backward threw', is typical of the register, and lacks the formality of high style diction. The middle style is at times close to polite speech, and verges on casual slang of a respectable kind. The description of her hair is concise and unemphatic in itself, but again we may detect a middle style aesthetic intensity; 'faire yellow locks' is just that much more descriptive than 'yellow lockes' in the high style version. This is a delicate variation of register, which the overlap in terms shows. The diction is on the whole rather informal: 'poursewd' and 'flew' (a casual metaphor), 'disperst' and 'puff of every blast', do not seem emphatic or poetic. They are of course far more formal than low or plain style diction, as we shall see. But here the contrast is between these middle style lines and the high style simile that follows; the contrast between the high style image of the pennon and middle style informality may be left to the reader. Spenser works in terms of local contextual variations; the lines that follow are formal, but also emphatic. The aesthetic world of the middle style, its moral and conceptual poise, are replaced by a ferocious natural splendour that terrifies the onlooker. The punning variation of 'faire yellow locks', 'hearie beames', and 'flaming lockes' is exactly the kind of patterning the mannerist writer would seek out. These variations reinforce the simile, but the high style epithets are far from aesthetic.

They describe in a general way, to bring out the splendour and energy of the natural phenomenon. Again, 'blazing starre' is not a specific idea; the general ideas of intensity and brilliance support the variation of 'flaming lockes'. The verbs too are formal: 'outcast' is much more formal than, for example, 'go ahead of', and 'dispredd' is already established as a high style verb. The last lines of the simile provide an audience and a warning, useful for the narrative development of the canto. Once again, the sense is generalised; we do not know who 'the sage wisard' is, nor do we need to know, and his warnings are vague, if threatening. The rest of the canto will explicate the actual truth of the matter; 'the sage wisard' is an heroic fiction of the high style simile, and has no existence in the primary narrative. The syntactic variation between the two halves of the stanza is less marked than the lexical shift, but we have to remember that the syntax of noun phrase, rather than clause pattern, is often equally important to a writer as an indexical marker of register. There is greater weight and force in the rhythmical grouping of noun phrases in the high style. The middle style lines linger on the visual and ornamental detail, the high style lines emphasise the effect of this sudden apparition. Spenser combines clarity of detail with general effect, and intensifies the subjective and emotional qualities in the episode. The apparition is disquieting, enigmatic (for the reader does not know the cause of it), and also elegant and diverting. Even terror can be a source of aesthetic pleasure in the mannerist approach to art.

In the low style, the figure of Occasion is typical of Spenser's method:

> And him behynd a wicked Hag did stalke,
> In ragged robes and filthy disaray;
> Her other leg was lame, that she no'te walke,
> But on a staffe her feeble steps did stay:
> Her lockes, that loathly were and hoarie gray,
> Grew all afore, and loosely hong unrold;
> But all behinde was bald, and worne away,
> That none thereof could ever taken hold;
> And eke her face ill-favoured, full of wrinkles old.   II. iv. 4

The figure is an emblem of the proverb, 'Take Occasion by the forelock', symbolising the fickleness of Fortune, and the isolated detail of the low style makes this clear. She is also an angry, spiteful creature, as the next verse relates. Occasion's hair and her baldness are a contrasive detail of a grotesque kind, and the diction in the passage is almost entirely distinct from the language of the other contexts. Only 'lockes' and 'loosely' have occurred elsewhere. In this low style context, 'lockes' is a cognitive usage; there is no contrast with a less formal alternative, such as 'hairs', or a more poetic item, like 'golden wyre'. With 'loosely', we can compare 'loosely disperst with puff of every blast' and 'loosely hong unrold'; the contrast is between formality and idealisation beside literal description. The syntax is cumulative, and there is often no explicit connection between clauses. Infrequent parallelism is marked by its vocabulary as plain style: 'In *ragged* robes and *filthy* disaray'. There is an absence of strong rhythmical control and the whole stanza seems additive and anecdotal at clause and phrase level. There is no enigmatic truth concealed in this image; Occasion is what she seems to be, a cantankerous old woman, and 'the roote of all wrath and despight'. The worlds of heroic will and of art are quite separate, distinct areas of experience, yet they and the plain style world of moral truth inhabit the same epic universe.

In the portrait of Acrasia, Spenser introduces variety and contrast by opposing art and moral truth, for Acrasia is a destroyer in spite of her attractions. This is a complex contrastive context, where the truth is only hinted at. Acrasia appears to be described in traditional middle style terms, with a conventional emphasis on art and paradox:

Upon a bed of Roses she was layd,
As faint through heat, or dight to pleasant sin;
And was arayd, or rather disarayd,
All in a vele of silke and silver thin,
That hid no whit her alablaster skin,
But rather shewd more white, if more might bee:
More subtile web Arachne cannot spin;
Nor the fine nets, which oft we woven see
Of scorched deaw, do not in th'ayre more lightly flee.   II. xii. 77

However, the paradox of art—'And was arayd, or rather disarayd'—conceals a moral truth. The careful qualifications of the middle style are apparently also conventional: '*shewd* more white, if more might bee', '*more* subtile web Arachne cannot spin; /Nor the fine nets, which *oft* we woven see . . . '. But the alert reader will realise that already the paradox is too refined, and Spenser's emphasis is on the deceptive quality of the experience. For the reference is to a trap (the literal meaning of 'subtle web' or 'fine nets'), as the following stanza makes explicit. There, the pretence of hinting at the truth is abandoned for a sharper contrast between natural appetite and visual deception:

Her snowy brest was bare to ready spoyle
Of hungry eies, which n'ote therewith be fild;
And yet, through languour of her late sweet toyle,
Few drops, more cleare then Nectar, forth distild,
That like pure Orient perles adowne it trild;
And her faire eyes, sweet smyling in delight,
Moystened their fierie beames, with which she thrild
Fraile harts, yet quenched not; like starry light,
Which, sparckling on the silent waves, does seeme more bright.
II. xii. 78

The conceit of her sweat 'like pure Orient perles' is ironic in context, and the contrasts in the plain style are especially critical. There is a colloquial turn of phrase in 'bare to ready spoyle/Of hungry eies, which n'ote therewith be fild' (in spite of the archaism of the verb), for the metaphor is expressive and a direct borrowing from speech. Spenser has taken it further in the antithesis of the line. The closing simile is plain style too, because it refers to an observed natural phenomenon. The language is precise and accurate ('the silent waves' are the sea at night), but again the emphasis is on the deception. Starlight does seem to be brighter than it is, because of the contrast with the dark sea. But it contains no heat or strength; it is only a reflection of a weak light. The simile has no heroic enlarging effect, and the middle style conceit of the pearls is made to appear tawdry and spurious beside its accuracy and literalism. The deceptiveness of Acrasia is swept aside by such shifts of style. Sonnet 37 in the *Amoretti* (1595) is a more conventional working out of the same argument, in less visual middle style terms.

In his description of Britomart, Spenser creates variation without ironic contrast; the plain, high and middle styles are supportive and reinforcing in sequence. It is easy to argue that this merely shows the writer taking the advantage of various tendencies in the language (for that is what he does do); we have still to account for the deliberate and delicate shift of tone in these lines:

> The wicked stroke upon her helmet chaunst,
> And with the force, whiche in it selfe it bore,
> Her ventayle shard away, and thence forth glaunst
> Adowne in vaine, ne harm'd her any more.
> With that her angels face, unseene afore,
> Like to the ruddie morne appeard in sight,
> Deawed with silver drops through sweating sore,
> But somewhat redder then beseem'd aright,
> Through toylesome heate and labour of her weary fight.
>
> IV. vi. 19

The first sentence is plain style: the technical vocabulary – 'ventayle' (the visor of the helmet), the moral plainness – 'the wicked stroke', and the common diction – 'chaunst', 'shard away', 'forth glaunst' – are markers of that register. The syntax too is coordinate and expository. The metaphors are those of common usage – 'which in it selfe it bore', 'glaunst/Adowne in vaine'. Then the writer shifts into a descriptive context of the high style. The language is poetic and conventional: 'angels face' (the world of heroic virtue), 'the ruddie morne' (a poetic term, generalised and elemental). The phrase 'Deawed with silver drops' both sustains the high style simile, and adds richness of contrast; 'the ruddie morne' and the 'silver drops' are elemental parts of the natural world, a morally more acceptable association than the world of art. Spenser is less tentative in his identification than in the portrait of Acrasia; compare 'Deawed with silver drops' and 'like pure Orient perles adowne it trild'. The syntax of the earlier context implies a self-conscious, decorative effect; the sweat looks like a necklace of pearls, when it isn't anything of the kind. Nature and art are mischievously fused together, without any moral purpose to sustain them. The real analogy with nature, the starlight on the water, is diminishing and critical. In the context of moral virtue, Spenser does not need to equivocate, and he moves into the plain style of moral truth in the last lines of this later stanza. We can contrast the effect of 'through sweating sore,/But somewhat redder then beseem'd aright,/Through toylesome heate and labour of her weary fight', with the similar syntax of 'through languour of her late sweet toyle'. The vocabulary of the middle style context is aesthetic and sensuous, formal in its harmonious phrasing. The second context is unpoetic ('sweating sore', 'redder', probably with a play on the earlier 'ruddie', 'weary fight'), colloquial ('beseem'd aright', 'toylesome heate and labour'), and explicit. Britomart is a vision of heroic virtue in action, not a deceptive trap for the unwary. Spenser follows this stern reminder of her heroic sense of duty with a shift into the middle style; through a typical paradox in the register, he again draws our attention to the natural excellence of Britomart:

> And round about the same her yellow heare,
> Having through stirring loosd their wonted band,
> Like to a golden border did appeare,
> Framed in goldsmithes forge with cunning hand:
> Yet goldsmithes cunning could not understand
> To frame such subtile wire, so shinie cleare;
> For it did glister like the golden sand,
> The which Pactolus with his waters shere
> Throwes forth upon the rivage round about him nere.
>
> IV. vi. 20

By denying the validity of middle style analogies founded on art, Spenser is able to launch into a high style simile that embraces the heroic, elemental world of nature. The two parts of the stanza are linked by lexical cross references: 'golden border' – 'golden sand', 'such subtile wire, so shinie cleare' – 'waters shere'. There is too a syntactic patterning of the verse, where the middle style complexity of the first three lines matches the emphasis of the last three high style lines. But the mode in each is distinct; the weaker, stative and analytic mode of the middle style (in 'Having loosd', 'did appeare') contrasts with the stronger dynamic usage of the high style ('did glister', 'Throwes forth').

We have examined some examples of variation in both *The Shepheardes Calender* and *The Faerie Queene*. They demonstrate the mannerist techniques which Spenser has adapted to a literary context. But not all of his work has this type of variety; the sonnets are entirely middle style, and so are the *Epithalamion* and *Prothalamion*, and the *Fowre Hymnes*. *The Teares of the Muses* is an example of learned high style. *The Faerie Queene* also has many passages of traditional usage, where the particular style level is sustained without complex variation. Spenser's epic is very readable and although there are some obscurities in parts, most people are left with an overwhelming impression of clarity and exact discrimination. For Spenser is a moral-political type of writer; he creates a general context of pattern and order to advance certain beliefs which he imposes on experience. Most adverse criticism of his work is based on this aspect of his style, even when the critic appears to be attacking his ideas or his subject matter. Spenser can be dismissed as a decorative, ornamental stylist with nothing new to say. But this kind of approach is obviously wrong-headed and futile; Spenser is not a social-philosophical type of writer in our sense of the terms. His 'heroick stile' in *The Faerie Queene* is formulaic and restricted. He refines and reduces experience to useful patterns. This 'pleasing Analysis' is an intellectual device for demonstrating moral virtue; it makes no claims to describe experience for its own sake. The poem is designed to 'fashion a gentleman or noble person in vertuous and gentle discipline'. His sonnets also show the same tendency to patterning and formula for the sake of a moral argument. The middle style in which they are written has elegance and analytical power, but insufficient variation for most modern readers. William Shakespeare (1564–1616) develops a new realism in the sonnet tradition by introducing a wider range of low style imagery into the genre. He is often able to create a vivid sense of immediate experience which Spenser never attempts.

Sonnet 107 begins in a typical middle style manner:

> Not mine own fears, nor the prophetic soul
> Of the wide world dreaming on things to come . . .

The reference is philosophical and learned, as well as personal; the two ideas are brought together with an intensity that gives a rich enigmatic tone to the lines. Nothing is made too explicit, or too familiar. There is a complex harmony of sound and sense in both lines. The next two lines of the quatrain complete the sentence in a contrastive style:

> Can yet the lease of my true love control,
> Suppos'd as forfeit to a confin'd doom.[6]

These terms are unpoetic, legal imagery: 'lease', 'control', 'forfeit' and 'confin'd doom' refer to some debt that must be repaid by a certain date. They sound ironic and contrast strongly with the emotive value of the middle style: 'my true love', surely, is not a subject for commercial arrangements. Shakespeare introduces these low style legal terms to make exactly this impression. He exploits the traditional ideas of decorum in the sonnet genre for his own purpose. The poem is an ironic varied patterning of personal and public uncertainty about the future, and the connection between these two worlds is the plain style language of the law. The relief at finding that what appeared to be the end is not in fact the end is a familiar modern experience; the writer stands so closely involved with the moment of truth, as it were, that he seems to go beyond the conventional arguments of the sonnet form. In the second quatrain, he shifts into a high style form, proper to the public world of political and military prestige:

> The mortal moon hath her eclipse endur'd,
> And the sad augurs mock their own presage;
> Incertainties now crown themselves assur'd,
> And peace proclaims olives of endless age.

The grammar of the noun phrase is significantly high style: the formulaic use of the definite article, or the deletion of the article entirely (with powerful effect in the last line). The reader has the feeling that a great public crisis has passed off without the anticipated disaster. The diction is archaic and suggests ancient Rome; this is a further device for giving a sense of historical perspective in the poem. For the Roman empire was not invulnerable to time, and as the poet implies, neither is his love:

> Now with the drops of this most balmy time
> My love looks fresh;

There is irony in the superlative, since the uncertainties are so vividly recalled in the first quatrain. There everything seemed to be determined and settled with the inexorable certainty of the law itself. The writer is incredulous of the efforts of this public change of mood – 'my love *looks* fresh'. He knows this is a momentary deception: as he says in sonnet 104:

> So your sweet hue, which methinks still doth stand,
> Hath motion, and mine eye may be deceiv'd.

He returns to the middle style, with its ironic attitude to public achievement, in the final quatrain:

>   ... and Death to me subscribes,
> Since spite of him I'll live in this poor rhyme
> While he insults o'er dull and speechless tribes.

The middle style pun on 'subscribes' (both 'submits' or 'yields' and literally 'writes under', i.e. 'copies') is based on the Latin sense of the word; death can only triumph over those who leave no lasting monuments behind them. Even death, the poet argues, can only imitate him, and turn the poem into a monument to his beloved, which future ages will make live in their own speech. The writer will survive in the art of the work, and so death can only claim the illiterate and unsung as his victims. The heroic conquest is made trivial, although described in the high style. The low style grace note, 'this poor rhyme', is a way of returning the poem to the more immediate context, the address to the reader-lover:

> And thou in this shalt find thy monument
> When tyrants' crests and tombs of brass are spent.

The depth of feeling in the first quatrain becomes clearer when we realise that it is addressed directly to his mistress; the intimacy of tone in the middle style formality derives from this fact. In the final line of the poem, the writer's dismissive attitude to the heroic world of absolute certainty and assertion becomes explicitly contemptuous; 'spent' is a plain style colloquialism. The world of art is part of the real world, it is a fact of experience; the universal meaning of the high style asserts a permanence denied by experience, and so inferior to reality. The complexity of tone and the intricacy of argument in this sonnet is quite unlike the smooth formal patterning of Spenser's poetry. Shakespeare is translating an actual experience into art, in spite of the traditional topics involved; his poem retains the pressure of that experience, and the variation of tone is a response to his varying insights into self and art.

The new realism of Shakespeare's approach can be seen in many other sonnets. We can only select a few of the most interesting for analysis. Sonnet 35 is an example of Shakespeare's capacity to use even the most atrophied Petrarchan diction to new effect:

> No more be griev'd at that which thou hast done:
> Roses have thorns, and silver fountains mud,
> Clouds and eclipses stain both moon and sun,

And loathsome canker lives in sweetest bud;
All men make faults, and even I in this,
Authorizing thy trespass with compare,
My self corrupting salving thy amiss,
Excusing their sins more than their sins are:
For to thy sensual fault I bring in sense-
Thy adverse party is thy advocate-
And 'gainst myself a lawful plea commence:
Such civil war is in my love and hate
   That I an accessary needs must be
   To that sweet thief which sourly robs from me.

The first line has the formal syntax and vocabulary of the middle style; the careful marking of the adverbial by its initial placing, the specific, almost pedantic relative construction (useful for metrical harmony), and the poetic idealisation of 'griev'd' contribute to this effect. The familiarity of the personal pronoun is a middle style convention, but will be used to develop an increasingly honest directness in the argument. Shakespeare undermines the conventions of the middle style, replacing them with a tougher dialectic. The writer is attempting to speak the truth about an insight into his own motives; this at once takes the subject matter of the poem away from the conventional and safe areas of middle and low style diction. Neither are in fact adequate for the dialectical process he tries to define. These poetic images of roses, fountains, and buds, with their polite innuendoes, are quite misleading. The writer turns on himself and regrets this inevitable deception. But it is more than a deception; the writer also betrays himself by such apparently innocent authorial licence. For the honesty and truth of his relationship matters to him; it matters more than the debased language of poetic convention will allow him to state. He is forced into a middle style evasion as he recognises this fact: 'Myself corrupting salving thy amiss' – both he and his love are trapped in a process of mutual self-deception. The writer deceives both himself and his mistress by the very choice of language in the poem. 'And in our faults by lies we flatter'd be', Shakespeare concludes in sonnet 138. The middle style image of healing the wound of love is also the emblem of mutual betrayal. This is a very original and fiercely dialectic usage; so difficult is the image, that in the last quatrain Shakespeare translates it into a legal low style allegory. The legal idea of corruption is easier to grasp than the middle style conceit; the process of consciousness that is parodied in the low style is compressed in that middle style crux. Both images depend on the idea of a reciprocal relationship, where reactions on both sides at once affect the other. 'Two distincts, division none', as we find in *The Phoenix and the Turtle*. There is wit and exasperation in the conclusion; 'civil war' is a middle style pun on 'internal strife' and 'politely conducted hostilities', but in striking contrast to 'love' and 'hate', those primary low style realities. The use of antithesis across style levels is peculiarly effective here. The writer is forced, by deep compulsions, to be an 'accessary' to a crime; the final antithesis describes the crime in middle style terms. But the context sustains the low style description of process. At every turn in the argument, we have to recognise the mutual dependence of both registers on the writer's skill and controlling insight. Now it would be easy to say, from this example, that these two registers are not really there at all. That we are dealing with variations of sense which are perfectly normal and available to any writer in the sonnet tradition. The issue revolves around the meaning of 'variations of sense': the terms are distinct and antithetical in the poem. There is a poetic fiction, and an explanatory sequence of legal imagery. The first is part of sonnet tradition from Petrarch onwards; the second is clearly unpoetic, a novel introduction into the sonnet genre. They both represent precise and closely ordered sets of vocabulary. The reader and the writer both know this. There seems little doubt therefore that they are formal registers, which are naturally available to any writer, since they are part of the range of language use. One particular form happens to be restricted to poetry, the other happens to have two areas of use, one non-literary. We can understand the poem better if we regard them as registers, involving natural variations such as we might find in spoken usage. This helps us to see why the poem is so fluent and accessible to the modern reader, in spite of its artifice. It depends on natural principles of language use. Further, when we find the same types of variation elsewhere in the sonnet sequence, we are better equipped to understand them if we assume, as we should, that there is a certain element of determination in their use.

The scepticism which Shakespeare brings to the middle style is also found in his approach to the high style. At times, he can use the style without criticism, as in sonnet 7; this is an early formulaic treatment of a conventional theme. But elsewhere, as in sonnet 21, he uses the high style as a test of motivation:

> So is it not with me as with that Muse,
> Stirr'd by a painted beauty to his verse,
> Who heaven itself for ornament doth use
> And every fair with his fair doth rehearse,
> Making a couplement of proud compare
> With sun and moon, with earth and sea's rich gems,
> With April's first-born flowers and all things rare
> That heaven's air in this huge rondure hems.

The sarcasm of 'painted beauty' is obvious; the inferior writer's motive for art is false and Shakespeare parodies his style with zest. He exploits the emptiness and grandeur of the high style to establish his own sincerity and seriousness. The sestet associates truth and low style diction; the syntax is also more concise and meditative, as though what is written had been composed with more deliberation and forethought than the fluent but vacuous high style:

> Oh, let me true in love but truly write,
> And then believe me my love is as fair
> As any mother's child, though not so bright
> As those gold candles fix'd in heaven's air:
> Let them say more that like of hearsay well;
> I will not praise that purpose not to sell.

Such phrases as 'any mother's child', 'hearsay', and 'believe me' translate the poem into a colloquial context, where reality is tangible and familiar. The high style is no more than salesman's cant.

In sonnet 130 high style diction is contrasted with a reality that is more complex and paradoxical. All metaphor is an hypothesis, and if the writer withdraws his consent, it can become overtly inappropriate. In the sonnets we have been analysing, metaphor is seen as an attempt to define experience, but the writer's intentions in using it are often more complex than his language will allow. So he frequently relies on paradox and contrast to imply that greater complexity. Sonnet 130 is another example of this technique; poetic diction is transposed into the real world of the low style. This sets up a series of paradoxes which define an opposed pair of assumptions about experience. And out of these variations the truth emerges. But it cannot be stated without the two sides of the paradox:

> My mistress' eyes are nothing like the sun;
> Coral is far more red than her lips' red;
> If snow be white, why then her breasts are dun;
> If hairs be wires, black wires grow on her head:
> I have seen roses damask'd, red and white,
> But no such roses see I in her cheeks;
> And in some perfumes is there more delight
> Than in the breath that from my mistress reeks:
> I love to hear her speak, yet well I know
> That music hath a far more pleasing sound;
> I grant I never saw a goddess go-
> My mistress when she walks treads on the ground.
>   And yet by heaven I think my love as rare
>   As any she belied with false compare.

The arbitrary convention of the high style is focused by the set of negations. His mistress fails to live up to the idealised perfection of the language; indeed, she is, if this perfection is real, just the opposite. But there is a difference between language and truth. The high style conceits of 'snowy breasts' or 'golden wire' only bring out more clearly the reality. This has nothing to do with language: 'If snow be white, why then her breasts are dun;/If hairs be wires, black wires grow on her head'. These lines are absurd, and grotesque; but this, the writer implies, is what happens when you try to match up literary idealism with life. The colloquial syntax dictates the nonchalant tone of the piece: 'nothing like the sun' 'why then . . . ', 'But no such roses . . . ', 'I love to hear her speak . . . ', 'As rare As any she . . . ' (where 'she' is a colloquial substantival use of the pronoun). The language of the high style, so the writer implies, is emotionally false to reality. The real is not beautiful, and real people are seldom physically perfect. Genuine affection is not concerned with appearances. The writer's experience is more complex than these facile terms suggest. The couplet transposes high style language into low style colloquial emphasis: 'by heaven' is a common oath, not a poetic ideal, 'rare' has the high style sense of 'peerless, unique' in normal usage, but here, a contextual sense, in the witty realism of the poem, of 'unusual, special'. The form of address is the first use of 'love' in its full sense ('I love to hear her speak' has the weakened casual sense of speech). The final oxymoron, 'false compare' is a summary of the poem; 'false' can mean 'logically false', as in the poetic hypotheses of the first lines, or 'morally and emotionally false' as in the complex contextual sense which has been constructed through the poem.

In the last example, high style imagery was treated as low style literalism, and shown to be ridiculous in consequence. In some other contexts, there is a tendency to balance the varied views of reality in either register. 'A crow that flies in heaven's sweetest air' (70) is a contrast of low style realism and high style idealism; the crow is ugly, commonplace, and uncourtly, but the air is its natural habitat. In the same way, the poet argues, 'The ornament of beauty is suspect' (meaning 'suspicion'); the true mark of beauty is scandalous rumour and suspicions. This is a typical mannerist paradox, implying the truth is much more complicated than it is. Intricate, evasive statement of ideas is a mark of this approach to art. 'Bare ruin'd choirs where late the sweet birds sang' (73) contrasts the actual condition of the building in winter with its appearance in springtime. The courtly association of spring and young love is utterly conventional; the image gains depth and resonance by a further association of the 'choirs' with the bare branches of a tree. Both are low style realistic images, in contrast to the middle style convention. 'With Time's injurious hand crush'd and o'erworn' (63) combines a standard personification of the middle style ('injurious' means 'insulting') with a low style metaphor borrowed from the cloth trade. We can use imagery as a marker of register, as part of the subject matter of the style, if it is consistently related to particular areas of the language, as is the case in the sonnets. These dynamic shifts of stance focus on the real world and compare it whth the memory of the ideal, or the associations of an idealised courtly image.

A different example of this opposition across register is sonnet 94. The tone of this poem has attracted a lot of comment, but it can be most easily explained by reference to middle and low style variations. The opening lines are cryptic and pre-suppose familiarity with the courtly conventions of the middle style:

> They that have power to hurt and will do none,
> That do not do the thing they most do show,
> Who moving others are themselves as stone,
> Unmoved, cold, and to temptation slow-

The phrase 'power to hurt' is crucial, but it can only be understood as a middle style reference; compare Sidney's more explicit usage:

> His heart his wound received from my sight;
> My heart was wounded with his wounded heart;
> For as from me, on him his hurt did light,
> So still methought in me his heart did smart:
> Both equal hurt, in this change sought our bliss;
> My true love hath my heart, and I have his.

The word 'hurt' has a standard courtly sense, the wound of love received by the lover. In Shakespeare's cryptic reference to the idea we are made to consider motive, we do not remain in the middle style register with its courtly ritual of exchange and consolation. Indeed, there is no consolation, that is the point; the collocation of 'power to hurt' is antithetical in register–'power' has far too realistic a meaning for this idealised setting. The lover is dismayed by this self-absorption. The writer accuses his lover of 'niggarding' (the courtly rebuke of sonnet 1):

> They rightly do inherit heaven's graces,
> And husband nature's riches from expense;
> They are the lords and owners of their faces,
> Others but stewards of their excellence.

Those who are prepared to enter into relationships with others have in a sense already lost the complete self-possession of the unattached. They are at least aware of the need for human relations and love. They are not completely self-sufficient, but only 'stewards' of their own humanity; they do not 'own' themselves in this possessive and isolating way. The quatrain is low style, defining the emotional attitude in legal terms. 'Nature's riches' are the reserves of humanity and affection stored away unused; there is virtue in it, but it is an ironic admiration which the writer concedes. Certainly, the person addressed is 'to temptation slow' – but does the writer mean the word in a plain moral sense (his love might suppose it), or a middle style sense, meaning 'testing, trying out'? Is his love afraid to test the worth of her new admirer, or fearful of moral trespass? Both may be implied; the poem is an attempt to seduce by reasoned argument. It is a reckless piece of special pleading.

The writer appears to recast the argument in polite middle style terms, giving them their orthodox value:

> The summer's flower is to the summer sweet,
> Though to itself it only live and die;
> But if that flower with base infection meet,
> The basest weed outbraves his dignity:

The first two lines seem innocent enough, but the implications of the first quatrain, with its sexual resentment, cannot be so easily forgotten. What appears to be a platitude on its own, becomes, in the context of the argument, a way of re-stating the criticism. The 'summer's flower' has a natural beauty; in the middle style terms of the poem it represents his mistress. Beauty is fragile and corruptible, and can turn into something very nasty. The low style term 'temptation', with its covert middle style pun, is paired with the middle style term 'infection' ('staining, morally corrupting'). The writer implies that either the person he admires must trust him, or she will probably come across someone worse. The low and middle style terms of the poem interact to sustain the theme with its powerful subjective impulse. Shakespeare transfers the argument from statement to figurative analysis in the middle style; the argument itself gains depth and complexity through such contextual variation. In the final couplet, a middle style antithesis is paired with a low style statement, and the reader can feel the clash between civility and emotion in this variation:

> For sweetest things turn sourest by their deeds;
> Lilies that fester smell far worse than weeds.

Now both lines are statements, it is true, but the focus in the first is the contrast; the second is an example supporting the analysis. It is an emblem of moral corruption, but only real lilies can fester and smell. So Shakespeare exploits the different resources of the middle and low style to vary tone and expression. Both registers support the complex theme of the poem.

The parameter of situation or immediate purpose can be exploited to show the ideal world of the high or middle style in the context of the real world in the low style. Unlike the opposition across the parameter of subject matter, this is an implicit shift of stance, and easily overlooked by the modern reader. Sonnet 12 begins with an elegant variation between middle and low style: 'When I do count the clock that tells the time' (the first clause is formal, while the second is more colloquial). There seems no reason why we should attach much importance to such variety. But it becomes a significant pattern of variation as the poem develops. The second line is a high style antithesis which dominates the poem; it articulates the primary theme. 'And see the brave day sunk in hideous night' is a rich combination of poetic ideas. Generalisation and grandeur lend tragic weight to the image of shipwreck. Then the writer turns to a sequence of images which relates the high style of an ideal heroic world with the actual reality he can see around him: 'the violet *past prime*' (an emblem of all natural decay); 'sable curls o'er silver'd all with *white*' (where 'sable' and 'silver' are elemental high style terms, and 'white' is low style realism); 'lofty trees . . . *barren of leaves*' ('lofty' is high style, 'barren of leaves' figurative low style); 'Which erst from heat did canopy the herd', elegiac high style; 'summer's green all *girded up in sheaves*' (figurative low style in contrast to the elemental metaphor); 'Borne on the bier with *white and bristly beard* ' (the high style ritual of burial, or the low style gathering of the harvest, beside the low style detail of the cornstook). The variation of styles is carried on in the rest of the poem; two worlds are opposed, the one, the world of elegiac regret for transient splendours, the other, the world of practical calculation and action. 'And die as fast as they see others grow' is emphatic in its stark simplicity, beside 'Since sweets and beauties do themselves forsake'. The eloquent periphrasis of the middle style is almost a passive acceptance of a tragic truth; the low style describes without feeling. There is a further variation between the high style 'nothing 'gainst Time's scythe can make defence' and the more practical scrutiny, in the language of legal inquiry, 'Then of thy beauty do I question make'. In the low style world, something must and can be done; there is no escaping into images and eloquence. The writer accepts the reality of the human condition-'That thou among the wastes of time must go', but he also answers the elegiac tone of the high and middle style with realistic advice, get 'breed to brave him when he takes thee hence'. Death and Time can be defied by accepting their necessity, but not their power: 'breed' ('offspring') can make a real difference to the human condition. New life cancels out the inevitable death of the old, even if it cannot stop death itself. In its first occurrence, 'brave' is an heroic epithet in a high style line; in the last line 'brave' is a verb in a colloquial low style context. Thus the argument of the poem has been developed and inverted; what was tragic and splendid is turned into practical advice to marry and have children.

Sonnet 60 provides an example of all three style levels which create a triple context for the poem. It begins with a low style imitation of reality, defining a process observed by the writer:

> Like as the waves make towards the pebbled shore,
> So do our minutes hasten to their end;
> Each changing place with that which goes before
> In sequent toil all forwards do contend.

Again, we notice the variation in the last two lines, from low style statement to high style formal repetition. This is a feature of Shakespeare's style in the sonnets, but here it prepares us for the high style quatrain that follows. The heroic diction, 'sequent toil' and 'contend', anticipates the tragic inevitability of these lines:

> Nativity, once in the main of light,
> Crawls to maturity, wherewith being crown'd,
> Crooked eclipses 'gainst his glory fight,
> And Time that gave doth now his gift confound.

They describe a process like the waves falling on the shore, but the idea has been enlarged and extended to heroic dimensions. The whole pattern of human experience is implied. The last line, however, has a distinctly middle style tone. Its antithesis and personification, without any heroic associations, places it at a lower level of style. The third quatrain analyses in middle style the paradox of experience; the sublime grandeur of struggle gives way to the gradual decline of beauty under the murderous assaults of time:

> Time doth transfix the flourish set on youth,
> And delves the parallels in beauty's brow,
> Feeds on the rarities of nature's truth;
> And nothing stands but for his scythe to mow.

The refined cleverness of this passage is in marked contrast to what precedes it; the imagery is slightly obscure, enigmatic and conceptualised. We are not meant to examine too closely the individual images, but only gather the general effects of time on beauty. It is a necessary concluding analysis, but in a distinct form. The writer's purpose has been to show us a familiar image from common experience, to enlarge and amplify that image to a wider context, and then to return to a more analytical and conceited middle style conclusion. The final couplet is a conventional expression of the idea that art is more permanent than nature, and certainly the variation of style in the poem suggests that the artist can adapt nature very easily for his own purposes. This selfconscious manipulation of an idea is a virtue of mannerist art in all its forms.

The parameter of roles provides Shakespeare with some of his most delicate stylistic variation. Sonnets 71, 74 and 81 are the best examples. In each the contrasting pattern of familiarity and formality is the focus of the poem. In sonnet 71 Shakespeare even repeats the same ideas from one quatrain to the next, but in a contrastive register. He begins the poem with an eloquent middle style admonition:

> No longer mourn for me when I am dead
> Than you shall hear the surly sullen bell
> Give warning to the world that I am fled
> From this vile world with vildest worms to dwell:

The syntax has a fullness and ease of rhythm that goes with the courtly disdain for mortality. Death is seen as a social disgrace, not a physical fact: 'surly sullen bell' and 'vile world . . . vildest worms' are middle style phrases. The quatrain is an elegant periphrasis for the simple statement 'when I am dead'; that terse reference is low style, but the idea is repeated in a consolatory middle style formula. The same technique of contrast and repetition is extended into the other two quatrains. The next one is low style (although the deferential personal pronoun, 'you', places the writer's sincerity against a formal background):

> Nay, if you read this line, remember not
> The hand that writ it, for I love you so
> That I in your sweet thoughts would be forgot
> If thinking on me then should make you woe.

Some middle style diction is interwoven: 'your sweet thoughts' and 'make you woe' show a formal concern for the lover's feelings. But the low style elements in this quatrain can be best seen by contrast with the last quatrain:

> Oh if, I say, you look upon this verse
> When I perhaps compounded am with clay,
> Do not so much as my poor name rehearse,
> But let your love even with my life decay.

At once a delicate but definite contrast emerges between 'if you read this line' – 'if . . . you look upon this verse'; 'If thinking on me . . .' – 'Do not so much as my poor name rehearse'; 'I in your sweet thoughts *would be forgot*' – 'let your love even with my life decay'; between the last quatrain and the first we can also find the contrast of the familiar and factual 'when I am dead', beside the formal periphrasis, 'When I perhaps compounded am with clay'. This particular contrast is a repeated variation, which has already occurred in the first quatrain, and gives the poem its elegiac tone.

Variation across the parameter of mode is a more abstract device of emphasis in the sonnets. Shakespeare may want to focus the immediacy of experience beside the aesthetic idealisation of the middle style, as in sonnet 2:

> Then being ask'd where all thy beauty lies,
> Where all the treasure of thy lusty days,
> To say within thine own deep sunken eyes
> Were an all-eating shame, and thriftless praise.
> How much more praise deserv'd thy beauty's use
> If thou couldst answer: 'This fair child of mine
> Shall sum my count, and make my old excuse',
> Proving his beauty by succession thine!

Or he may wish to assert the self-confidence of his own character in a plain unaffected manner, as in sonnet 121:

> 'Tis better to be vile than vile esteem'd,
> When not to be receives reproach of being,
> And the just pleasure lost which is so deem'd
> Not by our feeling but by others' seeing.
> For why should others' false adulterate eyes
> Give salutation to my sportive blood!
> Or on my frailties why are frailer spies,

Which in their wills count bad what I think good?
No: I am that I am, and they that level
At my abuses reckon up their own;
I may be straight though they themselves be bevel;
By their rank thoughts my deeds must not be shown,-
Unless this general evil they maintain:
All men are bad and in their badness reign.

The sestet is typical low style syntax: additive, exemplifying, and emphatic in its phrasing and colloquial diction. The subtle paradoxes of the octet, with their subjective insight, are part of the cynicism of the middle style world. The tone of the two parts is contrastive and forced, unlike the elegant and sincere variation of sonnet 71. There is a contrast too between the clever morphological and phrase structure parallelism of the first seven lines, and the blunt parallels at clause level in the sestet. 'Which in their wills count bad what I think good?' is a deliberate deviation from the middle style of the octet; it conceals a pun on the author's name, and has a low style simplicity of diction.

3 Donne and Dryden

The *Dialectique* of Pierre de la Ramée, published in Paris (1555), had a considerable influence on literary style in the sixteenth and seventeenth centuries.[1] Something of this influence has been noticed in the scepticism of Spenser and Shakespeare towards the high and middle styles. But to understand more exactly the changes brought about by Ramistic logic, we have to consider first the earlier view that Aristotle took of the relation between language and logic.[2] This view had been accepted throughout classical antiquity and the medieval period, and tended to support the rhetorical tradition of style as advanced by Cicero and Quintilian. Aristotle of course wrote at a time when the tradition of the three styles had not been developed in its fullest form. He took a broad view of the relations between language and logic; while he saw that language and reasoning were fundamental properties of rhetoric, he made certain general distinctions between different kinds of reasoning or 'logic'. There was the 'logic' of science (demonstrative logic), used in formal disputations, where inductive and deductive syllogisms could be used to test the truth of propositions. Science, for Aristotle, described things necessarily true. There was also the 'logic' or reasoning of opinion, called dialectic; matters discussed in this context were probably true, but could not be demonstrated with certainty. In rhetoric, Aristotle considered there was another kind of 'logic'; this form of reasoning was based on probabilities, and directed towards persuasion. It allowed implicitly for idealised literary registers such as the persuasive middle style and the emphatic high style, where the factual or the real were not directly at issue. A fourth kind of reasoning was to be found in poetry. Poetry, according to Aristotle, had a distinct pedagogic function. In his view, it ought to go beyond the particular example of the real world to an ideal version of experience that conveyed universal moral truths. This also allowed for idealised registers of literary language; moral truth can be seen more clearly in a selection from experiential reality. Poetry was not in these terms a realistic art in any modern sense; it was an example of the possible, not the probable, although governed by probability or necessity in a complex way. Aristotle clearly held a wide and loose definition of 'logic'. He made a number of empirical observations about its role in various contexts, and drew attention to the variety of its functions. His comments are scattered throughout his work, and he did not gather them together for consideration in one place. He seemed to imply a complex range of distinctions that resisted further analysis. This arose from the nature of the problem he was dealing with. These distinctions between different kinds of logic were an attempt to clarify the complex relationship between language, reasoning and truth. Now the relation between reasoning and truth (a descriptive function of language) is no simple matter. It depends in many cases on the point of view of the reporter; the context, whether literary, scientific or political, will always determine the kind of truth advanced. However, could one kind of reasoning be in fact distinguished from another? Weren't they all, in the final analysis, the same kind of reasoning, even if they put forward different kinds of truth? Pierre de la Ramée realised this, and argued that the operations of the intellect were all of one character. The same faculty of reason was at work in all contexts in one way or another. So these distinctions seemed unnecessary. Aristotle's inquiry was far too subtle and tentative to be tolerated in an age of political and religious controversy. There was a general demand for accessible thought and certainty rather than knowledge. Pierre de la Ramée and his followers simplified and distorted Aristotle's views in the interests of a superficial clarity. Moreover, Aristotle's ideas had long before become the property of obscurantist and pedantic minds, and his genius had been long lost sight of in degenerate medieval logics. An attack on Aristotle appeared to be an attack on the old learning, and a discovery of new truths about man's mind. Yet although in a sense all this was the case, a new approach to literary language emerged from the controversy. The idealism of Aristotle's view of poetry and literature in general was replaced by a new realism. The importance of the plain or low style in the seventeenth century owes a great deal to Ramistic logic.

If the intellect operated in the same way in all contexts, then the most formal logical context could be said to be the primary basis for all language use. All 'logic' was demonstrative logic. This highly normative view of language restricted all meaning to its conceptual skeleton. A poetic image in the high or middle style was nothing more, according to Ramistic logic, than a literal statement in disguise. The mind responded to images, so it was argued, by analysing the 'cryptic argument' concealed in the image. This 'cryptic argument' was the literal sense in the context. This was an obvious simplification of associative meaning in poetry; inevitably, in spite of the theory, such areas of meaning could not be kept out of the local context of the image. Yet images could be made to depend more on the conceptual relationship than on an associative sense; there could be a tendency to avoid figurative language that contained no argument about the main topic. Decoration became suspect, and was regarded, as we have seen in Shakespeare and Spenser, as an evasion of the real truth, and perhaps a spurious argument in disguise. Otherwise, what need was there for such imagery in place of direct statement? Rhetoric began to take on its modern meaning of deception. But how could the mind know what was the truth, because even literal statements can be false? Pierre de la Ramée did not worry too much about such difficult questions; the natural reasoning powers of the mind, applied automatically to the issue at stake, would find out the truth without difficulty. The inner light of 'natural reason' would give the essential guidance required. Once the mind had understood the meaning of an image (i.e. the literal sense in the context), the truth or falseness was at once apparent. Truth was not a matter for reasoned argument; it was an instinctive property of the mind's reasoning faculty. There was also only one kind of truth, in the same way that there was one kind of reasoning. The complex relation between language and reality did not raise difficulties, because it was ignored. A syllogism only presented the argument more clearly; it did not test the truth of statements in any way. This was a complete caricature of Aristotle's intention. In fact, Ramistic logic was a method of organising persuasive arguments; it was not an instrument of inquiry into the truth. Ramistic 'dialectic' was a parody of Aristotle's 'logic of demonstration', not his 'logic' of opinion or rhetoric (which in any case had no overt structure). Some of the original material in Aristotle's logic was preserved, such as the places of logical invention for argument, from cause, effect and so on. But all in the service of persuasive argument, not for the discovery of truth. The idealistic distortion of Aristotle's view of poetry was replaced by a new concern for conceptual clarity in image, and formal structure in argument. Pierre de la Ramée had also published his work in French instead of Latin, the contemporary language of scholarship, and had emphasised the importance of the vernacular as a fit vehicle for learning. All men, he argued, practise the exercise of reason in their daily lives; the logician only formalises the usage. His examples of logical places of argument and syllogisms are drawn from vernacular translations of classical poetry, and again show his literal acceptance of the term 'natural logic'. All language has a conceptual base, so any examples may be interpreted as examples of reasoning. But the literary interests of Ramistic logicians are crucial to an understanding of their main purpose; they intended to influence the style of all serious discourse in their time, and the predominant style of such discourse was literary. The vernacular embodied a new intellectual seriousness, which was reflected in seventeenth-century writers especially. In this period the plain style is used with more seriousness than in medieval and early Renaissance writing. There is a new conceptual complexity in literary language, and all three styles undergo an enriching transformation.

John Donne (1572–1631) goes beyond the paradoxical scepticism of Shakespeare's sonnets; he treats the middle style as a strategy in the construction of complex plain style discourses. The middle style becomes the point of reference for a more subjective inquiry into truth. Ramistic logic, with its intuitive view of 'natural reason', makes possible such an approach to experience. If all can exercise reason at will, each person's insights are quite likely to be as valid and true as anyone else's. The inherited traditional images of the middle style were in any case no substitute for intuitive truths. But intuitions had to work on something; if they were entirely arbitrary, language became conceited and precious, in a plain style imitation of the artificial middle style. Some of Donne's poetry has traces of this tendency. The images are conceptually original, but do not correspond to any existential reality which might justify them. The subjective view must, to be convincing, show some genuine insight into reality. It is a consequence of the search for simple truths that Ramistic logic makes no clear distinction between different kinds of meaning, but reduces all meaning to one kind. Implicitly, all meaning is essential. Ramistic logic offers no distinctions of meaning to correspond with the categories of Aristotle. There is by the same token no attempt to distinguish between concepts and things in Ramistic logic.[3] This also allows the writer a great deal of freedom to make any associations of ideas and things that he wishes. The famous 'method' of Ramistic logic was an arbitrary and intuitive division of topics into pairings (or 'dichotomies'), or sometimes into triplets ('trichotomies') which were thought to share some generic category, itself entirely a creation of the writer. The idea of divisions and subdivisions was supposed to represent the actual structure of human thought in the brain; it was 'natural logic' in its 'natural pattern'. But it only arranged arguments in an apparently coherent order; no one could learn how to tell the truth about experience from such a method. This view of meaning as an intuitive aspect of reason, and its consequences in the ordering of discourses into arbitrary methods, encouraged writers like Donne to enlarge the received topics of the middle style with new material from the plain style. The rhetorical posture of distaste for the middle style and its values which we found in Spenser and Shakespeare, has become an open disagreement.

An example of this development is *The Good Morrow*:

> I wonder by my troth, what thou, and I
> Did, till we lov'd? were we not wean'd till then?
> But suck'd on countrey pleasures, childishly?
> Or snorted we in the seaven sleepers den?
> T'was so; But this, all pleasures fancies bee.
> If ever any beauty I did see,
> Which I desir'd, and got, t'was but a dreame of thee.
>
> And now good morrow to our waking soules,
> Which watch not one another out of feare;
> For love, all love of other sights controules,
> And makes one little roome, an every where.
> Let sea-discoverers to new worlds have gone,
> Let Maps to other, worlds on worlds have showne,
> Let us possesse one world, each hath one, and is one.
>
> My face in thine eye, thine in mine appeares,
> And true plain hearts doe in the faces rest,
> Where can we finde two better hemispheares
> Without sharpe North, without declining West?
> What ever dyes, was not mixt equally;
> If our two loves be one, or, thou and I
> Love so alike, that none doe slacken, none can die.[4]

The first verse is plain style. The language is close to speech in its rhythm and casual imagery. What appears to be a learned reference to the seven Christian youths who concealed themselves in a cave during a time of persecution, is in fact a commonplace image from a popular legend; the youths emerged many years later to find that Christianity had become the state religion. Perhaps Donne implies that his discovery of love's conquest of his life is equally startling, and took place in the same way without his knowledge. His mistress too is surprised by her new-found faith. The immaturity of earlier experience is at first conveyed through actions and not defined in concepts. Its unreflecting grossness is increased by this device. The use of questions for statement adds dramatic immediacy to the lines, as though the poet were thinking aloud. The last three lines of the verse do not analyse, but define ironically a new understanding of earlier experience. The arbitrary generic distinctions in these lines are typical of Ramistic logic; they are an intuitive reappraisal of experience which in this case happens to assert an existential truth. Exposition in the plain style becomes logical entailment: since beauty cannot exist apart from the new mistress, it must have been a dream of her in the past. Previous loves were not real, only now is real. The second verse is analytic and abstract. The topic of lovers looking at each other is a traditional middle style conceit; it forms the basis for the last two verses. But Donne develops and expands the formula. The casual additive sequence of the first verse is replaced by a formal definition of emotional and intellectual order. Donne transforms the middle style conceit, with its trivial content, into a statement about the intellectual significance of emotional experience. Only animals watch each other out of fear (there are other irrational kinds of experience, he says, which we lovers do not share); love brings order and meaning to the lover's experience. He understands his own humanity in all its rational commitment. And he shares this knowledge with his mistress. Love controls and satisfies the anarchic natural instincts. These ideas are presented in an enigmatic form – 'out of feare' and 'love of other sights' are middle style in their decorum. There is also the fear of unfaithfulness and disloyalty which love removes. The completeness of true affection is another discovery for the lovers. Donne takes this up in 'one little roome, an every where'; he uses a plain style spatial paradox for an emotional truth. The vocabulary is unpoetic and the syntax of this phrase is close to speech; it has the casual intensity of a genuine insight. The robust syntactic parallelism of the closing lines in this verse is also plain style; the writer assumes a nonchalant, dismissive tone. The lines have emphasis of a natural kind, while remaining loose and additive; in fact, they are a characteristic division of topic into 'triplets' or 'trichotomies' in Ramistic logic. There are three different kinds of worlds: the 'new worlds' of those who travel and explore uncharted seas, the worlds which maps represent as an image of the real world, and the two worlds of the lovers, which can become one. Again, the 'real' world is the world of love, not those other worlds which have little interest for the lovers. They have a world in themselves; those other worlds are remote possibilities or mere images. They are not real, and cannot be possessed. The refusal to distinguish between concepts and things in Ramistic logic gives power and depth to these insights. The language operates at a level where rational distinctions of meaning are quite useless and dry out the essential truths. But in the last verse Donne returns to the middle style formula and has some trouble working it out in literal terms. The exposition is inevitably plain style, and not very explicit, although in Ramistic logic an image had a definite literal meaning that could be set out to explain it. A heart, which is round, is 'projected' like a map in a 'flattened' form ('true plain hearts') into the face reflected in the lover's eye. Equally, there is no guile in the lover's heart, and his expression reveals his true feelings. The reflecting eye makes the face round like the hemispheres of a globe. This 'reflection' provokes further thought. This is not a globe, but a 'heart-face', so it does not have literal points of the compass. Each face and heart appears in the other's eye, so the two hemispheres make one world. Donne moves first to the concept (or image) of the map as 'face-heart', then away from it to the concept of the 'heart', their mutual love. He exploits the idea of a map as the projection of the real world, to give new meaning to a tired formula of the middle style – 'My face in thine eye, thine in mine appeares'. These 'hemispheres' may however have emotional compass points. Perhaps 'sharpe North' and 'declining West' implicitly suggest this, although the connection in the thought is not clear. But the last lines return to the idea of change and decay as natural processes, and their cause. The analogy with emotional experience is made clear in the conclusion. Love dies when the necessary tension or responsiveness between the lovers decays. The terms of this philosophical analogy are physical, but stand for a concept. Again, the failure to distinguish meanings is an advantage for the writer. Such concrete verbs as 'mixt', 'slacken' and the repeated 'die' are markers of the plain style. The simple expository syntax is also part of the register. A scientific truth, as it was known then, is conveyed in simple non-technical language. Love, like all things in the world, obeys the natural laws of existence. Again, 'natural logic' has led to this conclusion; the poet has reasoned his way through the imagery of the middle style to a plain style technical fact of existence. He has found out the meaning of his experience of love. The expository parallelism echoes the previous verse; the method in this discourse is essentially to create generic analogies for emotional experience, and place them beside the experience itself. Each verse moves from the particular moment of mutual recognition, through more general topics, back to the particular truths of mutual experience. Donne uses an inductive method of argument to discover truth; but these truths are not open to question or dissent. They either convince on sight or can be dismissed as implausible. There is no appeal to reasonableness; the sheer energy of the demonstration is meant to convince.

John Dryden (1631–1700) begins writing in the speculative Ramistic style, but modifies this in his later work. Yet he remains throughout his poetry indebted to the analogical acuteness which Ramism encouraged. In his later work, an illusory belief in order and stability discourages subjective intuitions. 'Natural reason' is interpreted as a common basis for inquiry and consensus amongst men of 'good sense' and acceptable political opinions. Individualism was often the result of unstable judgement and could lead to treason, as Dryden suggests in *Absalom and Achitophel*. Reason becomes in his work a social and political concept, and the revolutionary idealism of Donne's approach disappears. For Donne, natural reason makes the world meaningful by struggle and effort of the will, resolving apparent contradictions in paradoxical truths; for Dryden, natural reason translates received opinion into acceptable form. However, in his first published work, Ramistic logical invention is still the dominant influence. *Upon the Death of Lord Hastings* (1649) is a formal exercise in the conventional genre of the elegy. The subjective analogies of Donne's lyric are based on existential truths; here Dryden relies on the internal relations of sense within the concepts – he is not writing out of any personal experience. His subject is the poetic art itself. The poem is notorious for the description of the smallpox that killed Hastings, but few modern critics have bothered to consider the artistic decorum of this disagreeable passage:

Was there no milder way but the Small Pox,
The very Filth'ness of *Pandora's* Box?
So many Spots, like *naeves*, our Venus soil?
One Jewel set off with so many a Foil?
Blisters with pride swell'd; which th'row's flesh did sprout
Like Rose-buds, stuck i'th' Lily-skin about.
Each little Pimple had a Tear in it,
To wail the fault its rising did commit:
Who, Rebel-like, with their own Lord at strife,
Thus made an Insurrection 'gainst his Life.
Or were these Gems sent to adorn his Skin,
The Cab'net of a richer Soul within?
No Comet need foretel his Change drew on,
Whose Corps might seem a *Constellation*.   53–66[5]

The passage divides into a series of distinctive registers. The middle style of the love lyric (53–8); the plain style of explicit medical detail (59–62); the middle style of courtly praise (63–6). The passage is elegantly varied in image, and controlled by inventive argument. The smallpox is first conceived as an erotic ornament (Hastings has already been likened to Ganymede, who was snatched from earth in his youth to be Zeus's cup-bearer); the spots are *naeves*, moles which add to his beauty, as they add to Venus's charms. They are a foil to the jewel of his body. They swell with pride at carrying out such a task; they are rose-buds on lily skin. To the modern reader all this is repulsive and unnatural. But it is an example of natural reason at work. The poet shows his art in contriving these analogies; he makes artful what was hideous fact. The sequence of images is an impersonal argument about the ideal of beauty; the ugliness of disease, Dryden argues, becomes its opposite, beauty, in such a context. As he says in an earlier line, 'Is *Death* (Sin's wages) Grace's now?' The poem argues out this statement in detail. Beauty transforms even the disease that brings death into something beautiful. The lines are a ghastly consolation for lost youth; but the horror is transmuted by art. The modern reader clings stubbornly to his distaste for all this; we remain unconvinced by displays of lucid argument. We don't think it carries conviction; but the exactness of the analogy is impressive. Dryden has more faith in art, and the artist's authority, than we do. He also believes, like Donne, in the intuitive rightness of these analogies; he expects the reader to see they are right, *because* they can be seen to have a conceptual relation with the main topic. The poem is meant to persuade by such clear linking, even if it isn't true. Art is not concerned with normal ideas of truth; rather, the artist's interpretation of experience is the final authority. He makes truth, he doesn't find it already made for him. The unifying element is his 'natural logic', however arbitrary it seems today. In the plain style passage, Dryden tries to blend the unpleasant detail of medical fact with the social status of the youth. Again, the modern reader rejects this artifice; but he cannot deny that it shows some skill in contrivance. We no longer think much of such skill if it does not reveal something new about both sides of the analogy. We expect truth as well as art; the anachronism of this has already been pointed out. The pun on 'rising' translates the medical image into the political image of rebellion. The disease has destroyed a peer of the realm. From here the poet can consider his worth as a Christian gentleman; the spots are 'gems' for a box containing sacred reliques. Or the disease is a classical transformation into the eternal beauty of stars, like some youth beloved of the gods. The single topic of the illness has yielded a range of elegant arguments. None of them is true, in the sense that Donne's poem conveys truth. They are still art of a kind. Their elegance consists in their exact reasonableness as art, and the way they translate commonplace detail into formal pattern in a variety of styles. While any idealistic distortion seemed futile to a Ramist, because it was false to natural reason and the way it worked, an image could be justified in the middle style if its *argument* had some relevance to the main topic. We noticed the dominance of conceptual relations in this passage; the images are traditional middle style, only their application is original. But Dryden shows their relevance, and in doing so demonstrates his art. Although smallpox killed the young lord, his own beauty turned even disease into an additional grace. And the symptoms of the disease also lament his death.

In the first example of Ramistic logic in Donne's poem, the subject contained some existential truth; in Dryden's poem, the conceptual invention has no existential base. A disease is not a person, and cannot have feelings, nor is it an aid to beauty. This 'category error' is startling but not insightful or persuasive. Dryden's art has no relation to experience; it is a purely formal exercise in paradox. The Ramistic writer is always in danger of arbitrary analogies that suggest more or less than he intended. Dryden abandons this approach to art in his later work; the firm logical coherence of image remains. He achieves clarity and order within a more secure context of meaning. The conventionality of his satire is founded on public opinion, and his own judgement is usually at the service of the accepted view. Donne for his part continues to develop subjective insights in his later work, although arbitrary analogy is controlled in the religious poems by many traditional images. Donne remains most effective in the plain style, as we would expect of a Ramistic writer, and some of his *Holy Sonnets* have unexpected and powerful images of his own invention in that style. At the same time, some middle style images develop into a new complexity in his work. Dryden, because he discards the subjective assumptions of Ramism, is free to write in the baroque as well as the neo-classical high style; his plain style in the later work is closer to the classical tradition of caricature than Donne's version of the register.

In *Lovers Infinitenesse* Donne interprets the middle style emblems of love as commercial tokens in the stock exchange. This plain style development of traditional images creates a multiple context work. Irony and cynicism become dominant tones in the work; nevertheless, the poem ends with a statement of genuine affection. Donne reasons his way out of cynicism into a shrewder truth about human relationships; the middle style is inadequate because it does not correspond to reality. 'Natural logic' is a more secure guide to the truth, however paradoxical. The poem begins in an elegant analytical mode of the middle style, but this tone rapidly becomes more cynical as the commercial imagery from the plain style intrudes into the discourse:

> If yet I have not all thy love,
> Deare, I shall never have it all,
> I cannot breath one other sigh, to move;
> Nor can intreat one other teare to fall.
> And all my treasure, which should purchase thee,
> Sighs, teares, and oathes, and letters I have spent,
> Yet no more can be due to mee,
> Then at the bargaine made was ment,
> If then thy gift of love were partiall,
> That some to mee, some should to others fall,
> Deare, I shall never have Thee All.

Elegant formality in the opening periphrasis lasts for the first four lines; the diction is also formal, and courteous to the person addressed. The parallelism of syntax in phrase and clause imposes a gracious decorum on the language. But the poet is describing a moment of emotional exhaustion in the relationship. The middle style terms, 'Sighs, teares, and oathes, and letters . . . ' are focused by contrast with a group of commercial or legal terms, 'purchase', 'spent', 'due to mee', 'bargaine', 'gift of love', 'partiall', 'fall'. Donne has applied the techniques of reasoned analysis to the traditional images, and shown up the competitive reality behind the courtly emblems. The subjective intuitions of Ramistic logic lead him to reveal his basic insecurity in the affair. His love is too expensive for him in terms of emotional cost; perhaps she has as well limited her commitment to him, while he has exhausted his own resources. 'Infinitenesse' takes on associations of infidelity. The change from 'Deare, I shall never have it all' to 'Deare, I shall never have Thee All', is a shift from courtly middle style to a more suggestive plain style usage. His mistress's intentions are ambiguous – what was meant 'at the bargaine', he wonders? A courtly lover should never doubt his mistress's integrity like this. But the realism of the discourse derives from the probing rationality of the speaker; Donne assumes, like all Ramistic writers, that his natural reason can discover the truth about experience by direct inquiry. The commercial and legal analogy still has currency today, and the modern reader is under less pressure to recognise the artifice of these lines. Donne's insights are also more truthful to experience than Dryden's analogies; Ramistic logic can deny experience, and sometimes escape from truth in paradox, but Dryden's images deny an existential fact, and no paradox can overturn that. Again, a disease is something we can see the effects of, but a human relationship is in some ways an abstraction, a set of potentialities that are constantly re-affirmed if they are to survive. So metaphor is easier to accept in the second example; there is no natural language to describe relationships.

In the second verse, Donne considers the temporal aspects of love. The plain style context of the real world, in which love must grow or fade, and be exposed to tests of loyalty and endurance, is remote from the middle style courtliness of traditional images. There is a sharp clash of tone in this verse between these two registers:

> Or if then thou gavest mee all,
> All was but All, which thou hadst then,

> But if in thy heart, since, there be or shall,
> New love created bee, by other men,
> Which have their stocks intire, and can in teares,
> In sighs, in oathes, and letters outbid mee,
> This new love may beget new feares,
> For, this love was not vowed by thee.
> And yet it was, thy gift being generall,
> The ground, thy heart is mine, what ever shall
>   Grow there, deare, I should have it all.

The commercial imagery of the first verse is sustained in terms borrowed from the business world; 'stocks intire', 'outbid', as well as legal terms, 'gift', 'generall' (contrasting with 'partiall' before), 'ground'. Love's infiniteness is defined in the sense of a property relation, for if the lover has been given his mistress's heart, whatever affection grows there should be his. Again, Donne extends and develops an atrophied middle style metaphor in logical and realistic terms; the abstraction is severe and spurious, in fact. The cause of this 'new love' is not the lover, nor is the lover who speaks its object. This aspect Donne does not pursue, nor could he. The claim is ironic and indefensible; the legal argument has no relevance to the existential truth of love (can love by definition be divided and separated so easily?), although it tells us about sexual jealousy. The image is deliberately faulty, so that the final verse unfolds the true relationship:

> Yet I would not have all yet,
> Hee that hath all can have no more,
> And since my love doth every day admit
> New growth, thou shouldst have new rewards in store;
> Thou canst not every day give me thy heart,
> If thou canst give it, then thou never gavest it:
> Loves riddles are, that though thy heart depart,
> It stayes at home, and thou with losing savest it:
> But wee will have a way more liberall,
> Then changing hearts, to joyne them, so wee shall
>   Be one, and one anothers All.

The poem, it now emerges, is developed around the conflicting ideas of 'partiall' and 'generall' gifts of love. But neither of these opposites are adequate definitions of a process; they are suited only to describe a legal relationship that is static and unique. A true 'liberall' gift of love, which allows for 'new growth' and 'new rewards' is not a gift in the legal sense at all; rather, it is an exchange of gifts which involves no loss to either party. The paradox is presented in terms of a contradiction, but the existential truth saves it from meaninglessness. The final image is fairly conventional and uninteresting to the modern reader, but even here the logical acuteness of Ramistic argument can be seen. The lovers are joined together in a deeper union than the conventional middle style image of exchanging hearts can suggest; through a plain style image Donne states the more complex truth. The lovers are 'one' and 'all' at the same time, for they are 'one anothers All'. The essential mutuality of love is conveyed by colloquial grammar and plain diction. The structure of the poem gives that simple language a definite conceptual force. The propositional forms of Ramistic logic dominate each verse; the poem is an argument, and at times an analysis, in plain and middle style. But the middle style analysis is always extended by a plain style argument; 'natural logic' controls the imagery, and Donne is always in command of his material, never accepting it at face value.

Donne shows himself to be a social-philosophical poet in our definition; the truths he deals with so accurately cannot be stated in simple or direct terms. Nor is the traditional imagery of love acceptable as a true account of his insights into its nature. Dryden, on the other hand, is a moral-political writer; he avoids the subjective pursuit of reason and relies on conventional responses to experience. These responses are controlled by a keen sense of relevance, which can at times seem artificial and forced. His skill is in selection and manipulation of images for new argument. He is more interested in form than content. His portrait of Achitophel is characteristic of his techniques in his later work:

> Of these the false *Achitophel* was first:
> A Name to all succeeding Ages Curst.
> For close Designs, and crooked Counsels fit;
> Sagacious, Bold, and Turbulent of wit:
> Restless, unfixt in Principles and Place;
> In Power unpleas'd, impatient of Disgrace.
> A fiery Soul, which working out its way,
> Fretted the Pigmy Body to decay:
> And o'r inform'd the Tenement of Clay.

> A daring Pilot in extremity;
> Pleas'd with the Danger, when the Waves went high
> He sought the Storms; but for a Calm unfit,
> Would Steer too nigh the Sands, to boast his Wit.
> Great Wits are sure to Madness near ally'd;
> And thin Partitions do their Bounds divide. 150-64

Dryden exploits the formal order of the heroic couplet for contrastive effects in all three styles. The first line appears in syntax to be emphatic and laudatory, yet the plain style epithet 'false' destroys the illusion of the high style. The paradox of ability and self-destruction combined is the chief argument of the passage. The adjectival phrase in l. 151 is inverted for high style emphasis, but the plain style 'curst' is the opposite of the expected sense. Dryden uses a moralised diction to devalue high style implications. There is little overt comment; natural reason carries its own insinuations in this method of argument. If the reader can understand the conventions, he must realise what Dryden is saying. In ll. 152-5, the same device of contrast occurs. 'Designs' and 'Counsels' are positive terms, proper to rational discourse and public affairs. But 'close' and 'crooked' destroy such possible meanings, while 'fit' is sarcastic in context. The high style of public life becomes translated into the cunning of a dangerous man out to ruin the state for no real reason. Achitophel is 'sagacious' and 'bold', as a wise counsellor of state should be, but there is a fundamental instability in his mind. His judgement cannot rest on determinate principles or settled purposes. Dryden suggests his irrationality by contrasting the belief in power and the stoicism of the wise politician with the whimsical and petulant reactions of Achitophel: 'In Power unpleas'd, impatient of Disgrace'. The contradictions are stated by placing contrary adjuncts with each noun; Ramistic logic exploits the literal implications of meaning within the middle style of court politics. 'Power' and 'Disgrace' have specific and precise senses that Achitophel attempts to ignore by his attitude. In ll. 156-8 the plain style is a brutal reference to Shaftesbury's small person; diminishing by physical caricature is one of Dryden's favourite devices. But we should notice how it is reinforced by registerial variation: 'a fiery soul' has heroic, high style associations, while 'Pigmy Body' and 'Tenement of Clay' are plain style metaphors. The 'Pigmy Body' and 'Great Wits' is another satirical thrust, a typical Ramistic partition or dichotomy of opposites. In l. 159 we are led to think

Dryden will pay some conventional tribute and lose the satiric wit of earlier lines. But 'daring' turns out to have irrational implications. This 'pilot' is out to save the ship of state by the most dangerous tactics, and *seeks* the storms, or the sandbanks, if there are none. His personal whims come before the safety of the state, and he perverts statecraft 'to boast his Wit'. Again, echoes of the earlier lines occur; 'pleas'd with the Danger', 'for a Calm unfit' contrast with the opposite senses, 'In Power *unpleas'd*', 'For close Designs, and crooked Counsels *fit*'. But assertion by contrary is the common pattern of these contradictions; Achitophel is a study of elemental unreason in an extreme form. The final couplet, the most famous in the whole of Dryden's work, is indeed particularly damaging if read correctly. Dryden defines 'wit' by reference to its contrary, 'madness'. For 'wit' is an extreme form of reason that verges on madness in some cases. Dryden never denies that there is some show of reason in Achitophel's actions, but it is so paradoxical, he suggests, that it is almost in league with madness of some kind. A comforting thought for the enemies of Shaftesbury. The high style metaphor of state alliances, and the understandings between neighbouring powers, is translated into a description of the relation between faculties of the mind. By a pun on 'partition', meaning both territorial boundaries and the logical division of a *whole* into its constituent parts, Dryden manages to suggest the interdependence of this kind of wit and madness. And the partition is 'thin', that is 'slight, insubstantial'. Who would be able to tell when madness had taken over in this display of paradoxical 'wit'? Dryden exploits the equality of things and concepts in Ramistic logic to make damaging innuendoes. But the passage is remarkable for its formal control of argument and proposition, its clear grasp of contradiction and paradox as a basic device in the discourse; Dryden deals with no complex and irreducible experience, but with conventional responses to unreason and instability. Each image is entirely conventional, but the cumulative relevance is devastating. The experience is defined by contrast with a clear moral and political norm; there is no exploratory search for the truth as in Donne. The truth is known and part of the common ground between reader and writer.

We can now see more clearly the general principles of variation between the social-philosophical and the moral-political writer. In all cases so far in this book, we have found that the multiple context is typical of the former, while the latter uses contrastive or single contexts. Why should this be so? It follows from the approach each type of writer has to the problem of meaning. The social-philosophical writer is more exploratory, more subjective in his approach; the established meanings of words in natural language use are of course given. He does not write a 'private' language of utterly unintelligible meanings; but he does tend to use meaning in an oblique and ironic way. The subjective assessment of experience implies a refusal to accept established images at their face value; there is a search for a more complex and personal response. The multiple context provides the kind of graded variation that can supply shades of meaning, where clear statement may be too simple for the comment a writer wants to make. The moral-political writer needs clarity and contrast to make his points; he must dispel the illusion that there are levels of meaning between those he has chosen to exploit. He has a particular view to advance which must command understanding and assent; it must not seem a view put forward by a mere individual, but an opinion expressed by a spokesman for a group or class. The subjective and exploratory use of meaning must therefore be suppressed; conventional images are to be expected, for they are already common currency. How he uses them must also be unmistakeable. No one must be allowed to read the portrait of Achitophel and go away with the idea that Shaftesbury was an original genius, whose pragmatism might have succeeded if it had been timed right. Such qualifying and speculative reasoning has no part in the moral-political outlook. The writer must know what he wants to do, be unequivocal about its rightness, and demonstrate his lucid control of the means to the end. This kind of writing is much closer to propaganda than many critics will admit. The writer has designs on his audience; he wants them to share his opinion and final judgement. He does not show them how his view is formed, that would be too subjective and intrusive of his own thought. He shows the audience instead a brilliant sequence of conclusions which may be quite untrue; they must however carry conviction and authority. The social-philosophical writer exploits the actual indeterminacy of meaning in natural language use (within certain fairly obvious distinctions of sense); the moral-political writer uses language as though each word had a precise and unequivocal sense in all contexts.

Another example of variation in Donne and Dryden is worth considering. In *The Apparition*, Donne translates the middle style formulas into a dramatic episode in the plain style:

When by thy scorne, O murdresse I am dead,
And that thou thinkst thee free
From all solicitation from mee,
Then shall my ghost come to thy bed,
And thee, fain'd vestall, in worse armes shall see;
Then thy sicke taper will begin to winke,
And he, whose thou art then, being tyr'd before,
Will, if thou stirre, or pinch to wake him, thinke
  Thou call'st for more,
And in false sleepe will from thee shrinke,
And then poore Aspen wretch, neglected thou
Bath'd in a cold quicksilver sweat wilt lye
  A veryer ghost then I;
What I will say, I will not tell thee now,
Lest that preserve thee; and since my love is spent,
I 'had rather thou shouldst painfully repent,
Then by my threatnings rest still innocent.

The conventional metaphors of courtly love are taken literally in true Ramistic fashion. The poet warns that, 'killed' by his mistress's scorn, he will return to haunt her bed after death. His 'solicitations' will change from the attentiveness of a courtly lover to the insidious malice of the voyeur. Donne vents some of his spleen in a humiliating account of his former mistress and her new lover. She suffers a kind of symbolic death in *her* lover's rejection of her advances, and in a punning literal sense becomes a '*veryer* ghost' than the shadow watching her. The plain style description of her actions and state contrasts with middle style metaphors of courtly tradition. She is only a 'fain'd vestall'. 'Poore Aspen wretch' and 'cold quicksilver sweat' describe her more truthfully. Again, the Ramistic dislike of imagery shows in the implicit opposition of senses. But the contrast is not made structurally explicit, as it would be in Dryden. The writer leads the reader into the inference, he makes no open statements. The middle style sense of 'solicitations' is turned into a plain style sarcasm in his account of what she does. But these echoes of middle style conventions, in a new context of ironic realism in the plain style, are no more effective than his own more civil approaches to his former mistress. She too is scorned as he was. He at least has the gentility to die properly, while she merely 'dies' in a punning plain style sense. Even the topic of the lover's advice (so freely given in many an Elizabethan sonnet) is transformed into a weapon of revenge. He refuses to say anything before he actually does appear by her bed (the poem is set in the future tense), as he wishes her to suffer first, before she 'repents'. And the eloquence of the traditional middle style is dismissed as 'threatnings'. In fact, all the devices and metaphors of courtly language are transformed into literal meanings. The plain style stance of the writer invests these new terms with complex subjective values; the intuitive aspect of meaning is amplified, while in the middle style it was contained by the traditional values. Implicitly, Donne shapes the poem by a set of dichotomies in middle and plain style. The dialectic of persuasion is fused with the 'logical' demonstration of the distinct senses; Donne dramatises meaning in a Ramistic form, by a synthesis of two separate Aristotelian logics. Finally, we may note that the poem begins and ends with a pair of phrases: 'by thy scorne', 'by my threatnings'. These middle and plain style terms balance each other across registers, and represent another pair of 'dissimilar' arguments in Ramistic logic.

In Dryden, such variations of sense are more clearly patterned even in the plain style. In the portrait of Zimri, dissimilar arguments are used to demonstrate his irrational and impulsive nature:

> A man so various, that he seem'd to be
> Not one, but all Mankinds Epitome.
> Stiff in Opinions, always in the wrong;
> Was every thing by starts, and nothing long:
> But, in the course of one revolving Moon,
> Was Chymist, Fidler, States-Man, and Buffoon:
> Then all for Women, Painting, Rhiming, Drinking;
> Besides ten thousand freaks that dy'd in thinking.
> Blest Madman, who coud every hour employ,
> With something New to wish, or to enjoy!
> Rayling and praising were his usual Theams;
> And both (to shew his Judgment) in Extreams:
> So over Violent, or over Civil,
> That every man, with him, was God or Devil.   545–58

Ramistic logical treatises are divided into one part consisting of the invention of arguments, from the traditional places, and a second part, called disposition, or judgement, the arrangement of arguments in order within a discourse. This referred to the construction of axioms (the placing of one concept with another in a proposition), and syllogisms (the ways of arranging axioms). Here the pun in l. 556 refers to the placing of concepts in axioms: Zimri is incapable of discriminating reasonably, he can only use one form of judgement. So it is only right that he should suffer an extreme and paradoxical fate: 'He left not Faction, but of that was left'. Political factions, notorious for their tendency to schism, were unable to cope with his extreme instability.

We should now turn to other examples of register in these writers. Donne translates the high style into Ramistic form in one of the *Holy Sonnets* (VII):

> At the round earth's imagin'd corners, blow
> Your trumpets, Angells, and arise, arise
> From death, you numberlesse infinities
> Of soules, and to your scattred bodies goe,
> All whom the flood did, and fire shall o'erthrow,
> All whom warre, dearth, age, agues, tyrannies,
> Despaire, law, chance, hath slaine, and you whose eyes,
> Shall behold God, and never taste death's woe.
> But let them sleepe, Lord, and mee mourne a space,
> For, if above all these, my sinnes abound,
> 'Tis late to aske abundance of thy grace,
> When wee are there; here on this lowly ground,
> Teach mee how to repent; for that's as good
> As if thou'hadst seal'd my pardon, with thy blood.

The octet has all the generalising and emphatic features of the high style, in a religious context. But the effect is one of exact logical categorising, in the artificial class logic of a Ramistic Table, or outline of method. Donne divides up the human race by different kinds of death; he makes up arguments from cause, and classifies accordingly. The sestet is plain style, in its colloquial meditative syntax and vocabulary; the phrasing and rhythm of speech contrasts with the eloquent sustained rhythm of the octet. But even there the concern for realism endemic in Ramistic theory can be found, in the famous image, 'At the *round* earth's *imagin'd* corners . . .'. Natural reason is the image of universal truth. The earth's shape is no mystery of religion. The sonnet's structure is also an example of Ramistic 'method' of argument; the poet moves from the most general facts – the final doom of mankind – to the most particular – his own spiritual condition at that moment. The contrast is striking, but the poem is not an example of contrastive contexts; both contexts are complementary. The true humility of the Christian soul rests in considering the possibility that his own sins are greater than everyone else's ('if above all these . . .'); this act of contrition is meaningless if the rest of humanity has not somehow been included in the meditation. A general thought has a particular reference by logical entailment.

In *MacFlecknoe* (1682), Dryden uses the high style in contrastive contexts. He also adapts the conceptual approach to meaning in Ramistic 'logic' for satirical purposes. The high style is used here for solemn emphasis, but the main subject is in fact dullness and nonsense:

> *Shadwell* alone my perfect image bears,
> Mature in dullness from his tender years.
> *Shadwell* alone, of all my Sons, is he
> Who stands confirm'd in full stupidity.
> The rest to some faint meaning make pretence,
> But *Shadwell* never deviates into sense.
> Some Beams of Wit on other souls may fall,
> Strike through and make a lucid intervall;
> But *Shadwell*'s genuine night admits no ray,
> His rising Fogs prevail upon the Day: 15–24

So Dryden succeeds in amplifying the plain style idea of nonsense as though it were a carefully defined concept, which can only be preserved at enormous cost in will power and effort. Only Shadwell can maintain this heroic standard. Again, in what follows, unreason appears as natural as reason, and as important:

> Besides his goodly Fabrick fills the eye,
> And seems design'd for thoughtless Majesty:
> Thoughtless as Monarch Oakes, that shade the plain,
> And, spread in solemn state, supinely reign.
> *Heywood* and *Shirley* were but Types of thee,
> Thou last great Prophet of Tautology.   25–30

The religious context of the last couplet associates 'natural' reason and God, but it is the God of Unreason. In fact, Shadwell was no mean writer; Dryden exploits the redundancies of the high style, without analysing in middle style form the precise deficiencies in his rival's art. Yet the poem is one of the most effective and amusing of Dryden's work, from which Pope learnt the techniques of *The Dunciad*. The rigorous pursuit of destructive analogies is one of Dryden's great strengths. Ramistic invention is the firm basis of his art, in its precision of imagery and sustained structure.

In *The Medal* (1682) and *Religio Laici* (1682), Dryden writes in a firm, conventional plain style; these poems argue abstract issues that cannot be reduced to a number of central images. The limits of natural reason become a source of satirical imagery in both works. The conciseness of image in both poems is a source of lucid strength; Donne's plain style *Satyres* seem far more difficult to read, and obscure in image, beside Dryden. The subjective imagery of Donne's plain style is not very useful in argument and statement, and he equals Dryden's work only in his third satire. It is significant that in poems of the moral-political type, Donne seems to struggle with his material; he lacks the clear general thought of defined ideals such as Dryden had. Because Donne wrote in the first quarter of the seventeenth century, his work shows few traces of the baroque style of poetry that became fashionable in later decades. John Dryden, however, attempts the new visual style of the counter-reformation. The high style of baroque is to be found in the elegy to *Mrs. Anne Killigrew* (1686), and the dedicatory poem to the Duchess of Ormond in *The Fables* (1700). The variety and profuseness of visual image in these two poems is a new departure in style for Dryden. Argument and persuasion have been abandoned for decorative richness. The high style is not a register in which argument and analysis can be made, nevertheless Dryden suggests in the elegy at least that the reader should qualify his response to this exuberance. There is a delicate humour in the poem which reminds us that Dryden stayed as sceptical of mere visual imagery as any good Ramistic logician should.

4 Milton and Pope

We can best examine the influence of Ramistic logic on John Milton (1608–74) and Alexander Pope (1688–1744) by comparing two famous elegies, Milton's *Lycidas* (1638) and Pope's *Elegy to the Memory of an Unfortunate Lady* (1717). Milton's poem is an example of strict classical decorum; in a sequence of single contexts in middle and plain style he laments the loss of his friend drowned in the Irish sea. The poem is written in a similar form to Spenser's *Epithalamion*; a series of complex stanzas articulate the themes of loss and consolation, with a satiric aside on those who could have been better lost in place of his friend. Milton's attitude to the pastoral conventions he uses is modified and controlled by the reality of his grief, and this realism in the work dominates the traditional styles. Unlike Spenser, Milton adopts a middle style form for most of the pastoral, and avoids Chaucerian archaism. Milton exploits the traditional images of grief and loss by implying their inadequacy, while at the same time rendering them in the most delicate and pure form. It is important also to notice the role of syntax in this work; Milton creates a powerful surging rhythm to suggest strong feeling behind the conventional gestures of mourning. These devices of style in diction and syntax make the poem profoundly ambiguous in its use of the conventions, and many critics have described it as a mannerist work in its subjective and disturbed feeling.[1] However, while the writer's attitude may be regarded as emotional and strained, there is no need to regard the style as anything but a characteristic product of the synthesis between Ramistic logic and traditional rhetorical decorum. The formality of middle style diction, image and syntax is everywhere balanced against the accuracy of plain style truth. Milton is struggling all the time to express the truth of his experience alongside the traditional language of grief. Let us trace this element in the poem.

It opens with a traditional gesture: the poet makes a garland to wear as he sings. In Spenser's *October* eclogue in *The Shepheardes*

Calender the reference is much clearer and more conventional (although in his archaic plain style):

> Thou kenst not, Percie, howe the ryme should rage,
> O! if my temples were distaind with wine,
> And girt in girlonds of wild Yvie twine,
> How I could reare the Muse on stately stage.... 109-12

But Milton's garland is untimely; the fruits are 'harsh and crude' ('unripe'), and 'with forc't fingers rude' he must 'Shatter' the leaves 'before the mellowing year'.[2] The clash between the convention and the real seasons of the year is emphatic and central to the argument. This is no garland of rejoicing, but a symbol of grief and suffering:

> He must not float upon his watry bear
> Unwept, and welter to the parching wind,
> Without the meed of som melodious tear.   12-14

In this formal middle style context the phrase 'welter to the parching wind' is particularly poignant. For it conveys the reality of his friend's death by powerful implication, cutting through the conventional as though it were inadequate for the truth. It is a plain style phrase, describing the corpse floating in the water, abandoned by all human pity. Only an inanimate thing like a log or a corpse would be a grammatically acceptable subject for the verb 'welter'. We see how the conventions of the middle style are recognised as conventions beside the unbearable truth which can only be indirectly suggested. But the middle style represents a way of translating the unbearable into art, and so into speakable truths. Hence the pastoral conventions of the next three stanzas. But these are remote images of the reality to which the poet returns in the next lines. He traces the actual geography of the disaster, albeit in middle style terms, and the accuracy of these references reminds him of the illusion of art: 'Ay me, I fondly dream!/Had ye bin there – for what could that have don?' He goes on to cite the famous example of Orpheus torn to pieces by the Maenads; there too myth contains a truth close to the reality of the poem. Perhaps it is relevant to the argument of this analysis that 'goarie scalpe' was changed to 'goary visage' in the final draft of the poem, for 'scalpe' has a plain style informal tone, while 'visage' sustains the middle style diction of the passage, and reduces the more physical associations of despoiling the corpse. What follows is a conventional disgust for the poetic calling; it doesn't seem to need the kind of subjective interpretation it has often been given. (To support this we may turn to the *October* eclogue in *The Shepheardes Calender*, ll. 7–24.) Here in Milton's poem it is the sense of wasted talent that strikes the poet; a life dedicated to higher things has been unnaturally cut short before true recognition. Again, by a typical departure common in the logic of invention, Milton considers those who could have been more easily spared for the sake of this young poet. The satirical plain style is a classical version of the register, quite different from the sober realism of the earlier plain style usage. There is an element of caricature in its strong language, reminiscent of the biblical plain style we find in passages of invective in Donne's sermons. The fierceness of the ridicule, and the anger in the writer's attitude is entirely in keeping with the pity and grief he feels, although the style is colloquial and contrasting with the middle style pastoral. Yet it is a pastoral form of the satire, and as such within the general subject matter of the poem. When Milton returns to the idealised lyricism of the middle style in the next stanza there is less complexity of feeling; the singer's garland is, like his song, harsh and out of season, but the 'Laureat Herse' deserves a finer tribute of spring flowers. Again, Milton recognises, even as he finishes the tribute, that it is unreal and inadequate beside the truth: 'For so to interpose a little ease,/Let our frail thoughts dally with false surmise.' These images of flowers palliate grief, but are they in any sense a consolation to the dead poet? This is the kind of reaction we would expect to find in a Ramistic writer. For an image is only an argument in disguise, and the literal meaning of these pastoral conventions is impossible. The 'herse' or 'bear' does not actually exist; Lycidas does not 'lie' anywhere, and the truth is quite other. His burial place is the sea, with its endless tidal movement; only the dolphins can perhaps guide the 'hapless youth' to a final resting place. The realism of this passage is powerfully enforced in the accuracy of language: such lines as 'whilst thee the shores and sounding Seas/Wash far away, where e're thy bones are hurld . . .' have a plain style directness which faces the truth without losing decorum. Again, 'Where thou perhaps under the whelming tide/Visitst the bottom of the monstrous world' has an emphasis through the plain style terms 'Visitst' and 'whelming' which can only be called piteous. So it is natural that Milton should add 'Look homeward Angel now, and melt with ruth'. Only now can the consolations of art be replaced with divine inspiration, for art has been shown to fail the poet even as he attempts to believe in it. The poem ends in a consolatory middle style denying the facts of death at sea, and returning to the pastoral world of the opening; but it is evening and the poet's song is over as the shadows close around him. The enigmatic image of death and change as the day passes balances the forced gesture of the opening lines. What caused rebellion and grief has become translated into an image of natural order, and grief is assuaged by the silent passage of time. What makes the poem remarkable, however, is the sustained struggle with the conventions of the middle style pastoral, and Milton's refusal to abandon the truth of experience for a traditional commonplace. Why, in conclusion, is this elegy so different from Dryden's notorious early work? After all, Dryden is writing in a typical Ramistic manner as well. The answer is that while Dryden has no existential fact to draw on in his invention, Milton has a personal involvement with his subject matter. He writes from the heart.

Pope's *Elegy to the Memory of an Unfortunate Lady* is written in a sequence of single contexts from all three styles. We notice at once the virtual disappearance of the pastoral middle style, and its replacement by an elegant politeness of a new kind. There are of course traces of the earlier convention:

> Yet shall thy grave with rising flow'rs be drest,
> And the green turf lie lightly on thy breast:
> There shall the morn her earliest tears bestow,
> There the first roses of the year shall blow . . .   63–6^3

But this is more in the nature of eloquent reminiscence; it does not carry the central themes of the work. The traditional lyricism of the middle style is less important to Pope than a new formulation of that style based on the social milieu. The central theme of the poem is the importance of friendship, social status, and the ties of family honour. The register is far more conceptualised than in its earlier pastoral form:

> So peaceful rests, without a stone, a name,
> What once had beauty, titles, wealth, and fame.
> How lov'd, how honour'd once, avails thee not,
> To whom related, or by whom begot;

> A heap of dust alone remains of thee;
> 'Tis all thou art, and all the proud shall be!   69–74

These abstract terms replace the imagery of an earlier period with complex social ideals; they always no doubt existed in fact, but they are rarely so explicit in literature. There is, too, a hint of that ironic perception of the social setting which is so typical of Pope's poetry. Indeed, irony is a technique of argument in defence of the lady in an earlier passage:

> What tho' no friends in sable weeds appear,
> Grieve for an hour, perhaps, then mourn a year,
> And bear about the mockery of woe
> To midnight dances, and the public show?   55–8

The traditional middle style terms are translated into a reality that denies their value. It is better not to be mourned at all than to be treated in this way; the social slight is, Pope implies, too much for a genuine person. So irony becomes the ground for a polite compliment to the integrity of the lady's character. The syntax in these lines is colloquial and relaxed; Pope does not attempt to contrive a formality such as we found in Milton's elegy. There is a balancing formality in the parallelism of the lines preceding this passage, but the tone is distinct, and the diction reminds us that this is part of the high style register which is a major feature of the poem:

> What can atone (oh ever-injur'd shade!)
> Thy fate unpity'd, and thy rites unpaid?
> No friend's complaint, no kind domestic tear
> Pleas'd thy pale ghost, or grac'd thy mournful bier;
> By foreign hands thy dying eyes were clos'd,
> By foreign hands thy decent limbs compos'd,
> By foreign hands thy humble grave adorn'd,
> By strangers honour'd, and by strangers mourn'd!   47–54

There are some elements of the middle style in such a passage; 'complaint', 'domestic tear', 'decent limbs' are in the conventional form of the style. But the ritual of burial is presented in high style epic terms, like a Homeric funeral. The dominant image is pagan and classical; it neutralises grief and composes the feelings of the bereaved. Such terms as 'ever-injur'd shade', 'fate', 'rites', 'pale ghost' and the repetition of 'foreign hands' and 'strangers' give a generality and dignity to the final episode of an unhappy life. Pope exploits such a neutral register for the opening lines of the elegy, where he has the difficult task of breaking into the painful subject without causing offence to those who knew the lady better than he. The delicacy of control here is maintained by using the vagueness of the high style and its dramatic impact to disguise the disagreeable details of tragic death:

> What beck'ning ghost, along the moonlight shade
> Invites my step, and points to yonder glade?
> 'Tis she! – but why that bleeding bosom gor'd,
> Why dimly gleams the visionary sword?   1–4

In this way Pope adapts the high style conventions to a social purpose; the reader knows this is a fiction, but it is an acceptable fiction given the reality that is urbanely implied. This may seem remote from the severely logical argument of Ramistic invention, but we should notice the careful use of limited detail in these lines, and the fact that they point to an actual event with unequivocal directness. The high style in such a context is paradoxically realistic and truthful; no imagery disguises the experience, rather the imagery here contains and transforms experiential truth. Quickly the writer moves into the middle style analysis that gives a firm conceptual frame to the work:

> Oh ever beauteous, ever friendly! tell,
> Is it, in heav'n, a crime to love too well?
> To bear too tender, or too firm a heart,
> To act a Lover's or a Roman's part?   5–8

The motives for the lady's suicide are not clear, but the writer must make them sound admirable, and he transforms them into idealised arguments about love. The lady shows a Roman virtue in her determination, 'The glorious fault of Angels and of Gods'. Like Milton, Pope considers those who lack these particular qualities of character:

> Most souls, 'tis true, but peep out once an age,
> Dull sullen pris'ners in the body's cage:
> Dim lights of life, that burn a length of years

> Useless, unseen, as lamps in sepulchres;
> Like Eastern Kings a lazy state they keep,
> And close confin'd in their own palace sleep. 17–22

Pope does not use the classical low style with its satirical vein, but there is an element of caricature in this analogy. It is a plain style Ramistic invention, similar to many such images in Dryden, and derives its effect from the conceptual accuracy of its use. The subject matter is remote from the immediate theme of the elegy. But the variety and liveliness of these analogies, and their fusion of concepts and things into a witty association of ideas, is a relief from the tragic tone of earlier lines. Pope is prepared to vary tone, and hence register, far more than Milton, mainly because he is less directly involved in the experience he describes. This may account for the slight sense of strain in lines 29–46. The passage shows an eloquent variation between high style indignation (a social transformation of the style) and a traditional middle style compliment to the lady's beauty. One image combines wit and sarcasm in a novel invention in the high style: 'frequent hearses shall besiege your gates'. The metaphor is derived from Homeric images of battle, and the hearses take on a malevolent animism. There is a kind of jaunty assurance in the couplet:

> Thus, if eternal justice rules the ball,
> Thus shall your wives, and thus your children fall. 35–6

Pope does not wish to appear as cruel and unfeeling as those he rebukes, so he turns the attack by a slight suggestion of parody. This tendency to underplay the register he works in is to be seen again at the end of the poem, where his sincerity gains by the careless tone of the final couplet. This removes any impression of pomposity from what could have been a frigid and unfeeling statement in middle style:

> Poets themselves must fall, like those they sung;
> Deaf the prais'd ear, and mute the tuneful tongue.
> Ev'n he, whose soul now melts in mournful lays,
> Shall shortly want the gen'rous tear he pays;
> Then from his closing eyes thy form shall part,
> And the last pang shall tear thee from his heart,

Life's idle business at one gasp be o'er,
The Muse forgot, and thou belov'd no more! 75–82

The impression we gain from this analysis is how closely Pope controls tone in his use of traditional registers; the control derives from an extraordinary acuteness to meaning in natural language use. Like Milton, Pope looks outside the traditional parameters of literary language to the dominant facts of general usage. To that extent at least, both of them may be said to show, in a profound way, the influence of Ramistic traditions on the inherited styles of writing. At the same time each maintains the distinctive features of the traditional styles, although some of their functions have been modified.

Elsewhere in the minor poems we can find further examples of the new realism of style in both writers. Milton's poem *On the Morning of Christ's Nativity* (1629) is written almost entirely in the high style; it celebrates the great occasion in formal and splendid language. But the precision of image which is such a striking feature of the poem indicates that the high style is modified by a new conceptual accuracy. Each image at once generalises and remains exact and close to the experience described. There are many memorable lines: 'The Star-led Wizards haste with odours sweet', 'The Nymphs in twilight shade of tangl'd thickets mourn', 'No nightly trance, or breathed spell,/Inspires the pale-ey'd Priest from the prophetic cell', 'the chill Marble seems to sweat'. This is of course an example of the Spenserian influence on Milton, the compound adjectives being a particular feature of the style. But the tradition has been modified by a sharper sense of relevance than Spenser achieved in his own work. There are, too, occasional shifts into plain style, as when the Shepherds appear 'simply chatting in a rustic row'. Again, when Milton allows himself a plain style image to describe the sun, we see the other side of Ramistic influence in this poem. The realism of the high style images is sustained by close approximation to the experience described; the plain style image argues an approximation that modern readers deny. But the same techniques of conceptual accuracy are at work in both sets of images. The sun in bed, 'Curtaind with cloudy red' as he 'Pillows his chin upon the Orient wave' is an apparent breach of decorum. But in the plain style it is a lively image of a familiar and commonplace happening; there is no breach of decorum if the tradition is read correctly. Further, we may read this shift in style as an attempt to resolve the discrepancy between the humble circumstances of Christ's birth and the general tone of the poem. While 'the Orient wave' may be high style, the sun has a domestic context of a kind suitable to the real setting.

While Milton's use of the high style can be described as reaching a new precision of meaning, Pope exploits the possibilities of varied meaning in registers. In *Eloisa to Abelard* (1717) he complements a deliberately mechanical form of the middle style with a subjective and tormented high style. The balanced syntax of the middle style describes Eloisa's surroundings, which are beautiful but alien to her state of mind. Because she speaks these lines they express the depression of the thwarted lover more eloquently than direct statement would:

> The darksome pines that o'er yon rocks reclin'd
> Wave high and murmur to the hollow wind,
> The wand'ring streams that shine between the hills,
> The grots that echo to the tinkling rills,
> The dying gales that pant upon the trees,
> The lakes that quiver to the curling breeze;
> No more these scenes my meditation aid,
> Or lull to rest the visionary maid.   155–62

Her true feelings can only be expressed in an emphatic high style passage that follows immediately upon this middle style sequence:

> But o'er the twilight groves and dusky caves,
> Long-sounding isles, and intermingled graves,
> Black Melancholy sits, and round her throws
> A death-like silence, and a dread repose:
> Her gloomy presence saddens all the scene,
> Shades ev'ry flow'r, and darkens ev'ry green,
> Deepens the murmur of the falling floods,
> And breathes a browner horror on the woods.   163–70

The weight of noun phrases in this passage is balanced to some extent by the series of clauses dependent on the main subject, but the main impression left on any reader is one of sustained syntax overriding line ends and couplet structure. The contrast with the earlier lines is striking for this syntactic reason alone, but it is also reinforced by the changes in diction. The earlier lines use diction that is aesthetic and pleasing; here the diction is restricted to lexical sets related to darkness, stillness, and horror. The generality of this language is high style, but also embodies the subjective truth in Eloisa's mind; the very vagueness of reference is a strength. Pope is not always successful in his use of the high style: an early work like *Windsor Forest* seems far too unoriginal in its use of the register, although it is on a political theme that Pope was not very interested in. In a later work, *The Essay on Man, Epistle IV*, written in 1734, Pope shows the same sense of the grotesque we noticed before in his *Elegy*. But the tone of this passage is very far from that early work; there is a vein of bitterness and hatred running through a series of shifts into plain style denunciations. The writer is working off some personal grudge against an individual under the guise of a general attack; he does so through a complex multiple context:

> Mark by what wretched steps their glory grows,
> From dirt and sea-weed as proud Venice rose;
> In each how guilt and greatness equal ran,
> And all that rais'd the Hero, sunk the Man:
> Now Europe's laurels on their brows behold,
> But stain'd with blood, or ill exchang'd for gold:
> Then see them broke with toils, or sunk in ease,
> Or infamous for plunder'd provinces . . .
> What greater bliss attends their close of life?
> Some greedy minion, or imperious wife,
> The trophy'd arches, story'd halls invade
> And haunt their slumbers in the pompous shade.   291–304

The antitheses are made dramatic by shifts in register: 'wretched steps' is plain style, 'glory' high style, for example. Sometimes the antithesis works across the couplet, so that an heroic high style line, such as 'Now Europe's laurels on their brows behold', precedes a plain style truth. The closing lines describe in ludicrous terms the persecution of these conquerors of provinces by domestic servants or worse still by an overbearing wife. Only Pope could have chosen that high style context for such domestic humiliation, and it follows aptly on the high style pretensions of the public life. Pope uses the decorum of subject matter to overturn and expose the ideal of heroism and the deceptions of grandeur. In the evening of their lives, these heroes are persecuted in surroundings that can only remind them of their past achievements ('the pompous shade' is the place where some hero sleeps, surrounded by his trophies and emblems of victory). It is this inventive approach to the traditional styles which makes Pope one of the most original of writers. The courtly middle style which determined so many contexts in earlier writers has been replaced by eighteenth-century politeness in his work, but the high and plain styles still offered much opportunity to a thoughtful and resourceful mind. And the new middle style, based on the social milieu of the respectable, gave much material to the observant and the reflective. These features of the traditional and contemporary styles can be seen in their mature development in *The Dunciad* (1743) and *The Rape of the Lock* (1714).

But before we turn to such works, we should consider the chief features of style in Milton's major poetry. For in a way, the range of style in *Paradise Lost* is closely similar to the stylistic choices of *The Dunciad*; both works exploit the range of material allowed by the plain style, both have sustained passages of high style. Milton's epic is of course of wider range, and there are occasional lyrical sequences in the middle style. But on the whole it is a remarkably austere epic style that Milton adopts. While Milton deals with a sequence of single contexts, as the epic genre requires, Pope characteristically creates multiple contexts of great complexity. He goes beyond the more schematic contrastive contexts of his model in Dryden's *MacFlecknoe*. But the plain style is the main source of originality in the poem. The reason for these parallel developments in style may be found in the influence of Ramism: the scepticism about metaphor and traditional lyrical imagery, the preference for direct statement as a morally more acceptable stance for the writer, the concern to be understood – all these tendencies are to be found in the Ramistic theory of language. As Milton remarks in his first pamphlet (1641), 'The very essence of truth is plainness and brightness; the darkness and crookedness is our own.'[4] His view of art was equally unequivocal, and in keeping with the Ramistic emphasis on natural reason as the source of all truth: 'For doubtless that indeed according to art is most eloquent, which turns and approaches nearest to nature, from whence it came; and they express nature best, who in their lives least wander from her safe leading, which may be called regenerate reason.'[5] How, then, did these ideals translate into artistic practice in *Paradise Lost*?

We should first take note of the remarkable change in style between *Comus* (1634) and *Paradise Lost* (1674). The first poem is written in a careful imitation of Elizabethan and Jacobean poets.

Many influences have been detected in the work. There are high style passages close to Spenser's epic, for example, ll. 420–51, and other passages that read like an imitation of Shakespeare's metaphoric version of the high style, for example ll. 705–35. There are also, as we would expect in an allegorical debate of this kind, many passages of middle style analysis, where the theme is argued out (e.g. ll. 736–54, 452–74, 512–79). The protagonist of virtue speaks in a hectoring plain style (ll. 755–98). Milton abandons this range of style in his epic; it has been suggested that he deliberately models his style upon Italian ideas of the epic genre.[6] Certainly, there is a clear shift in style range between the two works. We now have to consider some typical examples of the three styles in the later work.

Paradise Lost consists of speech and narrative; examples of each style level occur in both forms. In speech, the dimensions of formality and familiarity in high, middle or plain style are often more marked and observable than in the narrative, but it is frequently the case that speech does not differ markedly from narrative in this regard. We rarely get any sense of the dramatic and immediate in Milton's use of language in this work: the registers operate independent of natural language use. This is a considerable change from the realism of *Lycidas*; the epic genre imposes a distancing effect on literary language. The formal intimacy of tone in the elegy, where the poet speaks in his own voice, is inappropriate for the epic. In the high style, Satan's address to Uriel (III, 654–80) is the traditional language of petition; it contrasts with the analysis of a middle style debate, when Mammon discusses alternative courses of action with his peers in Hell (II, 229–83), and with the plain style directness of Satan's words when he discovers Hell (I, 242–63). These represent extremes of variation in the poem. The complex subordinations of syntax in the high style are matched by the general diction, with its laudatory epithets, and absolute formality of phrase:

> Uriel, for thou of those sev'n Spirits that stand
> In sight of Gods high Throne, gloriously bright,
> The first art wont his great authentic will
> Interpreter through highest Heav'n to bring,
> Where all his Sons thy Embassie attend;
> And here art likeliest by supream decree
> Like honour to obtain, and as his Eye
> To visit oft this new Creation round;

> Unspeakable desire to see, and know
> All these his wondrous works, but chiefly Man,
> His chief delight and favour, him for whom
> All these his works so wondrous he ordaind,
> Hath brought me from the Quires of Cherubim
> Alone thus wandring.

There is no need to itemise all the typical features of high style in this passage, but it is worth pointing out the extent of emphasis in the use of intensifiers (e.g. 'likeliest', 'Unspeakable', 'gloriously') and superlatives. Emphasis is also achieved by the use of absolute senses, especially in adjectives, as 'high Throne', 'great authentic will', 'supream decree', 'wondrous works'. The syntax delays the main clause while secondary clauses weave a pattern of respectful praise for the person addressed. This pattern is repeated in the secondary clause associated with man, who is also, as a creation of the Almighty, worthy of praise. The use of periphrasis is also a central feature of the style; nothing is said simply or directly, and rhythm justifies the repetition of statement for elegant variation (e.g. 'All these his wondrous works . . . All these his works so wondrous . . .). The speaker's real attitude is concealed behind this formality: Milton adds immediately after the address, 'So spake the false dissembler unperceiv'd'. Clearly he takes the view that artifice in language is suspect, as concealing plain truth. God always speaks in a harsh logical plain style (for example, III, 173–202).

When Mammon speaks to his peers in the great debate in Hell (II, 229–83) he uses the middle style. The speech is courteous in tone, as to equals; there is less emphasis and more analysis than in Satan's words to Uriel. The syntax is carefully finished and balanced, but there is little redundancy of phrase or clause. A typical passage from the speech would be the first few lines:

> Either to disinthrone the King of Heav'n
> We warr, if warr be best, or to regain
> Our own right lost: him to unthrone we then
> May hope, when everlasting Fate shall yield
> To fickle Chance, and *Chaos* judge the strife:
> The former vain to hope argues as vain
> The latter: for what place can be for us
> Within Heav'ns bound, unless Heav'ns Lord supream
> We overpower?

The close reasonableness of this passage is typical of Milton's analytical middle style. The argument is advanced clause by clause in a sequence of propositions: the two alternatives are posed to the audience, and then the speaker shows why each is impossible. There is no need for Mammon to state the obvious, that 'everlasting Fate' can never change; it follows from the epithet he uses. The conciseness of the demonstration, and the swift pursuit of reasoning throughout the whole passage, with its attendant sarcasm and irony, is a traditional formulation of the covertly diverting middle style. Mammon has a talent for the epigrammatic phrase: 'preferring hard liberty before the easie yoke of servile Pomp', 'Our torments may in length of time become our Elements', 'seek our own good from our selves, and from our own live to our selves'. But he lacks courage and will-power, which are the specific attributes of Satan in his first speech in Hell (I, 242–63). His words ring with defiance and hard determination, and Milton achieves this effect with blunt, clipped monosyllables, and simple statement without appeal to reason or any qualification of sense:

> Is this the Region, this the Soil, the Clime,
> Said then the lost Arch-Angel, this the seat
> That we must change for Heav'n, this mournful gloom
> For that celestial light? Be it so, since he
> Who now is Sovran can dispose and bid
> What shall be right: fardest from him is best
> Whom reason hath equald, force hath made supream
> Above his equals.

The sarcasm of 'what shall be right', and the paradox of 'force hath made *supream* Above his *equals*' are close to natural language use in their sharpness and sting. The looseness of connection in the last clause indicates anger and resentment; reason and power are opposed as antonyms, when we know they aren't. We notice the frequency of modal forms of the verb, commonly found in speech of a colloquial kind: 'can', 'must', 'shall', 'should'. Clauses are simple and there is little subordination throughout the passage as a whole. There is a careful change of tone when Satan, at the end of his meditation, turns to consider his fellow angels, and shifts into an elegant middle style:

> But wherefore let we then our faithful friends,

> Th'associates and copartners of our loss
> Lie thus astonisht on th'oblivious Pool . . .

This follows the line, 'Better to reign in Hell, than serve in Heav'n'; the elliptical syntax in the plain style contrasts with this elegance of formal address that Satan adopts to his followers.

In the narrative parts of the poem we find the visual element that has attracted so much comment. But here again the variation between the three styles can be detected, and can be analysed. The sustained rhythm of the high style, and its heavy nominality, mark such passages as the description of Satan's shield and spear, and his scattered followers (I, 283–313), but the realism of this passage is notable. The heroic similes refer not to classical myth, but to near contemporary history, and famous examples from the natural world. We must allow Milton to treat the sacred history of the Jews as equally authentic. The influence of Ramistic logic may be detected in this choice of material. When Milton has to describe the gathering of the troops in Hell (I, 531–71) he uses realistic effects of light and darkness to suggest the splendour of the scene, but the heroic image is undermined by a reference to the mental suffering of these doomed angels. At every turn in this epic, Milton is preoccupied with the moral truth, like Spenser, and cannot allow an untruthful impression to stand unqualified, however much decorum may dictate what is a proper style for that particular subject matter. The middle style is reserved in the narrative section of the poem for the idealised portrait of nature before the Fall; Eve's speech to Adam is in fact typical of this style (IV, 641–56). This is one example of the overlap between some examples of speech and the narrative norms of style, for Eve in her innocence is an almost impossible figure to present. In a sense she is simply part of the ideal world of Nature that she describes with such pedantic brilliance. The most obvious passage of middle style narrative occurs in Book IV, 216–68, the description of Eden itself. The essential feature of this style is, as we have seen already, the analysis of the natural world so that it comes to resemble art rather than nature. Even as Milton denies the role of art in the making of the Garden 'not nice Art . . . but Nature boon', he is forced to rely on artistic traditions about the Garden's appearance. The similes that follow this passage (ll. 268–85) are middle style lyrical analogies which invoke classical myths for the most part. They are very different in tone from the harsh natural imagery in the high style passages: there truth must be accurate and close to observable reality, while here, since no one can find an analogy in the natural world for Paradise, Milton is driven back onto learned reference. There are also middle style passages in the account of Hell: the description of Pandemonium (I, 710–30), or the admiration of those who enter the great building (ll. 730–7); the fable of Mulciber (ll. 738–46), or the simile of the elves (ll. 781–8). These passages are interwoven with plain style narrative, e.g. the construction of the great hall (ll. 692–709), or sarcastic qualification of the classical myth (ll. 746–51). The gathering of the host for the council is another plain style insertion (ll. 752–76); the simile of the bees is rich with exact detail from an observed occurrence. Milton's plain style is marked by technical terms proper to the subject: 'Spade and Pickaxe', 'trench a Field', 'cast a Rampart', 'scummd the Bullion dross', 'sound-board', 'every Band and squared Regiment', 'new rubd with Baum'. On one occasion, the description of Satan's flight to the throne of Chaos (II, 927–67) is made to contrast sarcastically with Satan's own high style reference to it (II, 402–13). The delusions of heroism, when it is in truth only rebellion, and essentially unheroic, could not be made clearer. In the list of devils (I, 392–530) the plain style language is always denigratory and demeaning, so that Satan's raising of their spirits at the end of this long passage is repulsive and discordant. His stature as a leader must surely be diminished by the account given of his troops.

Now we should return to Pope's mature work and see how this tradition of plainness and realism in literary language was exploited. The politeness of eighteenth-century middle style is no obstacle to exact observation and penetrating comment. There is formality and realism in this passage from the *Epistle to a Lady* (1735):

> 'Yet Cloe sure was form'd without a spot'—
> Nature in her then err'd not, but forgot.
> 'With ev'ry pleasing, ev'ry prudent part,
> Say, what can Cloe want?' She wants a Heart.
> She speaks, behaves, and acts just as she ought;
> But never, never, reach'd one gen'rous Thought.
> Virtue she finds too painful an endeavour,
> Content to dwell in Decencies for ever.   157–64

After the atrocities of Milton's devils, this may sound rather trivial;

Milton and Pope

we are in another universe. Milton is concerned with moral absolutes, while Pope is recording social truths of an ephemeral kind. The polite conversational style of this passage disguises the precision of sense and the seriousness of the idea. Pope's belief that social values are in the end moral principles gives weight to the style. But he perceives the moral issue through the social relations of daily life. He attacks those who translate morality into artifice, and lose sight of the purpose behind true civility. This is a form of the middle style which seems a long way from the learned lyricism of Milton; we cannot claim that there has been any direct development. The middle style passage from *Eloisa to Abelard* represents a closer continuity of the lyrical tradition. Mammon's speech to his peers in Hell has something of the exactness and wit of this eighteenth century version of the middle style. Pope analyses and presses home his argument with urbane assurance; the same epigrammatic terseness occurs in both passages. In *The Rape of the Lock*, Pope combines the high and middle styles to create a sophisticated multiple context. The poem is both a compliment to the young lady, Mrs Arabella Fermor, and a plea for restraint and good sense in social relations. The whole affair has, Pope implies, got a little out of hand. The high style expresses the subjective self-esteem of the protagonists, especially Belinda; the middle style provides the witty perspectives of the older poet, outside the social milieu of the younger set. This association of compliment and wit is seen at its best in the opening of Canto II, ll. 1–18:

> Not with more glories, in th'etherial plain,
> The Sun first rises o'er the purpled main,
> Than, issuing forth, the rival of his beams
> Launch'd on the bosom of the silver Thames.
> Fair Nymphs, and well-drest Youths around her shone,
> But ev'ry eye was fix'd on her alone.
> On her white breast a sparkling Cross she wore,
> Which Jews might kiss, and Infidels adore.
> Her lively looks a sprightly mind disclose,
> Quick as her eyes, and as unfix'd as those:
> Favours to none, to all she smiles extends;
> Oft she rejects, but never once offends.
> Bright as the sun, her eyes the gazers strike,
> And, like the sun, they shine on all alike.
> Yet graceful ease, and sweetness void of pride

> Might hide her faults, if Belles had faults to hide:
> If to her share some female errors fall,
> Look on her face, and you'll forget 'em all.

Pope analyses the whole incident in terms of a parallel between the sun rising in splendour and Belinda going out for a picnic on the river. The grandiose analogy is of course not meant seriously. There is a playful parallelism between the heroic imagery and the actual person: 'the bosom of the silver Thames' is paralleled by 'her white breast' and the 'sparkling Cross', the sun and her eyes are wittily compared to her disadvantage, and in the last line we are perhaps to understand that her beauty is as blinding as the light of the sun. The passage can be read as an act of homage to the beautiful and the wealthy; closer reading shows many small ambiguities that suggest gentle criticism. Belinda wears a 'sparkling Cross', 'Which Jews might kiss, and Infidels adore'. We remember that for the Jews, a cross is not a sacred object, and infidels are by definition unlikely to adore an alien religious symbol. Therefore, the cross cannot be a religious symbol at all, but only a piece of jewellery that sets off her beauty to perfection. But is Pope saying she is a goddess, or just a slightly vain young woman? Again, if her mind is as 'unfix'd' as her eyes, is this for lack of good sense, or because she has yet to choose a husband? The sun shines on everyone in an impersonal, neutral way; Pope perhaps means that Belinda's brightness is rather artificial and insincere. There is a kind of inanity about her consistent enthusiasm. But do Belles have to hide their faults, or is Pope saying that Belles are faultless? These possibilities of meaning are left open in the text; the middle style achieves a new formulation of its traditional function as a covertly diverting register. But we must not think that Pope writes with malice or sarcasm in this poem; the high style conveys a genuine compliment. Belinda is young and attractive, but delightfully unaware that she is an entirely conventional young woman of the time. The sustained delicacy of humour in the poem is created by using the high and middle styles as complementary contexts. Both contain certain truths about the situation in the work, but they are partial truths; together, they show the self-deception and the passion for what they are. The world of art is a selection from reality designed to explain experience, not simply to record it.

In the plain style, Pope shows traces of the earlier tradition of wit we find in Dryden; this associative play of mind is of course typical of the Ramistic theory of language. For example, in this passage from the *Epistle to Bathurst* (1733), the variety of idea derives from logical concepts of meaning:

> Riches, like insects, when conceal'd they lie,
> Wait but for wings, and in their season fly.
> Who sees pale Mammon pine amidst his store,
> Sees but a backward steward for the Poor;
> This year a Reservoir, to keep and spare;
> The next, a Fountain, spouting thro' his Heir,
> In lavish streams to quench a Country's thirst,
> And men and dogs shall drink him till they burst.   169-76

Cohesion in this passage depends on strict logical relations between the propositions; the images are in themselves quite disparate and arbitrary, and are subordinate to logical ideas of containment, and potential and revealed movement. The wastefulness of the heir to this fortune is implied in the final image: his wealth is spent indiscriminately. There is little observation in such a process; the literal meaning is merely exemplified in a series of images which repeat the idea. The statement of the idea carries conviction by its varied form. Another example of logical concepts shaping a passage can be found in the *Epistle to Burlington* (1731); in this passage Pope argues by placing opposite or inappropriate senses together:

> Lo! what huge heaps of littleness around!
> The whole, a labour'd Quarry above ground.
> Two Cupids squirt before: a Lake behind
> Improves the keenness of the Northern wind . . .
> The suff'ring eye inverted Nature sees,
> Trees cut to Statues, Statues thick as trees,
> With here a Fountain, never to be play'd,
> And there a Summer-house, that knows no shade.
> Here Amphitrite sails thro' myrtle bow'rs;
> There Gladiators fight, or die, in flow'rs;
> Un-water'd see the drooping sea-horse mourn,
> And swallows roost in Nilus' dusty Urn.   109-26

Again, the passage is obviously plain style; it is a sequence of statements without analysis or emphasis. Each isolated detail has its effect, and reinforces the main idea.

In *The Dunciad* (1743) this technique of plain style cohesion is pursued further than in any other work. Pope also employs the high style in this poem to increase the outrageous energy and power that dullness and commercial values seem to have acquired almost without anyone noticing it. 'And unawares *Morality* expires', he remarks at the end of the poem. Morality, in his sense of a lively social commitment to Christian values, has nothing whatever to do with commercial considerations. There is a hideous decorum in the energy and squalor of many scenes in the poem; the high style conveys the power of this new force in society:

> This labour past, by Bridewell all descend,
> (As morning pray'r, and flagellation end)
> To where Fleet-ditch with disemboguing streams
> Rolls forth large tribute of dead dogs to Thames,
> The King of dykes! than whom no sluice of mud
> With deeper sable blots the silver flood.
> 'Here strip, my children! here at once leap in,
> Here prove who best can dash thro' thick and thin,
> And who the most in love of dirt excel,
> Or dark dexterity of groping well.
> Who flings most filth, and wide pollutes around
> The stream, be his the Weekly Journals bound,
> A pig of lead to him who dives the best;
> A peck of coals a-piece shall glad the rest.' II, 269–82

We can see here the effect of reinforcement which the multiple context produces when limited to the two extremes of style. For the high style, with its natural emphasis and generality, gives exceptional force to isolated plain style detail, while the plain style defines the banal reality of the pretensions. It also gives figurative meaning to the heroic episode; the Notes to the poem explain the allusions to contemporary scandal sheets. Later in the poem, when Pope describes the effects and progress of the great yawn of the goddess, Dullness, the plain style becomes the dominant register (IV, 605–18), but the poem ends in a parody of Miltonic high style, transformed into the abstract ideals of the eighteenth century. Pope's objection to the new writers was that they were popular and politically unsound. The plain style attacks implicitly their popular support, and contrasts with the polite middle style Pope uses for respectable social figures in *The Rape of the Lock*. But the range of invention in the plain style is clearly more original and varied than the material Pope invents within the decorum of the middle style. His work moves consistently away from the inherited norms of literary language towards a greater inventiveness based on his own intuitions of appropriate language. This is also clear in his original use of high style contexts. At this point we end discussion of the three traditional styles in poetry, because after Pope little more could be done within these inherited norms of style. The future development of poetic language lay in the direction of increased accuracy of observation, less reliance on logical invention, and more complex forms of lyricism.

Part II: Prose

5 Sidney and Bacon

The achievement of the Renaissance was the reconquest of classical form in all the arts. For Renaissance writers the central problem of prose style was how to construct an elegant and ordered discourse in the vernacular that was equal to the brilliant prose styles of classical literature. The elaborate sentence patterns of Cicero could be imitated in English, and so could the dense, pithy style of Tacitus. Sir Philip Sidney (1554–86) used Cicero as the model for his prose style, while Francis Bacon (1561–1626) adopted the concise style of Tacitus. Both writers are influenced by the new emphasis on 'natural logic' in the sixteenth century, and their interpretations of high, middle and plain style contexts show a new conceptual complexity. Imagery is no longer decorative, as it was for Lyly and earlier writers.[1] In this development we may see the influence of Pierre de la Ramée and his many followers. Sidney himself was known to be interested in Ramistic logic, and his *Apology for Poetry* (1581–3)[2] shows knowledge of Ramistic method in its structure, and in its treatment of topics.[3] The revised *Arcadia* (1593) is almost certainly the result of a wish to make the original Elizabethan romance something more fashionable and modern, an heroic poem in the high Renaissance tradition.[4] Bacon's *Essays* (1597–1625) are written in the tradition of Montaigne's *Essays*, but are far more concise and pedantic in style; Bacon balances and opposes arguments in a characteristic form of Ramistic method. The intimacy of tone in Montaigne's style is absent, and the reader is held by the precision and insight of statement. Bacon's personality is kept out of the discourse, and he plays down rhetorical invention. In *The Advancement of Learning* (1605), Bacon constructs a whole work on the method which in Ramistic logic was held to be inherently persuasive. Here again arguments are balanced against each other in a rapid sequence of concise statements.

We should begin with the new *Arcadia* (1593), where we can find examples of all three style levels in an epic context. The tendencies towards categories and arbitrary divisions which are typical of

Ramistic logic can be seen in each register. This imposes a rationalising framework on the traditional forms of style. Emphasis in the high style, analysis in the middle style, and narrative in the plain style are transformed into strenuous argument. But the distinctive features of each style are maintained: in the rationalised contexts, emphasis is achieved by emphatic contradiction, analysis is developed through paradoxical and qualifying argument, narrative and exposition are presented in a set of complementary propositions. The characteristics of the high style can be shown in this passage:

> But thus the day passed (if that might be called a day) while the cunningest mariners were so conquered by the storm as they thought it best with stricken sails to yield to be governed by it: the valientest feeling inward dismayedness, and yet the fearfullest ashamed fully to show it, seeing that the princes (who were to part from the greatest fortunes) did in their countenances accuse no point of fear; but encouraging them to do what might be done (putting their hands to every most painful office) taught them at one instant to promise themselves the best and yet to despise the worst. But so were they carried by the tyranny of the wind and the treason of the sea all that night, which the elder it was, the more wayward it showed itself towards them: till the next morning (known to be a morning better by the hourglass than by the day's clearness) having run fortune as blindly as itself ever was painted, lest the conclusion should not answer to the rest of the play, they were driven upon a rock, which (hidden with those outrageous waves) did, as it were, closely dissemble his cruel mind, till, with an unbelieved violence (but to them that have tried it) the ship ran upon it; and seeming willinger to perish than to have her course stayed, redoubled her blows till she had broken herself in pieces and, as it were, tearing out her own bowels to feed the sea's greediness, left nothing within it but despair of safety and expectation of a loathsome end. 12–34/262[5]

The paragraph is an eloquent imitation of the large-scale rhythms of the periodic sentence. Clauses and phrases are used to sustain and balance the onward movement of the passage until the final sequence. Sidney relies on a series of incompatible statements for emphasis: 'so *conquered* by the storm . . . *yield to be governed* by it'; 'the *valientest* feeling *inward dismayedness*'; 'the *fearfullest ashamed* . . . to show it'; 'to promise themselves the *best* and yet to despise the *worst*'; 'the *elder* it was, the *more wayward* . . .'; '*redoubled her blows* till she had *broken herself in pieces*'; '*despair . . . expectation*', 'safety . . . *a loathsome end*'. The generality of sense typical of the high style restricts the detail in the passage to a number of dominant images; they are all conventional emblems of disaster and misfortune. In the context they create a set of general references to the downfall of princes and states which is the prime purpose of the narrative at this point. The shipwreck is only the pretext for this political meditation on how disaster should be faced and defeated even if it overwhelms the hero. Emphasis is maintained in this long sequence by a series of intensifying devices; superlative adjectives used as nouns are common ('the cunningest, the valientest, the fearfullest'), emphatic adverbs frequent ('*so* conquered', 'thought it *best*', '*fully* to show it', 'at one instant', '*all* that night', 'as itself *ever* was painted', '*closely* dissemble', and many adjectives have a strong unqualified sense ('stricken', 'cruel', 'outrageous', 'unbelieved' = 'unbelievable'). The style is also generally nominal; the analytic genitive of the noun phrase or parallel pairings are preferred for reasons of rhythm and balance ('the tyranny of the wind and the treason of the sea', 'despair of safety and expectation of a loathsome end', 'by the hour glass than by the day's clearness', 'no point of fear', 'the rest of the play'). It is a stative form of style; there is no analysis except for the purpose of emphasis. The analysis is secondary and the overriding intention is to state the heroic resolution of the princes in the face of disaster. There is in fact very little detail in passage. For detail would only distract from the larger meaning of the image, which teaches valour and resolution, and contrasts with ideas of cowardice and fear. Analysis implies the exploration of states of mind, which is entirely absent from this context, except in the most diagrammatic form. It is however a delicate version of the high style: there are more densely written forms of the style in the new *Arcadia*. Here is a passage where emphatic contradiction is exploited for the main argument in the context:

> The clashing of armour, the crushing of staves, the jostling of bodies, the resounding of blows, was the first part of that ill-agreeing music which was beautiful with the grisliness of wounds, the rising of dust, the hideous falls and groans of the dying. The very horses, angry in their masters' anger, with love and obedience brought forth the effects of hate and resistance, and

with minds of servitude did as if they affected glory. Some lay dead under their dead masters, whom unknightly wounds had unjustly punished for a faithful duty. Some lay upon their lords by like accidents, and in death had the honour to be borne by them, whom in life they had borne. Some, having lost their commanding burdens, ran scattered about the field, abashed with the madness of mankind. The earth itself (wont to be a burial of men) was now, as it were, buried with men; so was the face thereof hidden with dead bodies, to whom death had come masked in divers manners. In one place lay disinherited heads, dispossessed of their natural seignories; in another whole bodies to see to, but that their hearts, wont to be bound all over so close, were now with deadly violence opened: in others, fouler deaths had uglily displayed their trailing guts. There lay arms, whose fingers yet moved as if they would feel for him that made them feel; and legs, which contrary to common reason, by being discharged of their burden, were grown heavier.   2–24/469

Emphasis in the high style has become in this example a matter of logical contradiction: 'that ill-agreeing music which was *beautiful* with the *grisliness* of wounds . . .', 'with love and obedience brought forth the effects of hate and resistance', 'unjustly punished for a faithful duty', 'burial of men . . . now, as it were, buried with men'. There are examples everywhere. But why should Sidney adopt such a narrow formulation of the high style? It seems to be the result of trying to state the irrational and the emotive in logical terms, through propositions that can be analysed into their constituent parts. For the Ramistic view of invention was that it could only be dialectical, not rhetorical; the only kind of imitation was the imitation of arguments. These arguments were thought up by the writer before he began his work, and set out in the work. This doctrine of 'conceptual imitation' is very far removed from the idealism of Aristotle's doctrine of *mimesis*. We have to be careful not to imagine that Sidney was a pure Aristotelian: when he refers to the doctrine of imitation, he makes clear that it is designed to 'teach and delight'. The ideal 'golden' world of the poets is a didactic device, to instruct and persuade the reader by reasonable argument. The delightful images are designed to make 'our erected wit . . . *know* what perfection is' through argument, and they are not 'castles in the air' as Sidney dismissively puts it.[6] He is even more opposed to the ideas of aesthetic pleasure for its own sake, which he takes to be immoral.[7] Because William Temple, a rather obtuse Ramistic logician, thought Sidney was wrong to cite the doctrine of imitation in a Ramistic treatise on poetry, there is no necessity for us to accept today that Sidney was not therefore a Ramistic logician.[8] All Temple's attempts to catch Sidney out in a misunderstanding of Ramism can be shown to be mistaken. It is true that Sidney says that 'the poet, he nothing affirms, and therefore never lieth'.[9] On its own this statement looks like a suggestion that poetry does not consist of a sequence of arguments, which is the Ramistic view. Temple therefore criticises this assertion. But what does Sidney actually say? A few lines later, he makes a distinction between the truthfulness of a statement and the making of statements. Sidney argues that the poet does not labour to tell us 'what is or is not, but what should or should not be'. But the moral intention is still enacted through a sequence of arguments, as we have seen. Sidney presents the point in a way that misled Temple. Again, earlier in the work, when Sidney says that 'moving' or 'persuasion' is 'of a higher degree than teaching' because it is the 'cause and effect' of teaching, we must not conclude that he means this to refer to the teacher.[10] The person who is being taught has the desire to learn, in the ideal context, as he makes clear. And Ramism laid great stress on the presentation of arguments in such a way that they were as persuasive as possible. So the learner is moved by a desire to learn, as was implicitly recognised in the emphasis placed on method in Ramistic logic. What he learns persuades him of its truth by its method of presentation as he learns it. Sidney is perfectly within the tradition of Ramistic logic in the narrow sense in which he means 'moving'. We can see this from his comments on the methods of persuasion used by the philosopher and the historian in the same part of the *Apology*. They do not show the way to moral enlightenment for they are too dependent on particular truths, and cannot get away from those truths to the general principles which the mind can best grasp, as Ramistic logic held. The poet's task, for Sidney, was to discern 'the inherent reason within universal nature'.[11]

Now we should turn to Bacon and see what he made of the high style in his more concise usage. He keeps a much closer control over argument than Sidney; he seldom uses antithesis, and the onward movement of his sentences is usually achieved in the high style contexts by a heaping up of propositions with no ornament or figure. The nominality of the high style is evident from this group of sentences:

There be therefore chiefly three vanities in studies, whereby learning hath been most traduced. For those things we do esteem vain, which are either false or frivolous, those which either have no truth or no use: and those persons we esteem vain, which are either credulous or curious; and curiosity is either in matter or words: so that in reason as well as in experience there fall out to be these three distempers (as I may term them) of learning: the first, fantastical learning; the second, contentious learning; and the last, delicate learning; vain imaginations, vain altercations, and vain affectations; and with the last will I begin.

1–12/28[12]

Bacon proceeds by a series of definitions to begin his discussion; he appeals to common experience and common meanings of words. The passage is an emphatic set of definitions which convey the authority of the writer and the close relation between human motives and weaknesses and intellectual activity. The frequency of parallelism at clause and phrase level is typical of Bacon's linear style. It shows his dependence on the Ramistic method of division and sub-division to develop a topic. It also keeps the writing concise and dense with meaning; there is almost no redundancy in this version of the high style. Meaning and form are brought as closely together as possible, in the actual pattern of natural reasoning, or natural logic, the dichotomy itself.[13] The adjectives are categorising and general in sense, and there is close cohesion of vocabulary; the parallelism of phrase establishes the lexical sets. The ellipsis in the syntax towards the sentence end adds pace and emphasis in a familiar movement of the periodic sentence pattern. At each stage the writer develops his argument by a set of pairings: 'false or frivolous', 'no truth or no use', 'credulous or curious', 'matter or words', 'reason' – 'experience'. The triplets at the end of the sentence also add weight to the final movement of the rhythm. To compare this sentence with Sidney's high style passages may seem inappropriate: the passages are on widely different topics. Bacon's topics are non-literary and outside the genre of the epic poem (in prose or verse), but the sentence rhythm and the formality of diction make all these contexts equivalent. In the sentence following his introduction, Bacon shows a close understanding of the high style in its more traditional form. Here the syntax is less concise and phrasal; Bacon uses clauses to heap up arguments gathering pace throughout the sentence:

Martin Luther, conducted (no doubt) by an higher providence, but in discourse of reason, finding what a province he had undertaken against the bishop of Rome and the degenerate traditions of the church, and finding his own solitude, being no ways aided by the opinions of his own time, was enforced to awake all antiquity, and to call former times to his succours to make a party against the present time: so that the ancient authors, both in divinity and in humanity, which had long time slept in libraries, began generally to be read and revolved.   12–22/28

Devices of emphasis are less obvious but equally frequent: 'what a province', 'being no ways aided', 'to awake all antiquity' (hyperbole for emphasis), 'former times' (generalising), 'long time', 'generally'. The reinterpretation of the standard metaphor, 'awake all antiquity', in the subsequent phrase, 'which had long time slept in libraries' (meaning 'which had been left unread on the shelves for years') is an example of the cohesive use of metaphor favoured by Bacon. This second metaphor is surely plain style, for it introduces a note of disdain and perhaps even contempt; Bacon does not admire the style or influence of the classics, and that is one of the central points of the work. The classics (for the most part) provided a pernicious stylistic model: 'men began to hunt more after words than matter'. His own style in the *Essays* is studiously dense with meaning. The fusion of concepts and things into an equivalent relation, which we have seen is one of the features of Ramistic logic in Donne and Dryden, was also, it is clear from the two colloquial metaphors given above, common in Bacon. He loves to describe intellectual operations or conditions in terms of physical activities. He reserves his worst sarcasm for the medieval schoolmen, or philosophers; like Pierre de la Ramée, Bacon saw them as responsible for the grave deterioration in learning he observed around him. Again, the emphatic parallelism defines the high style, along with the generality of sense and the delaying of the main verb. These are features of the Ciceronian periodic sentence favoured by Sidney, yet here they seem more concisely exploited for a sharper, more impatient commentary:

This kind of degenerate learning did chiefly reign amongst the schoolmen: who having sharp and strong wits, and abundance of leisure, and small variety of reading, but their wits being shut up in the cells of a few authors (chiefly Aristotle their dictator) as their persons were shut up in the cells of monasteries and colleges, and knowing little history, either of nature or time, did out of no great quantity of matter and infinite agitation of wit spin out unto us those laborious webs of learning which are extant in their books. For the wit and mind of man, if it work upon matter, which is the contemplation of the creatures of God, worketh according to the stuff and is limited thereby; but if it work upon itself, as the spider worketh his web, then it is endless, and brings forth indeed cobwebs of learning, admirable for the fineness of thread and work, but of no substance or profit. 26/31–9/32

The metaphor of imprisonment is handled in a jocular way, but it is certainly diminishing; the wit consists in the analogy between physical and intellectual confinement, an association of the abstract and the concrete we would expect to find in a Ramistic author. The second sentence is a more delicate version of the high style, but the same features of main verb delay, and heavy subordination occur. There is a lot of heavy nominal structuring in the sentence, including the adjectival phrase, 'admirable for the fineness of thread and work', which introduces a slower rhythm before the final sharp, dismissive phrases. Yet very little information has been presented in these two sentences; the medieval philosophers receive no recognition for their achievements in many fields of learning. Bacon seems to think that these simple natural metaphors, because they are based on natural reason, have a strength and power of persuasion that needs no supporting argument. Here we see the fatal weakness of Ramistic logic, in that it had no method of examining and testing the truth of propositions, and it made no distinctions between various kinds of truth. The presentation of argument, even in these crude terms in this passage, was thought to be implicitly persuasive. The reader's mind would know at once whether something was true or false in the act of grasping the meaning of the sentence. This is simply not the case, but Bacon writes as though it were. The rigorous use of contradiction and antithesis in Sidney's version of the high style is based on a moral concept of reason as an uncorrupted part of man's mind, capable of telling the truth about experience. Bacon, because he has no strong moral perspective in his work, uses reason to persuade through natural images and commonplace objects of daily life. They seem to him the limits of natural reason, and make up a kind of paradigm of natural logic.

Yet their analytical power is severely limited; Bacon will not argue and assert in the way Sidney does in the high style. He relies too much on the intuitive power of reason, while Sidney brings a relentless moral pressure to bear through reasoning. This difference can be seen most clearly in the way Bacon deals with the schoolmens' philosophical method:

> This same unprofitable subtility or curiosity is of two sorts; either in the subject itself that they handle, when it is a fruitless speculation or controversy (whereof there are no small number both in divinity and philosophy), or in the manner or method of handling of a knowledge, which amongst them was this; upon every particular position or assertion to frame objections, and to those objections, solutions; which solutions were for the most part not confutations, but distinctions: whereas indeed the strength of all sciences is, as the strength of the old man's faggot, in the bond. For the harmony of a science, supporting each part the other, is and ought to be the true and brief confutation and suppression of all the smaller sorts of objections. But on the other side, if you take out every axiom, as the sticks of the faggot, one by one, you may quarrel with them and bend them and break them at your pleasure.   10–26/32

In this passage we can see that Bacon is very suspicious, as well he might be, of the labyrinth of medieval logic, but he makes the mistake of suggesting that no analysis is necessary at all. That somehow, we already know what is a 'smaller' objection, and what is the larger purpose of the area of study, or the topic within that area, that we happen to be examining. He even says that axioms should not be examined separately, because he is deceived by his simple analogy with the bundle of sticks. As we know, in any area of study, and especially in the sciences, each proposition in an argument or theory has to be considered separately. The harmony of a science is altogether different from his idea of it. He uses the image of the bundle as a catch-all term to resolve a much more complex matter. Natural reason must be applied in a series of propositions, it cannot be exploited through one simple natural image. There is, too, the problem of Bacon's persistent failure to distinguish between abstracts and concrete senses or meanings. Where there is an existential truth, and no suitable language to express it in, as in many parts of the *Essays*, the natural imagery is often insightful and original. In the more general discussion of *The Advancement of Learning*, the limitations of natural imagery rapidly become apparent. The generality of this high style passage cannot disguise the dialectical weakness of the image. It is a powerful visual image, which Bacon would have thought acceptable in a non-literary context because of its persuasive force. He must have imagined it would carry conviction on sight, but instead it raises questions about his view of what a theory or a science is.

The middle style, with its idealism and lyrical subject matter, rarely occurs in Bacon. He has almost no room for any aesthetic view of life. In any case, the subject matter of his work is not related to the poetic imagery and elegant introspection of the traditional middle style. There are some passages to be found in his *Essays*, but they are rare. In Sidney, of course, the middle style is widely exploited, especially in the new *Arcadia*. But again, the form is modified by an increased use of argument and a new sense of patterning in syntax. For example, the description of Musidorus and his sorrow is a typical middle style interlude:

> Musidorus (who, besides he was merely unacquainted in the country, had his wits with astonished with sorrow) gave easy consent to that from which he saw no reason to disagree: and therefore (defraying the mariners with a ring bestowed upon them) they took their journey together through Laconia; Claius and Strephon by course carrying his chest for him, Musidorus only bearing in his countenance evident marks of a sorrowful mind supported with a weak body; which they perceiving, and knowing that the violence of sorrow is not, at the first, to be striven withal (being like a mighty beast, sooner tamed with following than overthrown by withstanding) they gave way unto it for that day and the next; never troubling him either with asking questions or finding fault with his melancholy, but rather fitting to his dolour dolorous discourses of their own and other folks' misfortunes. Which speeches, though they had not a lively entrance to his senses shut up in sorrow, yet like one half asleep he took hold of much of the matter spoken unto him, so as a man may say, ere sorrow was aware, they made his thoughts bear away something else beside his own sorrow; which wrought so in him that at length he grew content to mark their speeches, then to marvel at such wit in shepherds, after to like their company, and lastly to vouchsafe conference. 1–22/69

The sentences develop through a sequence of pairings, by clause and phrase: correlation and parallelism are the main devices of style in this leisurely analysis of grief and its gradual disappearance. There is a witty play of abstract and concrete senses ('only bearing . . . evident marks of a sorrowful mind supported with a weak body' matches the concrete sense of 'carrying his chest for him'); a tendency to use periphrasis for elegant rhythmical balance ('gave easy consent to that from which he saw no reason to disagree'); and a constant exploitation of graded sense (through comparatives, 'sooner tamed with following than overthrown by withstanding', 'never troubling . . . but rather fitting . . .', 'at length' . . . 'then' . . . 'after' . . . 'lastly' . . .). The passage is full of qualifying devices: 'merely', 'by course', 'at the first', 'for that day and the next', 'like one half asleep', 'much of the matter spoken unto him', 'something else beside . . .'. It is significant for the middle style register that these are nearly all adverbials, which maintain the verbal tendencies of the register, with its preference for clausal style. Noun phrases, where they occur, are less dominant and emphatic than in the high style. Imagery is more conventional, closer to the similes of poetic tradition, than the fierce metaphor of the high style. Such analogies as 'like a mighty beast' or 'like one half asleep' are not very striking or original; the reader notices the loss of emphasis in such conventional asides. They lack the absolute emphasis of the high style- 'the tyranny of the wind and the treason of the sea', 'tearing out her bowels to feed the sea's greediness'. For in the middle style, an image is secondary and subordinate to the analysis of idea or state of mind, while in the high style, an image conveys directly the experience and the writer's emphasis. Sometimes Sidney takes analysis to such an intricate level that the sentence becomes almost unreadable in its strait jacket of the Ciceronian periodic pattern. In this example periphrasis and analysis go hand in hand to make an extraordinary problem for the reader:

> The sweet minded Philoclea was in their degree of well-doing to whom the not knowing of evil serveth for a ground of virtue, and hold their inward powers in better form with an unspotted simplicity than many who rather cunningly seek to know what goodness is than willingly take into themselves the following of it. But as that sweet and simple breath of heavenly goodness is the easier to be altered because it hath not passed through the worldly wickedness nor feelingly found the evil that evil carries

> with it, so now the lady Philoclea (whose eyes and senses had received nothing but according as the natural course of each thing required, whose tender youth had obediently lived under her parents' behests, without framing out of her own will the forechoosing of any thing) when now she came to a point wherein her judgement was to be practised in knowing faultiness by his first tokens, she was like a young fawn who, coming in the wind of the hunters, doth not know whether it be a thing or no to be eschewed; whereof at this time she began to get a costly experience. 30/237–9/238.

The sentence is difficult because of the complexity of qualifying clauses, and the length of these clauses. There are many paradoxes presented in forms of comparison and qualification. The passage means, in simple terms, that Philoclea was uncertain what to do, and placed herself in a vulnerable position because of her inexperience. She is faced with the problem of adult choice in an ambiguous world. The topic is an eternal source of interest to the middle style writer, but it strikes the modern reader as rather trivial and thin as a subject on its own. Is this kind of innocence that interesting? Can it be real? Such questions should not be asked of the middle style context, for it provides no answer. There is an assumption, right from the beginning, that there is leisure for such considerations and interest in such matters. Analysis and introspection become a way of life.

Sometimes analysis can take on a dramatic visual aspect, as in this description of the discovery of the shipwreck:

> They steered therefore as near thither-ward as they could; but when they came so near as their eyes were full masters of the object, they saw a sight full of piteous strangeness: a ship, or rather the carcase of the ship, or rather some few bones of the carcase hulling there, part broken, part burned, part drowned – death having used more than one dart to that destruction. About it floated great store of very rich things and many chests which might promise no less. And amidst the precious things were a number of dead bodies, which likewise did not only testify both elements' violence, but that the chief violence was grown of human inhumanity; for their bodies were full of grisly wounds, and their blood had (as it were) filled the wrinkles of the sea's visage, which it seemed the sea would not wash away that it might

witness it is not always his fault when we condemn his cruelty. In sum, a defeat where the conquered kept both field and spoil; a ship-wreck without storm or ill-footing, and a waste of fire in the midst of water.   36/65–15/66.

Here the categorising tendencies of Ramistic logic support and order the discourse. The nominal qualification of the first sentence, 'a ship, or rather the carcase of the ship, or rather some few bones of the carcase . . .', with its attendant past participles, moves gradually from the general to the particular details. This is the natural method of Ramistic logic, but it also presents the gradual revelation of the tragedy to those approaching the scene of the disaster. The middle style conceit of the 'wrinkles of the sea's visage', and its explanation, is both artful and elegant. The covert image of an old man weeping is appropriate to this 'sight full of piteous strangeness', although the blood is a startling paradox, for it suggests that nature (in the example of the sea) has been harmed by humanity. This explains the paradoxes of the closing sentence; 'human inhumanity' is a paradox as unnatural as 'a waste of fire in the midst of water', although it is an abstract idea, while the main images in this passage are concrete and visual.

Elsewhere, the realism of Sidney's middle style, its wit and humour, together with its psychological acuteness, overcome the dangers of too refined an analysis:

> The cunning of his flattery, the readiness of his tears, the infiniteness of his vows, were but among the weakest threads of his net. But the stirring our own passions, and by the entrance of them to make himself lord of our forces, there lay his master's part of cunning, making us now jealous, now envious, now proud of what we had, desirous of more; now giving one the triumph, to see him, that was prince of many, subject to her; now with an estranged look making her fear the loss of that mind, which indeed could never be had: never ceasing humbleness and diligence till he had embarked us in some such disadvantage as we could not return dry-shod; and then suddenly a tyrant, but a crafty tyrant. For so would he use his imperiousness, that we had a delightful fear and an awe which made us loth to lose our hope. And, which is strangest, when sometimes with late repentance I think of it, I must confess even in the greatest tempest of my judgement was I never driven to think him excellent; and yet so

could set my mind both to get and keep him, as though therein had laid my felicity: like them I have seen play at ball grow extremely earnest who should have the ball, and yet every one knew it was but a ball.   7–26/336.

We can see how paradox, qualification, and colloquial images (but not of a rough or unpleasant kind, rather a sort of elegant slang) combine to make this analysis dramatic and truthful. The speaker knows both what she ought to think about her former lover, and how she did feel about him. The passage balances reasoned distinctions of sense against the irrational need for love.

These topics have no interest for Bacon. But in the *Essays* he occasionally uses a middle style literary metaphor, although on the whole he prefers the plain style colloquial image drawn from common speech. These images are the most well-known aspect of the *Essays*. They make points without analysis, by bringing together unlikely associations of ideas. For example, 'Suspicions amongst thoughts are like bats among birds, they ever fly by twilight', or 'Men fear death, as children fear to go in the dark', or 'All rising to great place is by a winding stair.'[14] This is the plain style shorthand that replaces the middle style analytical image. Because these images are drawn from common experience they seem to have more weight and carry more conviction than a literary image. They seem to embody natural logic in their casualness and informal assertion; for the literal meaning of these arguments is quite abstract. Does Bacon mean that suspicions are difficult to identify, because they seem like real, soundly based thought? Or does he mean that suspicions are only entertained when we are not thinking clearly? Is the fear of death a childish thing we inherit from our early years, or an elemental fear that no human being can escape? Is the turn of the stair an image of deviousness or an image of the varied interests such a successful career might encompass? Bacon does not expect us to delay long enough to inquire. The *Essays* depend to a great extent on this 'half-thinking'. I do not believe these images are meant to be enigmatic and thought-provoking, because the style is not designed for subtle and difficult ideas. The most successful essays are quite explicit in their argument, and there is rarely any ironic deception, which would in any case be more proper to the middle style. The great strength of the essays is the cohesion Bacon develops between one colloquial image and another. A good example of this is the essay, *Of Truth*.

The general structure of the essay falls into three parts – philosophical truth, theological truth, and truth in public life. Bacon begins the essay with a witty variation on the traditional opening for a topic. Instead of a definition, Bacon uses a philosophical 'question'; he expects the reader to be aware that Pilate knows he is playing the philosopher: '*What is truth?* said jesting Pilate, and would not stay for an answer.' In the next sentence, Bacon translates the general question into particular comments on a familiar human type: 'Certainly there be that delight in giddiness, and count it a bondage to fix a belief; affecting free-will in thinking, as well as in acting.' Between these two plain style sentences Bacon makes a close thematic link; for the subject of the essay is not so much truth in the abstract as truth in the human context, the essay form being essentially a social genre. So '*delight* in giddiness' continues the image of '*jesting* Pilate', while '*would not stay* for an answer' has a loose but witty transformation into its opposite, 'count it a *bondage* to *fix* a *belief*'. And Christ Himself stands for, and in fact is, the Christian faith incarnate. Had he waited, Bacon implies, Pilate would have received a sufficiently convincing reply to his question. But Pilate was conscious of his guile, and left deliberately, as the reader is reminded in the second sentence, '*affecting* free will in *thinking*, as well as in *acting*'. Bacon's gloss on St John's Gospel gives him in a beautifully concise example the triple theme of philosophical truth, political truth and theological truth. The philosophical scepticism of the pagan administrator faced with a sectarian, the political delicacy of the issue, and the sacred truth of the Christian religion, combine in one image.

Bacon moves on to the topic of philosophical truth explicitly. Again, there are echoes of the earlier sentences. 'And though the sects of philosophers of that kind be gone, yet there remain certain discoursing wits which are of the same veins, though there be not so much blood in them as was in those of the ancients.' There seems to be an associative link between 'certain discoursing wits' and 'jesting Pilate'; the use of a similar form for the adjective focuses the similarity of sense. Next, Bacon puns on the double meaning of 'veins' (i. literary topic, ii. human veins), and perhaps suggests darkly that Pilate was more blood-thirsty than the present sceptics, who at least cannot be accused of allowing public executions for the sake of their theories. The phrases 'delight in giddiness' and 'count it a bondage to fix a belief' are translated into their opposites in 'the *difficulty* and *labour* which men *take in finding out of truth*' (purposeful action beside the unsteadiness of constant change), and in the clause 'when it is found it *imposeth* on men's thoughts' (= 'to enjoin as a duty or law', the opposite of bondage). These ideas are not sufficient to explain why lies or deception are so popular amongst men; Bacon turns to the explanation that nature offers: lies, one Greek philosopher says, are valued for their own sake, through a 'natural though corrupt love of the lie itself'. But Bacon does not agree that lies do not give pleasure or commercial advantage: 'this same truth is a naked and open day-light, that doth not shew the masques and mummeries and triumphs of the world half so stately and daintily as candle-lights. Truth may perhaps come to the price of a pearl, that sheweth best by day; but it will not rise to the price of a diamond or carbuncle, that sheweth best in varied lights.' Again, the 'pearl of great price', the biblical image of the soul's salvation, echoing the sacred image of the opening lines, is contrasted with the more valuable diamond or precious gem. Lies are loved for their enhancing effects in the market place, and in the rooms of state. If men's minds were robbed of vanity and self-delusion, they would be 'poor shrunken things', 'unpleasing to themselves'. Even the theatre of the inner life must be lit with candles.

But Bacon turns from such considerations to theological truth, which he defines in terms that remind the reader of the first image in the essay. He divides up the idea of truth into several aspects: 'the inquiry of truth', 'the knowledge of truth, which is the presence of it', 'the belief of truth' — all topics which can be seen to relate to the words of Pilate to Christ. He refers to a passage of poetry in the literary middle style he seldom uses, in order to contrast the pleasures of the senses with the pleasures of reason and truth. 'Certainly, it is heaven upon earth, to have a man's mind move in charity, rest in providence, and turn upon the poles of truth.' There is a reference back to those who, in contrast, 'count it a bondage to fix a belief' and, instead, 'delight in giddiness'. In the final part of the essay, on the 'truth of civil business', Bacon exploits the commonplace image of counterfeit money as a symbol of dishonesty between men in commercial dealings. Again, the biblical images appear: 'these winding and crooked courses are the goings of the serpent; which goeth basely upon the belly, and not upon the feet'. Alloy in silver and gold coins 'may make the metal work the better, but it embaseth it'. We see again, as in the pun on 'veins', how quickly Bacon seizes upon the literal and figurative meanings of words to create cohesion. And the reference to biblical truth is of course implicit in the second image. Significantly for the structure of the essay, Bacon chooses an antithetical quotation from Montaigne, 'If it be well weighed, to say that a man lieth, is as much to say as that he is brave towards God and a coward towards man.' This provides the lead-in to the final tying together of the whole structure. For Pilate was in a sense acting out Montaigne's dictum in his very behaviour. He jests with God incarnate, and avoids facing the man he questions, as well as the rabble who demanded execution. The pagan philosopher's cynicism outfaces revealed truth in the same way as, at Christ's second coming, 'he shall not find faith upon the earth.'

Now in the plain style, Sidney uses rather less of the figurative imagery that Bacon relies on. Only in the *Apology for Poetry* do we find similar effects of style. They are used to place the hyperbole of self-interest, whether it be that of the horseman, the philosopher, or the historian. But there is less conceptual play in the plain style of these contexts; Sidney reverts to the traditions of classical decorum, and uses the technical terms of each profession to overturn its claims to authority and status. Let us begin with the horseman:

> And he, according to the fertileness of the Italian wit, did not only afford us the demonstration of his practice, but sought to enrich our minds with the contemplations therein which he thought most precious. But with none I remember mine ears were at any time more loaden, than when (either angered with slow payment, or moved with our learner-like admiration) he exercised his speech in the praise of his faculty.   5–12/95[15]

Perhaps the phrase 'according to the fertileness of the Italian wit' would have alerted a contemporary; 'enrich our minds' and 'contemplations' sound ripe hyperbole, perhaps overripe, and can 'precious' be entirely unironic? The next sentence confirms the suspicion: 'with none . . . were my ears more loaden' is appropriate language in one sense, for it describes the saddling of a horse, a natural association with the speaker referred to, the Italian squire who is teaching Sidney advanced horsemanship. But while it is only too appropriate to the subject and the speaker, it is scarcely suited to the manner of his address. The Italian squire seems to be treating Sidney and his companion like a couple of horses. Another example of transferred register from subject matter to manner of speech is the clause, 'he exercised his speech in the praise of his faculty', for squires normally exercise horses not language. The 'fertileness of the Italian wit' receives ample recognition before dismissal:

> He said soldiers were the noblest estate of mankind, and horsemen the noblest of soldiers. He said they were the masters of war and ornaments of peace, speedy goers and strong abiders, triumphers both in camps and courts. Nay, to so unbelieved a point he proceeded, as that no earthly thing bred such wonder to a prince as to be a good horseman. Skill of government was but a *pedanteria* in comparison. Then would he add certain praises, by telling what a peerless beast a horse was, the only serviceable courtier without flattery, the beast of most beauty, faithfulness, courage, and such more, that if I had not been a piece of a logician before I came to him, I think he would have persuaded me to have wished myself a horse. But thus much at least with his no few words he drave into me, that self-love is better than any gilding to make that seem gorgeous wherein ourselves are parties.   12–26/95

The passage divides into two registers, that in which a middle style poetic and philosophic diction contrasts with the colloquial register of the plain style. Such phrases as 'no earthly thing' have a colloquial force, as does 'but a *pedanteria* in comparison' (taking the words out of his mouth); in the middle style register we find many terms, 'masters of war and ornaments of peace' (a Ramistic dichotomy), 'a peerless beast', and 'beauty, faithfulness, courage'. The whole passage is in fact ordered on Ramistic lines, in the natural method; it proceeds from the general statements of definition in the first sentence, with its careful axiomatic narrowing of topic, to the description of horsemen and horses, by developing a list of their proper qualities in logical adjuncts. But the colloquial register contains the poetic: 'and such more' is colloquial syntax, announcing an ironic shift in the movement of thought. Sidney exploits the proper logical implications of the speech to render the whole thing absurd: 'if I had not been a piece of a logician before I came to him, I think he would have persuaded me to have wished myself a horse.' The elegant middle style periphrasis in the syntax leads suddenly to the plain style truth. Perhaps the phrase 'a piece of a logician' is also colloquial: it would certainly be so today. The final irony occurs in the remark, 'thus much at least with his no few words he *drave* into me'; Sidney suggests that even if he remained unpersuaded, the speaker treated him as he would treat a horse, by applying the spurs vigorously. The technical terms of the philosophers and historians are obvious targets for attack, and Sidney is generous in his use of their terms to overturn their pretensions. There is no need to cite examples here in detail, but such passages as 10-37/104 or 8-32/105 show what he can do with their own jargon.

In the *Arcadia*, he returns to a more artificial plain style. In his account of a battle between the rebels and their rightful lords, he indulges in much patterned sarcasm at the expense of these uncourtly soldiers:

> Yet among the rebels there was a dapper fellow, a tailor by occupation who, fetching his courage only from their going back, began to bow his knees, and very fencer-like to draw near to Zelmane. But as he came within her distance, turning his sword very nicely about his crown, Basilius, with a side blow, strake off his nose. He (being a suitor to a seamster's daughter, and therefore not a little grieved for such a disgrace) stooped down, because he had heard that if it were fresh put to, it would cleave on again. But as his hand was on the ground to bring his nose to his head, Zelmane with a blow sent his head to his nose. That saw a butcher, a butcherly chuff indeed (who that day was sworn brother to him in a cup of wine) and lifted up a great leaver, calling Zelmane all the vile names of a butcherly eloquence. But she, letting slip the blow of the leaver, hit him so surely upon the side of the face that she left nothing but the nether jaw, where the tongue still wagged, as willing to say more if his master's remembrance had served.   18-34/380

The contradictions in this passage are far less marked than the striking metaphors of the high style. Rather, Sidney allows contradiction to emerge as sarcasm, by implication throughout the passage. This is the effect of such complementary propositions as 'fetching his courage only from their going back', or 'being a suitor to a seamster's daughter, and therefore not a little grieved for such a disgrace'. In both cases, each side of the argument has some relation to the other; but the relation is absurd to courtly ears, if plausible to the peasant rebels themselves. The meanings involved are social and chivalric, not logical contradictions as in the high style. Again, when the tailor loses his nose and stoops to recover it, Sidney introduces a complementary patterning which is sarcastic rather than contradictory: 'But as his hand was on the ground to bring his nose to his head, Zelmane with a blow sent his head to his nose.' The rebels are thwarted at every turn by the greater skill and knowledge of their opponents. Hence the final image of just retribution for the uncourtly butcher; 'all the vile names of a butcherly eloquence' is a paradox, a near contradiction, rather than a simple antithesis. Zelmane gives a just and exact punishment for his offence, which seems more social than political. There is throughout this passage a careful complementarity in statement, showing the balancing of each offence or social absurdity with its proper reward.

Sidney also writes a forensic form of the plain style, where close argument and exposition are the prime features of style. The most remarkable example is the speech of Euarchus, towards the end of the work. It is a long and severe argument against the princes who are standing trial. The speech begins in chapter 7 of Book 5, and may be contrasted with the middle style eloquence of Pyrocles in chapter 9 of Book 1. These styles depend more directly on the traditions of classical decorum in the courtroom, although the middle style passage uses a poetic diction quite alien to that environment. They are less typical of Sidney's chosen formulation of the styles with its 'natural logic' and exploitation of antithesis. The *Arcadia* of 1593 has many passages of middle style analysis, for that represents the original romance narrative of the earlier version; the high style images are often an additional development, and the plain style is part of the original form. Sidney keeps to the traditions of classical decorum in a sequence of single contexts, each one clearly marked for style level. Bacon cannot be directly compared with him because his plain style language is suitable to the subject matter of his work, which is non-literary and philosophical. Nevertheless, Bacon adapts the Ciceronian sentence model for his own purposes in *The Advancement of Learning*, and exploits the complexity of plain style aphorisms in the *Essays*. Yet it is remarkable how quickly the poetic diction of the Renaissance fell into disuse, for scarcely another writer follows in the tradition of Sidney's work. Bacon and Sidney represent two contrastive moments in the high Renaissance and early Jacobean period in English prose style; it is clear that the moral and political impetus behind Sidney's work is less influential in the development of literary prose than the social and philosophical interests of Bacon.

6 Andrewes and Donne

Augustine himself had discussed the use of traditional rhetorical styles for sermons in his *De Doctrina Christiana* (IV, 12 ff).[1] The problem that sermons present for the student of style is that they are non-literary texts and so do not share the same vocabulary as the literary tradition. Yet they provide another example of the influence of the three styles within their own range of vocabulary and syntax. Language in the sermon is adapted to the oral context of the work; the syntax has a tendency to be linear, without extensive subordination, and the vocabulary is usually close to speech, even in passages of high style emphasis. There are also more specialised areas of diction which are however almost always glossed by the speaker so that there can be little room for error in understanding. Lancelot Andrewes (1555–1626) represents the early Elizabethan usage in sermon writing; he analyses the biblical text of a sermon into a series of topics, derived from the various meanings of separate words in the quotation. His sermons are an extended analysis of each topic, in logical order. Often there is an impression that the quotation has been lost in the gloss that he develops from it. He rarely uses the high style, and is content to vary his language between concise variants of middle and plain style usage. There is an evenness of tone about his work which is in marked contrast to the more turbulent and theatrical manner of Donne's sermons. For John Donne (1572–1631) has much greater variation in his sermon style. Partly, this is because he uses elaboration for emphasis, rather than the conciseness favoured by Andrewes; there is much greater variety in sentence length in Donne's work. But more especially, Donne uses a much wider range of metaphors in all three levels of style, and is prepared to dramatise his own experience in a way that Andrewes will not do. On the contrary, while Donne dramatises himself as the type of the Christian believer, with all his doubts and fears, Andrewes refers only to the broad commonplaces of life, and never attempts to speak from his own inner experience. Andrewes then has little need for the subjective emphases of the high style, while Donne will often exploit the register in its sacred form. Again, Andrewes does not use the fashionable theories of Pierre de la Ramée, while Donne frequently exploits the fusion of concepts and things in these theories for arresting arguments about the Christian life. The importance of studying style in sermons is that it shows the natural basis for the academic literary styles in common features of language. The influence of these particular styles in sermon writing was very short lived, and by the middle of the seventeenth century they had been virtually forgotten. Nevertheless, Andrewes and Donne represent the final flowering of an ancient Christian rhetoric which was founded on the earliest traditions of the Church.

We can begin by considering two passages of high style emphasis. This example from Andrewes is quite rare, and shows the conciseness of usage which marks all his work:

> Yes sure, his Complaint is Just, *Have ye no Regard?* None? and yet never the like? None? and it pertaines unto you? *No Regard?* As if it were some common ordinary matter, and the like never was? *No Regard?* As if it concern'd you not a whit, and it toucheth you so neere? As if hee should say: Rare things you regard, yea though they no wayes pertaine to you; this is exceeding rare, and will you not regard it? Againe, things that neerely touch you, you regard, though they be not rare at all; this toucheth you exceeding neere, even as neere as your soule toucheth you, and will you not yet regard it? will neither of these by it selfe, moove you? will not both these together moove you? what will moove you? will Pitie? Here is Distresse, Never the like: will Duetie? heere is a Person, never the like: will Feare? here is wrath, never the like: will Remorse? heere are sinnes, never the like: will Kindnesse? heere is Love, never the like: will Bountie? heere are Benefits, never the like: will all these? heere they be all, all above any *Sicut*, all in the highest degree. 23/163-7/164[2]

We can see how the tradition of emphasis in the high style is achieved through a series of commonplace devices from ordinary usage. The literary tone of the high style elsewhere in other prose works is quite distinct from this passage. For example, the colloquial intensifiers, 'yes sure, . . .', 'None?' 'Againe, . . .', 'not a whit', 'exceeding rare', 'exceeding neere', 'and yet never the like?', 'and the like never was?' The parallelism of the phrases also lends emphasis in spite of this apparent casualness of diction and syntax. But it is a linear style, with hardly any subordination. Andrewes holds the attention of his audience by the careful controlled development of argument, through a series of concise antitheses. Yet argument is not the primary impression of this passage, although it is part of its function. Rather, Andrewes is seeking to drive home the absolute nature of Christ's sufferings to an audience that has heard it all once too often before. The question and answer device at the beginning of the passage is matched at the end by a similar device, but the content has changed. While in the beginning, Andrewes enters the discussion as the commentator, glossing and developing the reasons for Christ's question, at the end of the passage, he becomes the inquisitor, demanding an answer in Christ's name, and in the name of his sufferings on the cross. The preacher becomes indignant at the coldness and intransigence which he pretends to detect (perhaps correctly) in his audience. These abstract nouns are absolute and unqualified, like the events and the person they describe; they are appropriate diction for the high style, in spite of their biblical plainness. They speak of the fundamental truths of the crucifixion. And they do so by a metonymic association of Christ and the values attributed to Him. This trope is however fairly restrained compared to the rich development of metaphor in Donne; we can contrast this high style passage of Andrewes with a passage in similar style in Donne. Here the metaphor is exuberant and dialectical; Donne advances his argument and exposition through the most dynamic emphasis:

> The creeping Serpent, the groveling Serpent, is Craft; the exalted Serpent, the crucified Serpent, is Wisdome. All your worldly cares, all your crafty bargaines, all your subtill matches, all your diggings into other mens estates, all your hedgings in of debts, all your planting of children in great allyances; all these diggings, and hedgings and plantings savour of the earth, and of the craft of that Serpent, that creeps upon the earth: But crucifie this craft of yours, bring all your worldly subtilty under the Crosse of Christ Jesus, husband your farmes so, as you may give a good account to him, presse your debts so, as you would be pressed by him, market and bargaine so, as that you would give all, to buy that field, in which his treasure, and his pearle is hid, and then you have changed the Serpent, from the Serpent of perdition creeping upon the earth, to the Serpent of salvation exalted in the

wildernesse. Creeping wisedome, that still looks downward, is but craft; Crucified wisedome, that looks upward, is truly wisedome.   6–22/235[3]

The primary technique in this passage is substitution and repetition for emphasis. Even the two short sentences at the beginning and end of the passage show this characteristic of Donne's prose: 'creeping', 'groveling' apply to the serpent of 'craft', the 'crucified' serpent is the serpent of 'wisdom', while at the end of the passage Donne transforms the idea of a serpent into a clause ('that still looks downward', 'that looks upward'), and applies the epithets to 'wisdom'. The first sentence introduces the main idea of the paragraph in a pair of definitions, the last sentence shifts the definitions into a new alignment. The high style sentence that intervenes between these two concise plain style sentences works as a device of elaboration and clarification, giving weight and emphasis in the paragraph. Emphasis in the plain style is a matter of thematic ordering of sense, while in the high style passage metaphor is enriched by amplification. If we look at the high style sentence we see there the same devices of repetition and substitution. Donne collects and enlarges his thought as he progresses through the sentence. The first sequence of verbal nouns has no direct grammatical support, it is a dummy subject, rapidly summarised and repeated in a concise form as the actual subject – 'all these diggings, and hedgings and plantings . . .'. In this way Donne imitates the periodic rhythms of the classical sentence pattern. He exploits the analytic genitive structure for further exposition: 'savour of the earth, and of the craft of that Serpent, that creeps upon the earth'. He substitutes a second prepositional phrase to introduce the original metaphor which began the paragraph. This development has close cohesion with the structure that follows: 'this craft of yours', with its analytic genitive, both mirrors what has preceded it, and what follows, 'the Crosse of Christ Jesus'. The parallelism of syntax marks the turning point in the sentence. The listener is invited to choose between these alternatives. In the last part of the sentence, a series of parallel imperatives in which the preacher admonishes the congregation, we find the same devices of repetition and substitution. Each imperative is followed by a comparative clause; the final movement of the sentence balances 'the Serpent of perdition' with 'the Serpent of salvation', and two non-finite clauses occur in parallel sequence. All these features are devices of emphasis designed to reinforce the large contrast of meaning between the first half of the sentence and this part. There is also a careful semantic cohesion found in the association of 'diggings, and hedgings, and plantings' with 'that field, in which his treasure, and his pearle is hid'. For diggings, hedgings and plantings are all aspects of agricultural labour, carried on in the fields of England, and so the contrast between the two parts of the sentence is increased, because the similarity is deliberate. Again, the rhythm of the sentence becomes freer in the second half because Donne reverts to clause patterns, and uses no verbal nouns; the sentence in the first half is dominated by the cluster of noun phrases which slows up the rhythm, while in the second half it is patterned on the initial clause, 'crucifie this craft of yours'. Donne balances noun phrases against clauses, and the second choice makes the sense clearer and easier to follow. A clause conveys information in a more accessible way than a complex noun phrase. Less attention is required from the listener to follow the sense.

This pattern of balance and contrast in the high style can be amplified to any degree in Donne's sermon style. In this example, substitution becomes the primary device of emphasis, within a larger context of parallel clauses:

> But, if thou canst take this light of reason that is in thee, this poore snuffe, that is almost out in thee, thy faint and dimme knowledge of God, that riseth out of this light of nature, if thou canst in those embers, those cold ashes, finde out one small coale, and wilt take the paines to kneell downe, and blow that coale with thy devout *Prayers*, and light thee a *little candle*, (a *desire* to reade that Booke, which they call the Scriptures, and the Gospell, and the Word of God;) If with that little candle thou canst creep humbly into low and poore places, if thou canst finde thy Saviour in a *Manger*, and in his *swathing clouts*, in his humiliation, and blesse God for that beginning, if thou canst finde him flying into Egypt, and finde in thy selfe a disposition to accompany him in a persecution, in a banishment, if not a bodily banishment, a locall banishment, yet a *reall, a spirituall banishment*, a banishment from those sinnes, and that sinnefull conversation, which thou hast loved more than thy *Parents*, or *Countrey*, or thine owne body, which perchance thou hast consumed, and destroyed with that sinne . . .   13–29/209

There is not room here to quote the whole passage, which continues for many lines. It is sufficient to note that the high style in Donne can be employed as a climax in the sermon, as well as a moment of emphasis in the discussion of minor points. The sustained syntax of this passage indicates that it is designed as the climax of the whole sermon; the argumentative pattern of the clauses and the common-place language are typical of the preacher's attitude to his congregation. For Donne, the preacher's task was to arouse the congregation from its moral torpor, and create a new determination to follow the path of Christian duty. Andrewes probably took the same view, but he holds our attention by less dramatic means. In this passage, there are some devices of substitution and repetition, but there is less emphasis in sentence rhythm:

> But we are not so much to regard the *Ecce*, how *great* it is, as *Gaudium*, what *joy* is in it; that is the point we are to speake to. And for that; men may talke what they will, but sure there is no *joy* in the world to the *joy* of a man *saved*: no *joy* so great, no newes so welcome, as to one ready to perish, in case of a lost man, to heare of one, that will *save* him. In danger of perishing; By sicknesse, to heare of one will make him well againe: By sentence of the law, of one with a pardon to *save* his live: By enemies, of one that will rescue, and set him in safetie. Tell any of these, assure them but of a *Saviour*, it is the best newes he ever heard in his life. There is *joy* in the name of a *Saviour*. 11–22/34

The devices of emphasis are colloquial and light: 'men may talke what they will, but sure there is no *joy* in the world to the *joy* of a man *saved*'. In this sentence, the initial disclaimer disguises the emphasis, making it seem natural and familiar. The formality of the high style has been abandoned for an intimate tone of address; what follows has more formality, though. The parallel noun phrases give renewed emphasis to the passage, introducing the association of 'joy' with 'news of salvation'. The repetitions press home the statement, through the syntax of phrase, '*no* joy *so* great, *no* news *so* welcome'. The division of topic into the kinds of danger a man might suffer is again a device of emphasis. It amplifies and expands the consideration of the joy which salvation brings. Again, substitution gives emphasis in the next sentence, with 'Tell any of these, assure them but of . . .'; the phrases are not over-formal, but they represent the high style in Andrewes' usage. The colloquial statement, 'it is the best newes he ever heard in his life' is also high style in this writer's work. It appears colloquial out of context; but the delicacy of an indexical marker of style must be weighed against the general level of registerial marking. In Andrewes it is always delicate, and we are entitled to regard this as an example of the high style. Here is another example of equal delicacy:

> And, to doe it *now*. For (as in a *circle*) I returne to the first word *Now* which giveth us our *time*, when we should enter our first *degree*: *Now therefore*. And, when all is done, we shall have somewhat to doe, to bring this to a *Nunc*, to a *time present*. But besides that, now at this *time*, it is the *time* that all things *turne*: *Now*, is the onely sure part of our *time*. That which is *past*, is *come* and *gone*. That which is *to come*, may peradventure *never come*. Till tomorrow, till this Evening, till an houre hence, we have no assurance. *Now therefore*. Or, if not *now*, as neere *now*, with as little distance from it, as may be; If not this *day*, this *time* now ensuing.   11–21/141

These concise clauses appear casual and in a plain style; in fact, within the context of the sermon this is a powerful structural emphasis in the high style. The language is colloquial and unliterary, but the echoing repetition of 'Now therefore' and 'now' carries a weight of emphasis. Andrewes exploits conciseness for emphasis in his sermon styles; Donne, by contrast, uses elaboration of phrase and varying sentence length for emphasis. One writer is tied to the construction of phrasal patterns of emphasis, the second to clausal patterns of emphasis. Both devices are common in speech; what is rare, is the elimination of the other alternative from each writer's usage. They both developed a very precise range of effects in every level of style, but the range is narrow and unlike the variety of modern prose usage. But the same view may be taken of Sidney or Bacon; one of the chief distinctions between modern prose styles and early writing such as this, is the relative consistency of style within particular levels and authors. The rhetorical patterns of language, and the doctrine of the three styles made for much greater consistency in writing than today. Now we should examine some examples of middle style in both writers.

In Donne, the middle style is marked by argued metaphor and extensive analysis in sentences of relative brevity. The Ramistic idea that concepts and things are equivalent can lead to some surprising metaphors; in this passage the concept of equality in death is demonstrated by the image of the ashes of an oak tree, or the dust from the graveyard:

> Death comes equally to us all, and makes us all equall when it comes. The ashes of an Oak in the Chimney, are no Epitaph of that Oak, to tell me how high or how large that was; It tels me not what flocks it sheltered while it stood, nor what men it hurt when it fell. The dust of great persons graves is speechlesse too, it sayes nothing, it distinguishes nothing: As soon the dust of a wretch whom thou wouldst not, as of a Prince whom thou couldst not look upon, will trouble thine eyes, if the winde blow it thither; and when a whirle-winde hath blowne the dust of the Church-yard into the Church, and the man sweeps out the dust of the Church into the Church-yard, who will undertake to sift those dusts again, and to pronounce, This is the Patrician, this is the noble flowre, and this the yeomanly, this the Plebeian bran? So is the death of *Jesabel* (*Jesabel* was a Queen) expressed; *They shall not say, this is Jesabel*; not only not wonder that it is, nor pity that it should be, but they shall not say, they shall not know, This is *Jesabel*.   25/212–7/213

Donne argues from the effects of the tree (on herds and men), and then from the effects of various people (both poor, who can be ignored, and royal, who cannot be looked at by common people), and contrasts these distinct logical effects with the similar effects of their dust, now they are gone. The argument has some logical strength in it, but it is typical of his middle style that he intensifies and adds further complexity. So when these dusts from the churchyard are swept into the church, and out again, by the cleaner, Donne finds more evidence of the equality of persons in death. The dust of rich and poor is the same; it cannot be distinguished by its effects, nor by its actual quality. The passage has wit of a grisly kind, but it is ordered by the directness of argument that contains the imagery. There is less repetition and substitution than in the high style passage; the rhythm is less marked, and there are fewer runs of noun phrases. The passage has a clean clausal structure in which one proposition is balanced off against another. The first sentence is illustrated and expanded in those that follow; but in this case, unlike the high style passage, the examples are not dynamic metaphors heaped together for emphasis. Here the argument is presented in an even, balanced way, through comparison and correlation.

Andrewes uses the middle style for analysis too, but he does not conduct that analysis through metaphor. In this famous passage, we can see the technique of division of topic being used to create an historical gloss on the sermon text:

> It is not commended, to stand *gazing up into Heaven* too long, Not *on Christ Himselfe ascending*: Much lesse on His *starr*. For, they sat not still gazing on the *starr*. Their *Vidimus* begatt *Venimus*; their *seeing* made them *come*; come, a great journey. *Venimus* is soone sayd; but a *short word*; But, many a wide and weary stepp they made, before they could come to say *Venimus*, Lo, heer *we are come*; *Come*, and at our jorneys end. To looke a little on it. In this their *Comming*, we consider, 1. First, the *distance* of the Place, they came from. It was not hard by, as the *shepheard's* (but a step to *Bethlehem*, over the fields): This was riding many a hundred miles, and cost them many a dayes journey. 2. Secondly, we consider the *Way*, that they came: If it be *pleasant*, or plaine and *easy*: For, if it be, it is so much the better. 1. This was nothing *pleasant*; for, through *deserts*: all the way wast and desolate. 2. Nor (secondly) *easy* neither: For, over the Rocks and craggs of both *Arabies* (specially *Petraea*) their journey lay. 3. Yet, if *safe*: But, it was not; but exceeding dangerous, as lying through the middest of the *Black Tents of Kedar*, a Nation of *Theeves* and Cut-throtes; To passe over the *hills* of *Robbers*; Infamous then, and infamous to this day. No passing, without great troop, or Convoy. 4. Last, we consider the *time* of their comming, the season of the yeare. It was no *summer Progresse*. A cold comming they had of it, at this time of the yeare; just, the worst time of the yeare, to take a journey, and specially a long journey, in. The waies deep, the weather sharp, the daies short, the sunn farthest off *in solstitio brumali*, the very dead of *Winter*. *Venimus*, We are come, if that be one; *Venimus*, We are (now) come, come at this time, that (sure) is another.
>
> 1–30/109.

It is this persistent literalism of Andrewes' mind which makes for heavy reading in some of his sermons. But the compensations for such an approach can be seen here; the scrupulous distinctions of argument, step by step, imitate the tortuous and difficult journey of the three wise men. The dramatic impression of effort, sustained and deliberate, is conveyed through the most obvious distinctions between word and deed. Andrewes believed that this was the central problem of faith, to translate belief into action, and so he has little time for fanciful arguments based on unlikely analogies. Donne's sermons are very much the work of an intellectual for whom ideas have a reality most people cannot grasp. It is likely that many of his sermons were delivered to rather select groups within the City or the Court. Although this sermon of Andrewes was delivered before the Court too, it shows the consistent quality of his mind: there is a moral severity behind such sarcasms as 'It is not commended to stand gazing up into Heaven too long', or 'It was no *summer Progresse*', or again, '*Venimus*, We are (now) come, come at this time, that (sure) is another'. Here is another more extended example of middle style in Andrewes; it reminds us that the note form of his most famous passage is a deliberate mode of analysis, which could be altered where he felt necessary:

> But, leaves are but leaves, and so are all earthly stayes. The fruit then, the true fruit of the Vine indeed, the true comfort in all heavinesse, is *Desuper*, from above, is divine consolation. But *Vindemiavit me*, (saith the Latine text) even that was in this his Sorow, this day, bereft him too. And that was his most sorowfull complaint of all others: not that his friends upon earth, but that his Father from heaven had forsaken him, that neither heaven nor earth yeelded him any regard; but that betweene the passioned powers of his soule, and whatsoever might any waies refresh him, there was a Traverse drawen, and he left in the estate of a weather-beaten tree, all desolate and forlorne. Evident, too evident, by that his most dreadful crie, which at once moved all the powers in heaven and earth, *My God, my God, why hast thou forsaken me*? Weigh well that crie, consider it well, and tell me, *Si fuerit clamor sicut clamor iste*, if ever there were crie, like to that of his: Never the like crie, and therefore never the like sorow. 12–29/153

In this passage we can observe the same careful process of distinction which sustains the previous example; there is more complexity of noun phrase and greater correlation of clauses. The richness of adjectival variation in the description of the journey is replaced, in this passage, by one central metaphor, the 'weather-beaten tree', leafless in the storm. There is far more abstraction too; 'the true fruit of the Vine', 'the true comfort in all heavinesse', 'divine consolation', 'the passioned powers of his soule' – these noun phrases have a formality and weight which is absent from the earlier passage. The biblical metaphor is traditional, and quickly glossed to give the contextual sense, 'divine consolation'. But the formality of the metaphor adds dignity to the context. So does the formality of the question, 'Weigh well that crie, consider it well, and tell me . . .'. There is formality in the periphrasis 'yeelded him any regard', and in the vocabulary, 'evident', 'desolate and forlorne', 'estate', 'dreadful'. In the earlier passage, such adjectives as 'pleasant', 'wast and desolate', 'infamous', 'exceeding dangerous' lend formality to the context. Yet it has to be admitted that there are more frequent occurrences of colloquial phrases in the description of the journey: 'looke a little on it', 'cost them many a dayes journey', 'so much the better', 'Theeves and Cut-throtes', 'A cold comming they had of it', 'the waies deep, the weather sharp, the daies short'. But these phrases are a typical feature of middle style usage; they represent the elegant colloquialisms of the experienced traveller, in an age when only the wealthy could travel far and for any length of time. The main thrust of the passage is not in exposition or narrative, but in analysis of the hard task the Magi had set themselves when they decided to follow the star. Here in the second passage, the writer is constrained by the seriousness of the topic, Christ's anguish on the cross, and the casual colloquialism would be quite out of place.

Another example from Donne will show how he sustains metaphor in a middle style analysis throughout a paragraph; the metaphor is the vehicle of his analysis, and not kept for illustration only, as it is in Andrewes:

> It is not then with Riches in a family, as it is with a nail in a wall, that the hard beating of it in, makes it the faster. It is not the hard and laborious getting of money, the fixing of that in a strong wall, the laying it upon lands, and such things as are vulgarly distinguished from moveables, (as though the world, and we were not moveables) nor the beating that nail hard, the binding it with Entailes, of Iron, and Adamant, and perpetuities of eternity, that makes riches permanent, and sure; but it is the good purpose in the getting, and the good use in the having. And this good use is not, when thou makest good use of thy Money, but when the Common-wealth, where God hath given thee thy station, makes use of it: The Common-wealth must suck upon it by trade, not it

upon the Common-wealth, by usury. Nurses that give suck to children, maintain themselves by it too; but both must be done; thou must be enriched so, by thy money, as that the state be not impoverished. This is the good use in having it; and the good purpose in getting it, is, that God may be glorified in it. Some errours in using Riches, are not so dangerous; for some imploying of them in excesses, and superfluities, this is a rust without, it will be fil'd off with good counsel, or it will be worn off in time; in time we come to see the vanity of it: and when we leave looking at other mens cloaths, or thinking them the better men for their cloaths, why should we think, that others like us the better for our cloaths; those desires will decay in us. But an ill purpose in getting of them, that we might stand of our selves, and rely upon our Riches, that is a rust, a cancer at the heart, and is incurable.   18/200–18/201

The conciseness of this passage, and its relatively unextended rhythms, are at once obvious. There is a reflective and analytical use of metaphor that cannot be equated with the high style passage above; the writer pauses and interrupts himself with reflective insertions, and there is a firm but unemphatic use of parallelism in phrase and clause. The argument of the passage, or rather the analysis of the image in this passage, is typical of Ramistic logic. An action of a commonplace kind is contrasted with an abstract idea, the continued possession and enjoyment of wealth, from one generation to the next. But why should the nail in the wall have anything to do with the other proposition? Donne makes no distinction between abstract and concrete, between concepts and things. This is what makes the passage sound strange to the modern reader; it must also have sounded strange to the contemporary listener. How could Donne justify such a usage? He transforms the physical action of knocking the nail into the wall into an analogy for the devices which men invent to keep wealth in their families. One proposition supplies the terms for the other: 'the hard beating of it in' – 'the hard and laborious getting of money', 'the fixing of that in a strong wall' – 'the laying it upon lands' (where the first image recalls the nail, and implies the investment of money in property), 'the beating that nail hard' – 'the binding it with Entailes, of Iron, and Adamant'. The analogy is carefully sustained throughout the sentence; but it is made to contrast with the moral issues, the good or evil purpose in getting wealth, and the good or evil or foolish use of wealth. The sequence of dichotomies which develop from the image of the nail are analytical, and paradoxical; for while the nail is beaten fast in the wall, the same set of actions in the other part of the analogy are, Donne claims, useless for retaining wealth. The paradox is that wealth must be used generously through business dealings to be retained in any worthwhile way, and this must be the purpose, Donne suggests, for getting wealth. The capitalist profit motive takes on a social formulation. The image of the nail is developed in another direction with the use of riches; the foolish use of riches is likened to rust which can be filed away. But the false motive for getting rich is likened to rust within the iron, 'a cancer at heart'. Again, the dichotomy of sense as with the contrastive pair of 'purpose' and 'use'.

Some dense examples of the high and middle style are worth considering. They throw into relief the striking variation between the two writers. In the high style, Andrewes uses conciseness, while Donne exploits the extended sentence for his high style emphasis. In the middle style, Andrewes uses parallelism of phrase and clause to analyse and balance out a reciprocal relation of sense, while Donne uses an image to develop an argument which bears on the sermon text. In the high style, we may compare this passage from Andrewes:

> If then he be *borne to us*, it is to some end. *Esay* tels us what it is, when he expoundeth *Natus*, by *Datus*, *Borne to us*, by *Given us*. Borne, to bee bestowed upon us. And if *given* us, *bestowed* upon us, then hee is *ours*. Ours as a *Saviour*, *ours* as *Christ*, Ours as the *Lord*. Ours His *Benefit*, His *Office*, His *Power*: His *Benefit* to *save* us, His *Office* to *undertake* us, His *Power* to *assure* us. *Ours*, His *salvation*, as *Jesus*, His *anointing*, as *Christ*, His *Dominion*, as the *Lord*. And if *He* be *ours*, then *all His* are *ours*. *Omnia ejus nostra sunt*. His *Birth ours*, and if His *Birth*, all that follow His *Birth*, *ours* too.   9–18/45

and this passage from Donne:

> But when I lye under the hands of that enemie, that hath reserved himselfe to the last, to my last bed, then when I shall be able to stir no limbe in any other measure than a Feaver or a Palsie shall shake them, when everlasting darknesse shall have an inchoation in the present dimnesse of mine eyes, and the everlasting gnashing in the present chattering of my teeth, and the everlasting worme

in the present gnawing of the Agonies of my body, and anguishes of my minde, when the last enemie shall watch my remedilesse body, and my disconsolate soule there, there, where not the Physitian, in his way, perchance not the Priest in his, shall be able to give any assistance, And when he hath sported himselfe with my misery upon that stage, my death-bed, shall shift the Scene, and throw me from that bed, into the grave, and there triumph over me, God knowes, how many generations, till the Redeemer, my Redeemer, the Redeemer of all me, body as well as soule, come againe; As death is *Novissimus hostis*, the enemy which watches me, at my last weaknesse, and shall hold me, when I shall be no more, till that Angel come, *Who shall say, and sweare that time shall be no more*, in that consideration, in that apprehension, he is the powerfullest, the fearefulest enemy; and yet even there this enemy *Abolebitur*, he shall be destroyed.   12–32/214

Both passages are heavily nominal. Andrewes however uses repetition as the main device of emphasis, associated with a varied use of parallelism at phrase level; Donne uses replacement of phrase to develop and amplify within larger clause sequences, all in parallel form. The subject matter is entirely different, but it falls within the large context of man's spiritual life, even in the face of death itself. Donne contrasts the physical facts of dying with the spiritual truth of salvation and resurrection; Andrewes repeats in eloquent variation the universality of Christ's purpose. Each writer adapts the style to the general level of variation in the text he writes; neither range of markers in this style would be acceptable in the other's work.

In the middle style, some examples of dense variation are also to be found. In Andrewes, this passage is more clausal than the high style example, it contains less conciseness and more periphrasis:

Of which wine so pressed then out of Him, came our *Cup*, the *Cup* of this day, the *cup of the New Testament in His blood*, represented by the blood of the grape. Wherein long before, old *Jacob* foretold, *Shilo* should *wash his robe*; as, full well He might have done; there came enough to have washed it over and over again. So you see now, how the case stands. That former, our cup due to us, and no way to Him, He drank for us, that it might passe from us, and we not drink it. Ours did He drink, that we might drink of His. He, the *cup of wrath*, that we, the *cup of blessing*: sett first, before *God* as a *Libamen*, at the sight whereof He smelleth a savour of *rest*, and is appeased. After, reached to us, as a sovereigne *restorative* to recover us of the Devil's poison (for, we also have been sipping at *calix daemoniorum* more or lesse, wo to us for it; and no way but this, to cure us of it).   15–29/233

The passage is shaped by the systematic qualification of sense at clause and phrase level, the chief marker of middle style writing. The passage analyses, without obvious emphasis, the reciprocal relations of God and man; the contrast of actions and effects are evenly distributed across the text. There is a tendency to use causal or result clauses to explain the analysis, along with more colloquial connections. There is some thematic ordering of sense, as in 'Ours did He drink, that we might drink of His', where the emphasis is analytical rather than rhetorical as in the more overt high style usage. Donne's more dialectical middle style is already familiar to us, but this example is particularly striking:

But he is *Idem Deus*; that God who hath begun, and proceeded, will persevere in mercy towards us. Our God is not out of breath, because he hath blown one tempest, and swallowed a Navy: Our God hath not burnt out his eyes, because he hath looked upon a Train of Powder: In the light of Heaven, and in the darkness of hell, he sees alike; he sees not only all Machinations of hands, when things come to action; but all Imaginations of hearts, when they are in their first Consultations: past, and present, and future, distinguish not his *Quando*; all is one time to him: Mountains and Vallies, Sea and Land, distinguish not his *Ubi*; all is one place to him: *When I begin*, says God to *Eli, I will make an end*; not onely that all Gods purposes shall have their certain end, but that even then, when he begins, he makes an end: from the very beginning, imprints an infallible assurance, that whom he loves, he loves to the end: as a Circle is printed all at once, so his beginning and ending is all one.   9–24/216

The clauses in this passage do not have a strong emphatic rhythm; there is an analytical definition about the temporal and causal clauses here. Donne organises his discussion in a series of dichotomies: 'begun' – 'proceeded', 'blown' – 'swallowed', 'out of breath' – 'burnt out his eyes', 'light of Heaven' – 'darkness of hell', 'all Machinations of hands' – 'all Imaginations of hearts', 'come to action' – 'in their first Consultations'; or in a run of trichotomies or triplets: 'past, present and future'; or in a pair of dichotomies: 'Mountains and Vallies' – 'Sea and Land'. This patterning of noun and verb phrases lends a formal order to the passage. The evenness of balance in the language between verb phrases and noun phrases is echoed in the correlation at the end of the sentence: '*not onely that all Gods purposes shall have their certain end, but that even then, when he begins, he makes an end*'. This pairing of correlatives is also part of the pattern, preparing for the final image of the circle with its unbroken links. There is some deliberate pairing of clauses also: 'all is one time to him' – 'all is one place to him', 'when he begins, he makes an end' — 'whom he loves, he loves to the end'. The parallel clauses focus the writer's analysis, and control the theme; the final clause picks up the statement at the beginning of the passage, with a change from 'mercy' to 'love'. Donne combines analysis of argument with its covert extension over a paragraph. The substitution of 'love' for 'mercy' is the technique of replacement that operates from phrase to phrase in the high style. Here, in the analytical middle style, argument is balanced and extended by examples from many different fields. The effect is a cumulative use of imagery for analysis.

In the plain style, there are relatively few passages to be found in either writer. For the sermon is an analytical discourse, with occasional emphases at important points in the analysis. The middle and high style are therefore the most common style levels. In this passage of plain style writing, Donne uses some technical terms from the law as well as a number of colloquial metaphors from Biblical contexts:

> Hee *would not* spare, nay he *could not spare himselfe*. There was nothing more free, more voluntary, more spontaneous than the death of *Christ*. 'Tis true, *libere egit*, he *dyed voluntarily*, but yet when we consider the *contract* that had passed betweene his *Father* and *him*, there was an *oportuit*, a kind of *necessity* upon him. All this *Christ ought to suffer*. And when shall we *date* this *obligation*, this *oportuit*, this *necessity*? when shall wee say *that* begun? Certainly this *decree* by which *Christ was to suffer* all this, was an *eternall decree*, and was there any thing before that, that was eternall? *Infinite love, eternall love*, be[4] pleased to follow this home, and to consider it seriously, that what liberty soever wee can *conceive* in *Christ*, to dye or not to dye; this *necessity of dying*, this *decree* is as *eternall* as that *liberty*; and yet how small a matter made hee of this *necessity* and

this *dying*? His *Father* cals it but *a bruise*, and but a *bruising of his heele (the serpent shall bruise his heele)* and yet that was, that the *serpent* should *practise* and *compasse* his *death*. Himselfe calls it but a *Baptisme*, as though he were to bee the better for it. *I have a Baptisme to be Baptized with*, and he was in paine till it was accomplished, and yet this *Baptisme* was *his death*. The *holy Ghost* calls it *Joy (for the Joy which was set before him hee indured the Crosse)* which was not a *joy* of his reward after his passion, but a joy that filled him even in the middest of those torments, and arose from them. When *Christ* calls his passion *Calicem, a Cuppe*, and no worse, (*Can ye drink of my Cuppe?*) he speakes not odiously, not with detestation of it: Indeed it was a *Cup, salus mundo*, a health to all the world. And *quid retribuam*, says *David, what shall I render to the Lord?* answere you with *David, accipiam Calicem, I will take the Cup of salvation*; take it, that *Cup of salvation*, his *passion*, if not into your *present imitation*, yet into your *present contemplation*. And behold how that *Lord* that was *God*, yet *could dye, would dye, must dye*, for your *salvation*.   1–30/388.

Such words as 'necessity', 'contract', 'obligation' have some legal associations. The images from the Bible, with their commonplace ideas, are quite distinct from the unusual images from daily life that Donne uses in the middle style, where analysis is primary. Here these images are traditional and do not admit of extensive analysis; they are plain style images of the most immediate kind. There is no uncertainty about how they relate to the argument of the sermon for they are already part of the Christian tradition. The sentences are concise and almost without subordination. The whole passage is expository and additive in character. Sentence connection is loose and colloquial where it occurs: 'nay', ' 'Tis true', 'And when . . . ', 'Certainly', 'Indeed it was . . . '. There is a frequent use of colloquialisms in the course of argument: 'a kind of necessity', 'when shall we date . . . ', 'be pleased to follow this home', 'how small a matter . . .','cals it but a bruise', 'practise and compasse . . .', 'as though he were to bee the better for it', 'a health to all the world'; there is also a frequent use of modals to advance the argument: 'Hee would not spare, nay he could not spare himselfe', 'should practise and compasse his death', 'what shall I render . . . ', 'yet could dye, would dye, must dye . . . '. These features of the passage are the indexical markers of the plain style. There are of course some middle style markers: 'voluntary', 'spontaneous' are precise complex words unlikely to occur in common usage; such phrases as 'when we consider', 'consider it seriously', 'till it was accomplished', 'arose from them', 'not odiously, not with detestation of it', seem more formal than the plain style metaphors. But they do not dominate the passage as the plain style markers do.

In Andrewes, the plain style passages are equally rare, but this passage is typical of their common features:

> But, when we do it, we must be allowed leisure. Ever, *Veniemus*; never *Venimus*: Ever, *comming*; never, come. We love to make no very great haste. To other things, perhapps: Not, to *Adorare*, the Place of the worship of *God*. Why should we? *Christ*, is no wild catt. What talke you of *twelve* dayes? And it be *fortie* days hence, ye shall be sure to finde His *Mother* and *Him*; She cannot be *churched* till then: What needes such haste? The truth is, we conceipt Him and His *Birth* but slenderly, and our haste is even thereafter. But, if we be at that point, we must be out of this *Venimus*: they like enough to leave us behind. Best, get us a new *Christmasse* in *September*: we are not like to come to *Christ* at this Feast. Enough, for *Venimus*.   10–22/111

The passage revolves around simple contrasts, supported by colloquial metaphors: 'we love to make no very great haste', 'Christ is no wild catt' (i.e. no natural wonder?), 'What talke you of twelve dayes?', 'ye shall be sure to . . . ', 'What needes such haste?', 'She cannot be churched till then . . . ', 'We conceipt Him and His *Birth* but slenderly', 'we must be out of this *Venimus* . . . ' (i.e. 'we must no longer talk about "we have come", the words of the sermon text'). The argument and exposition develops by additive devices such as rhetorical questions and colloquial connectors between sentences: 'But . . . ', 'Best', 'Ever', 'The truth is . . .' 'Enough' . . . . There are colloquial contrasts of sense: 'Ever . . . never', 'To other things, perhapps; Not, to . . . '. Again, we notice the greater conciseness of Andrewes and the more extensive sentence forms of Donne. Even in the plain style, Donne uses some synonymy, building up the clauses to some extent, while Andrewes uses a phrase structure for the development of his argument. The chief use of the plain style in the sermon is for exposition and adducing references from a variety of sources that are relevant to the particular point in the text. There is either a tendency to avoid the analytical metaphors of the middle style, as in Donne, or to avoid the note-making form of the middle style as in Andrewes. Donne quotes more freely and fully from other sources, so that his plain style passages are rather more frequent than Andrewes. But some modern editions of Donne's prose give rather more of the high style and the 'exotic' metaphors in the middle style; they suppress, in their selection, the plain style passages.[5] This accounts for the impression that Donne's prose is somehow more extravagant than in fact it is. Donne is far more influenced by the ideas of Ramistic logic, even in his prose, than Andrewes, and they have little in common in their approach to the sermon, except for the broad tradition of Augustinian rhetoric. We may assume that Andrewes merges these European traditions of Augustine with a common medieval English tradition of colloquial directness in his writing.

In conclusion, we can say that the discussion of *local* contexts in the three styles leads to some clear distinctions of *general* context in these writers. Donne works within the general context of the social–philosophical writer; he is concerned with the way we perceive moral truth, and the way we experience the paradoxes of life. These he exploits to good effect as evidence of Christian truth; there is a level of dogmatic assertion in his sermons, as in all sermons. Nevertheless, his imagination is more exploratory and intuitive than Andrewes'. There is more direct description of reality in Donne's work. In Andrewes, the closeness of analysis, the careful exposition and interpretation of meaning within the sermon text, seems to limit the range of discussion. The moral truth is always the primary objective in his work; he does not set out to startle or persuade by unusual images of experience. He excludes the associative range of general truths, found in common life, and concentrates the mind of his congregation on his own strongly-held beliefs. These he presents in a narrow range of vocabulary with great strength and clarity. The intellectual pressure in his work, as in the work of all moralists, is very high; there is a strenuous deliberation about his willed translation of sermon text into moral statement. Donne, on the other hand, develops his analysis by paradox and indirection, and appears to discover the moral truth by a series of momentary insights.

7 Dekker and Dryden

We have seen how fashionable religious and philosophical prose was influenced by the Ramistic tradition of 'natural logic'. At the same time, there were writers like Lyly or Andrewes who did not follow the fashion. Their work seems quite out of keeping with later sixteenth and early seventeenth-century prose. It is useful to remember that there are no consistent movements of style in literary language, and archaic styles may be developed and used even when there is one dominant fashion. But Lyly and Andrewes had few imitators; their styles were admired as much for the extreme consistency of their methods, as for the devices of style they made their hallmark. Like all strenuous stylistic effects, their cult of analogy or conciseness came to seem tiresome and arbitrary.[1] The value of the Ramistic tradition was that it could take many forms, and it captured some genuine insights into language use. Meaning can be advanced through figurative imagery, and the division between concepts and things can be regarded as trivial. Writers in this tradition were encouraged to look about them with greater care than before; the emphasis on the writer's own reason and judgement, instead of an emphasis on the importance of a tradition directing his views, gave greater freedom to the imagination. We have already seen a number of varied interpretations of the Ramistic tradition in prose. Sidney adapted the idea of division into dichotomies as a principal device of style, others like Bacon and Donne used this device with more discretion. Their chief debt to Ramism was in their use of commonplace imagery for conceptual argument and analysis. Donne also uses commonplace imagery in high style contexts for dramatic emphasis. Now Dekker and Dryden cannot be called Ramistic in the sense that they use any obvious features of the tradition as we have seen it so far. Yet, in Dekker's consistent use of logical invention as a device of amplification, and in Dryden's schematic use of conventional imagery, we can detect the same assumptions as those of earlier Ramistic writers.

Ornament for its own sake was no longer acceptable in prose, any more than it was in verse. The writer's meaning was the sole justification for his use of ornament, and imagery was to be subordinate to the ideas in the context, whatever level of style was being used. Thomas Dekker (c. 1572–c. 1637) and John Dryden (1631–1700) provide examples of this tendency in the more popular prose of the seventeenth century. They represent the less specialised use of the Ramistic tradition, in the genres of the essay, the political tract, and the pamphlet. Dekker works mainly through multiple contexts, while Dryden exploits single contexts to vary his meaning and make it clear. Dekker exploits the atrophied poetic diction of the middle and high styles for ironic purposes, while Dryden uses the vagueness of conventional metaphor to make plausible generalisations about literary topics. They are both commercial writers, unlike those we have considered so far, and their main intention is to entertain; they do not involve themselves in the difficult ideas of the philosophical or religious writers of their time. From a consideration of a number of contexts in each writer, we shall see that Dekker has the more exploratory imagination; Dryden is content to write in conventional terms. The strength of Dryden's styles is that they reflect a political consensus about the man of letters, or the royalist defending the King against Parliament. There was no need for him to be more explicit than he is for his views to be understood, whereas in a writer such as Donne, the originality of his ideas required explanation. Dryden does not intend to provoke his readers into demanding an explanation, and he uses metaphor cautiously, as though he recognises its limited value. He is aware that argument must be conducted in terms of statement, not through rhetorical imagery. Even so, he cannot avoid using conventional metaphor altogether. Often he finds an effective colloquial plain style image that conveys ideas in an accessible form for the common reader. The tradition of literary criticism he began is in a large measure the same today. The audience is assumed to be literate and educated in the broad general knowledge which an interest in literature supposes. A great deal of importance is attached to the tone of the writing. It is made clear that the writer does not expect to have to inform anyone of anything too specific. That would be ungentlemanly and didactic. The writer's response to the work or author under discussion is of primary importance; but his response must be conventional and tacitly embody established values and attitudes. Otherwise it is not good criticism. Beside Dryden, Dekker seems almost uncivilised in his readiness to pursue the personal response. Dekker's capacity to develop arguments from any association of sense he can contrive to introduce in the context is unlimited. He builds up panoramic sentences that have little cohesion of argument at a literal level, but can be justified as examples of logical invention in the rather subjective tradition of Ramistic logic. In Sidney, Bacon and Donne such logical invention is used for didactic purposes, while in Dekker the purpose is merely to entertain. He allows his wit free play, since he has no larger argument to advance in his work. Often he writes near nonsense to fill the page. For all these reasons we can conclude that Dekker is a social-philosophical type of writer, while Dryden belongs to the moral-political group. Dryden articulates the current values of a literary public, while Dekker deals in the cruder social values of any time, such as social status, resentment of the newcomer, ambition, interest in crime and criminals. Dekker's social satire has no firm moral basis and is close to documentary journalism.

Here is an example of Dekker's parody of biblical high style in a plain style contemporary context, where the subject matter itself defines the satire:

> But thou art gotten safe out of the civil City calamity to thy parks and palaces in the county, lading thy asses and thy mules with thy gold (thy god), thy plate and thy jewels; and, the fruits of thy womb thriftily growing up but in one only son, the young landlord of all thy careful labours, him also hast thou rescued from the arrows of infection. Now is thy soul jocund and thy senses merry. But open thine eyes, thou fool, and behold that darling of thine eye, thy son, turned suddenly into a lump of clay. The hand of pestilence hath smote him even under thy wing. Now dost thou rend thine hair, blaspheme thy Creator, cursest thy creation and basely descendest into brutish and unmanly passions, threatening in despite of Death and his plague to maintain the memory of thy child in the everlasting breast of marble. A tomb must now defend him from tempests. And for that purpose the sweaty hind that digs the rent he pays thee out of the entrails of the earth, he is sent for to convey forth that burden of thy sorrow. But note how thy pride is disdained. That weather-beaten sunburnt drudge that not a month since fawned upon thy worship like a spaniel, and like a bondslave would have stooped lower than thy feet, does now stop his nose at thy presence and is ready to set his mastiff as high as thy throat to drive thee from his

door. All thy gold and silver cannot hire one of those whom before thou didst scorn, to carry the dead body to his last home.

8-29/45²

The grandiose poetic metaphor of the Bible is concentrated into a distinct high style register against the caricature of low style realism. It remains caricature because it has the extravagant melodramatic heightening of the comic stance; it is also realistic because it depends on the accurate appraisal of actual responses in a real situation. The plague caused terror and confusion in the countryside surrounding London, and the reality of this experience, as well as the hatred between tenants and landlords, gives bite to this account. The passage is at first high style in its generality of sense and deliberate periphrasis (as in, 'the fruits of thy womb thriftily growing up but in one only son, the young landlord of all thy careful labours'). But 'thriftily', and 'landlord' strike a discordant tone, anticipating the realism that follows. And the remark 'thy gold (thy god)' argues that the writer is not well-disposed to the main figure in this episode. The disaster that overtakes him is a just retribution from the Almighty, and is described with exultant emphasis by the gloating 'moralist'. Such phrases as 'the hand of pestilence', 'the everlasting breast of marble', 'that darling of thine eye' are clearly high style. There is however a spurious grandeur about such remarks as 'A tomb must now defend him from tempests'. Dekker also adapts the periphrasis of the high style for satiric asides about the servants: 'the sweaty hind that digs the rent he pays thee out of the entrails of the earth', 'that weather-beaten sunburnt drudge that not a month since fawned upon thy worship like a spaniel'. These restrictive relative clauses are high style formulas, but they have the vocabulary and sense of the plain style reality in the context. Even 'the entrails of the earth' strikes the reader as a facetious metaphor which exploits the high style generality of sense in a comic manner. Further, the plain style figurative sense of 'fawned like a spaniel' anticipates the literal plain style of 'ready to set his mastiff as high as thy throat'. And that remark is parallel to the high style formula, 'like a bondslave would have stooped *lower* than thy feet'. Perhaps this is an example of a Ramistic dichotomy, where the literal and the figurative are treated as equivalent and antithetical arguments. Certainly, there is a lively play with senses in this passage in order to devalue the rhetorical imagery and place it in a satiric light. Dekker uses logical invention as the primary structure of his prose style.

We may compare this multiple context with a similar variation of style, in a range of single contexts, in Dryden:

> To begin, then, with Shakespeare: he was the man who of all modern, and perhaps ancient poets, had the largest and most comprehensive soul. All the images of nature were still present to him, and he drew them not laboriously, but luckily; when he describes any thing, you more than see it, you feel it too. Those who accuse him to have wanted learning give him the greater commendation: he was naturally learned; he needed not the spectacles of books to read nature; he looked inwards, and found her there. I cannot say he is every where alike; were he so, I should do him injury to compare him with the greatest of mankind. He is many times flat, insipid; his comic wit degenerating into clenches, his serious swelling into bombast. But he is always great when some great occasion is presented to him; no man can say he ever had a fit subject for his wit, and did not then raise himself as high above the rest of poets,
>
> *quantum lenta solent inter viburna cupressi.*
>
> The consideration of this made Mr. Hales of Eton say that there was no subject of which any poet ever writ, but he would produce it much better treated of in Shakespeare; and however others are now generally preferred before him, yet the age wherein he lived, which had contemporaries with him Fletcher and Jonson, never equalled them to him in their esteem. And in the last King's court, when Ben's reputation was at highest, Sir John Suckling, and with him the greater part of the courtiers, set our Shakespeare far above him.   I, 11/67–9/68[3]

The passage begins with a high style generality. Johnson described this whole passage as an example of good criticism, 'exact without minuteness, and lofty without exaggeration'.[4] For us, these lofty remarks may seem too vague, but Johnson was considering their general truth. Dryden's estimate of Shakespeare, given the values of the period, is a peculiarly accurate judgement. It has stood the test of time and needs little revision now. Shakespeare was not the untutored genius that Dryden and Johnson supposed him to be, but the sheer variety of his achievement is of course undeniable. This they were able to see, but their criticisms of his work, against the standard of neo-classical taste, are presented in this passage in a plain style. We recognise this shift in style from the shift in tone and indexical markers. From the almost unqualified statement of the first sentence, with its superlatives and general sense, we read on to the absolute statement of the next. But the qualification of meaning here detains the reader. Dryden shifts into a colloquial tone, using 'laboriously' in a colloquial sense, and contrasting it with 'luckily'. Dryden assumes that Shakespeare's art is the product of natural talent, not careful training. We may suspect some high style sense of 'laborious' in the back of his mind, for the writing of literature could be regarded as a epic task fit for heroic exertions. The meaning is not entirely clear. But the general sense is: Dryden wants to contrast the natural genius with the rules of art. Hence the paradox that he was 'naturally learned', which Dryden quickly expands by a careful plain style metaphor: 'he needed not the spectacles of books to read nature'. In the second sentence he shifts into the verbal mode of the plain style: 'when he describes any thing, you more than see it, you feel it too'. The sense is rather vague, as we might expect from the plain style. But there is sufficient meaning to allow the reader a nod of assent; all Dryden means is that Shakespeare writes in a vivid, precise way, which presents the object described to the mind's eye. The variation of style in Shakespeare is a cause for criticism in Dryden's canon of taste, and this part of the passage is also plain style. There is an additive, colloquial phrasing about this sentence: 'He is many times flat, insipid; his comic wit degenerating into clenches, his serious swelling into bombast.' The vocabulary is figurative and ill-defined; but again, the reader is given a plausible generalisation that loosely characterises Shakespeare's style, in terms of the neo-classical standards. Such phrases as 'the greatest of mankind' maintain the high style impetus running through the passage, as does the Latin quotation, with its classical associations, and its general emphasis. Again, the reputation of Shakespeare, to which Dryden rightly attaches great importance, is also presented in a high style, although the indexical markers are relatively light. For example, 'no subject of which any poet ever writ' (with its absolute unqualified sense), '*never* equalled them to him in their esteem', 'reputation . . . at highest . . . far above him'. The impression such prose creates is that it is more modern than Dekker because it is less densely marked for style level, as indeed most prose of the essay genre is. The levels of style are sequential, as in most single contexts. Sentence length too has a crucial effect on prose style. Dryden's sentences are rarely complex, and he hardly ever uses a panoramic sentence of the type Dekker prefers. Dryden

180   *Literary Language from Chaucer to Johnson*

controls much more carefully than Dekker the variety of information that he presents to the reader, and this too is a feature of modern prose style. Dryden is however very far from modern in his 'rigorous' handling of vague metaphor to control general argument; it is almost impossible in his work to find any specific statements about a piece of text, except in the most abusive plain style, where accuracy is unimportant. Yet he imposes on fairly conventional metaphor a heavy burden of meaning which it cannot always sustain. This passage is almost a sequence of platitudes, yet it gives the impression of an orderly discussion:

> Then he was more happy in his digressions than any we have named. I have always been pleased to see him, and his imitator Montaigne, when they strike a little out of the common road, for we are sure to be the better for their wandering. The best quarry lies not always in the open field; and who would not be content to follow a good huntsman over hedges and ditches when he knows the game will reward his pains? But if we mark him more narrowly, we may observe that the great reason of his frequent starts is the variety of his learning: he knew so much of nature, was so vastly furnished with all the treasures of the mind, that he was uneasy to himself and was forced, as I may say, to lay down some at every passage, and to scatter his riches as he went. Like another Alexander or Adrian, he built a city or planted a colony in every part of his progress, and left behind him some memorial of his greatness. Sparta, and Thebes, and Athens, and Rome, the mistress of the world, he has discovered in their foundations, their institutions, their growth, their height, the decay of the three first and the alteration of the last. You see those several people in their several laws, and policies, and forms of government, in their warriors, and senators, and demagogues. Nor are the ornaments of poetry and the illustrations of similitudes forgotten by him, in both which he instructs as well as pleases: or rather pleases that he may instruct.   II,18/9–4/10

The middle style reference to the gentlemanly sport of fox-hunting, and the high style survey of an imperial progress, serve as images of literary method. The first is a defence of digressions on structural grounds, that the reader will find a new aspect of the subject in the most unlikely reference, the second suggests the wealth of Plutarch's mind, which accounts for the variety of his learning. These metaphors are in a sense instructive; they do draw attention to certain aspects of Plutarch's *Lives*. They do explain and suggest reasons for particular literary impressions. But they do not analyse or explain by examples from the text; Dryden seems to rely on the idea that metaphor is cryptic argument, as Ramistic logic stated. But the analogies he advances are very conventional, and it is difficult to tell whether he thinks these metaphors have any real accuracy. They are both related to a journey, and there seems to be a common association of journeys with literary undertakings. What follows these images is a general summary of the main topics in the *Lives*, in the high style form that reminds the reader of a Ramistic table of method, for the subjects are divided up from the general to the particular. Dryden supports his metaphors by careful selection of the actual contents, as though he did not think the metaphors alone were adequate. They give a general idea of technique but give no information about subject. Elsewhere we can find similar examples of his belief in the factual at the expense of metaphorical sense; here the plain style appropriate to the genre of the work discussed, allows some specific examples:

> *Biographia*, or the histories of particular lives, tho' circumscribed in the subject, is yet more extensive in the style than the other two. For it not only comprehends both, but has somewhat superadded which neither of them have. The style of it is various, according to the occasion. There are proper places in it for the plainness and nakedness of narration which is ascribed to annals; there is also room reserved for the loftiness and gravity of general history, when the actions related shall require that manner of expression. But there is withal a descent into minute circumstances and trivial passages of life which are natural to this way of writing, and which the dignity of the other two will not admit. There you are conducted only into the rooms of state; here you are led into the private lodgings of the hero; you see him in his undress, and are made familiar with his most private actions and conversations. You may behold a Scipio and a Lelius gathering cockleshells on the shore, Augustus playing at bounding-stones with boys, and Agesilaus riding on a hobby horse among his children. The pageantry of life is taken away; you see the poor reasonable animal, as naked as nature ever made him; are made acquainted with his passions and his follies, and find the demigod a man. II, 33/8–17/9

Dryden shows a traditional knowledge of decorum, the appropriate language for particular genres of prose. This part of the text is middle style; there is a general formality of diction and syntax here that contrasts to some extent with the middle style colloquialisms of the last example. Dryden suppresses colloquial, if polite, middle style imagery in this passage. We notice the shift from middle to plain style towards the end. In place of literary definitions and careful, balanced relative clauses, we find a new familiarity in syntax and vocabulary. We can compare the formality of 'conducted only into the rooms of state' with the familiarity of 'led into the private lodgings . . .'. The domestic pursuits of the hero contrast implicitly with the public figure, the high style 'demi-god'. In plain style terms he is but a 'poor reasonable animal'. Metaphor would be distracting in such a context; the examples Dryden gives are far more enlightening for his argument. But they are only possible in the plain style. The essay genre generally requires the middle style with occasional passages of high style emphasis. Only when he deals with biography does Dryden feel himself required to cite actual examples and make some detailed reference to the text. This is however entirely motivated by the relative informality of the genre under discussion, and has nothing to do with Dryden's wish to strengthen his argument. In the middle style of the essay, such details are unacceptable except where they demonstrate the distinctions of literary genre. This is a permanent limitation on Dryden's range of reference, and a purely rhetorical one. There is little doubt that it has had extraordinary influence on the development of literary criticism in its present form.

When we turn back to Dekker again, we realise how much control and selection Dryden imposes on his material, and we can see the advantages of clarity even if it lacks precision. Dryden is always a lot easier to read than Dekker. This passage of high, middle and plain style in a multiple context shows the energy and disorder of Dekker's usage:

> It shall crown you with rich commendation to laugh aloud in the middest of the most serious and saddest scene of the terriblest tragedy and to let that clapper, your tongue, be tossed so high that all the house may ring of it. Your lords use it, your knights are apes to the lords and do so too, your Inn o' Court man is zany to the knights and – marry, very scurvily – comes likewise limping after; be thou a beagle to them all and never lin snuffing till you

have scented them, for by talking and laughing like a ploughman in a morris you heap Pelion upon Ossa, glory upon glory. As, first, all the eyes in the galleries will leave walking after the players and only follow you; the simplest dolt in the house snatches up your name and, when he meets you in the streets or that you fall into his hands in the middle of a watch, his word shall be taken for you. He'll cry 'He's such a gallant!' and you pass. Secondly, you publish your temperance to the world, in that you seem not to resort thither to taste vain pleasures with a hungry appetite but only as a gentleman to spend a foolish hour or two because you can do nothing else. Thirdly, you mightily disrelish the audience and disgrace the author. Marry, you take up (though it be at the worst hand) a strong opinion of your own judgement, and enforce the poet to take pity of your weakness and by some dedicated sonnet to bring you into a better paradise, only to stop your mouth.   14–34/100

Dekker's method is to create and establish a particular context of use and then transform its values by a shift of register. So the first sentence begins with a high style sequence, 'It shall crown you with rich commendation . . . '. The tone of this remark does not prepare us for the crude direction, 'to laugh aloud'; the phrase has a familiar and subversive meaning, which undermines the formal language of the rest of the clause. But it is only a momentary flicker of dissent; Dekker returns to the high style in the next sequence, 'in the middest of the most serious and saddest scene of the terriblest tragedy'. But the phrase is too emphatic, too fulsome and rhetorical. Parallel to the first plain style sequence, Dekker inserts another stylistic antithesis with the sequence, 'to let that clapper, your tongue, be tossed so high that all the house may ring of it'. The country-bumpkin for whom *The Gull's Horn-Book* was written is supposed to take this advice seriously, but there is also another audience, the sniggering lower middle classes of contemporary London. They would be delighted by the decorum of Dekker's plain style address to the yokel, and amused at his exploitation of the high style by such plain style effects. The satire on the lords and knights would not be ill-received either. Dekker disguises his attitude by pretending that all is plain style so that the poor fellow can understand him properly. The plain style sequence in the second sentence ends with a high style insertion: ' . . . laughing like a ploughman in a morris you heap Pelion upon Ossa, glory upon glory'. Like a Renaissance book of courtesy, Dekker gives sound practical advice for achieving the desired social goal (or so the gull is supposed to imagine). The logical invention of the passage is quite obvious; Dekker divides up what he wants to say into three points, the useful effects of the action he advises. The first effect is plain style, except for the middle style remark 'He's such a gallant!'; Dekker implies from his whole attitude in this work that this reaction is in fact most unlikely. Indeed, the gull would be lucky to escape a good drubbing for his conceit. The second advantage to be gained from laughing out loud at a serious play is that subtle pose of casualness that marks the true gentleman; but even here we find a conflict of view, for while 'publish your temperance to the world' sounds formal and serious, 'because you can do nothing else' sounds too accurate to be far from the truth. There is a formal disdain in the middle style metaphor, 'taste vain pleasures with a hungry appetite' beside the more colloquial middle style, 'spend a foolish hour or two'; but in the end, both attitudes are overturned. Again, in the third effect, Dekker plays around with ideas in the middle style: 'disrelish' and 'disgrace' are formal in structure and meaning, while 'a better paradise' and 'enforce the poet to take pity of your weakness' are also marked as middle style aesthetic or social terms. But there is also a plain style that gravels these assumptions of social poise and aesthetic discrimination: 'though it be at the worst hand', with its figurative sense ('though it is in the worst possible way'), and 'to stop your mouth' (does it mean the poet will ram the sonnet down his throat, or that he will try to get into the gull's favour by writing sonnets to him?). Dekker, then, handles a wide range of arguments that are loosely related under general headings; he does not have a more coherent direction in his writing of the kind we find in Dryden. It is largely this absence of loose cataloguing in Dryden's prose that makes it seem modern. In fact, he is very much of his time.

Here is another example of Dekker's panoramic sentence structures; he suggests suitable topics of conversation at lunch:

> If you be a courtier, discourse of the obtaining of suits, of your mistress's favours, etc.; make enquiry if any gentleman at board have any suit, to get which he would use the good means of a great man's interest with the King; and withal (if you have not so much grace left in you as to blush) that you are, thanks to your stars, in mighty credit (though in your own conscience you know and are guilty to yourself that you dare not, but only upon the privileges

of handsome clothes, presume to peep into the Presence). Demand if there be any gentleman whom any there is acquainted with that is troubled with two offices, or any vicar with two church livings: which will politicly insinuate that your enquiry after them is because you have good means to obtain them. Yea, and rather than your tongue should not be heard in the room but that you should sit like an ass with your finger in your mouth and speak nothing, discourse how often this lady hath sent her coach for you and how often you have sweat in the tennis-court with that great lord – for indeed the sweating together in France (I mean the society of tennis!) is a great argument of most dear affection even between noblemen and peasants.   6–23/94

The passage is a parody of middle style politeness; all the arguments put forward are disastrously ambiguous and so quite improper for the context. They sound however as though they might be acceptable; only the more experienced would know that they are entirely fatal for the speaker's claims to gentility. The passage begins in middle style, with occasional plain style insertions, such as 'peep into' or the aggressive repetition of 'good means'. But soon Dekker falls back on the plain style sarcasms of the rest of his work, as in 'that you should sit like an ass with your finger in your mouth and speak nothing', a parallel to 'rather than your tongue should not be heard in the room'. This last phrase is a middle style politeness in syntax, but it refers to a breach of decorum; even in Dekker's time loud voices were not regarded, one may assume, as a sign of breeding amongst the middle classes. The passage ends in crude plain style innuendo about the sexual appetites of lords and ladies. The structure of this passage is associative and random, like the previous example; Dekker appears to be writing at speed, and finding material for his work as he goes along. There is little formal patterning, although the sense of decorum is sharp and refreshing, especially in the parody of middle style. The variety of topic and the inventiveness of metaphor in this passage are distracting and tiresome when extended over a whole work. What succeeds locally in one context is in a cumulative sequence of contexts too predictable and mechanical. The inner reality of the gull is never explored; there are severe limits to Dekker's social and philosophical context. Although he is more exploratory than Dryden, his insights take him only a little way into his subject. *The Gull's Horn-Book* is a parody of a Renaissance book of courtesy, not a novel, so that the form itself of the work restricts and narrows its originality. Dryden of course is as much a prisoner of middle style assumptions in his essay. We tend to underestimate how much the formal requirements of genre dictate the substance of a writer's stylistic choice; this aspect has not been dealt with explicitly in this book, but it is one that requires investigation. The problem with such a topic is the complexity and range of variables you would have to identify in large-scale works; probably the rhetorical techniques of literary criticism will always give a better sense of a writer's performance than explicit models of a realistic but inaccessible complexity.

However, Dryden was able to develop a more coherent technique for controlling theme and argument in his own prose styles. We have seen that he does this by selection of a small number of metaphors or topics for discussion, and his treatment of these topics is always general and conventional. The metaphor requires no secondary explanation, as it often does in Dekker, and there is no need to explain the division of topics for they are evident from the general sense. The vitality of Dryden's prose derives from the close relation of metaphor and proposition, so that metaphor advances argument and moves the discussion of topics forward, instead of diverting attention onto side issues. This example from *A Discourse concerning Satire* is typical of his middle and plain style variations:

> How easy is it to call rogue and villain, and that wittily! But how hard to make a man appear a fool, blockhead, or a knave, without using any of those opprobrious terms! To spare the grossness of the names, and to do the thing yet more severely, is to draw a full face, and to make the nose and cheeks stand out, and yet not to employ any depth of shadowing. This is the mystery of that noble trade, which yet no master can teach to his apprentice: he may give the rules, but the scholar is never the nearer in his practice. Neither is it true that this fineness of raillery is offensive. A witty man is tickled while he is hurt in this manner, and a fool feels it not. The occasion of an offence may possibly be given, but he cannot take it. If it be granted that in effect this way does more mischief; that a man is secretly wounded, and though he be not sensible himself, yet the malicious world will find it for him: yet there is still a vast difference betwixt the slovenly butchering of a man, and the fineness of a stroke that separates the head from the body, and leaves it standing in its place. A man may be capable, as Jack Ketch's wife said of his servant, of a plain piece of work, a

bare hanging; but to make a malefactor die sweetly was only belonging to her husband. I wish I could apply it to myself, if the reader would be kind enough to think it belongs to me. The character of Zimri in my *Absalom* is, in my opinion, worth the whole poem: 'tis not bloody, but 'tis ridiculous enough. And he for whom it was intended was too witty to resent it as an injury. II, 31/136–23/137

The middle style of the opening sentences contrasts with the brutal delight in a good public execution. But both the aesthetic images of the middle style and the plain style analogy from common life are related to the main theme of the passage. The essence of good satire is the 'fineness' of the artist's methods in dealing with the subject. This theme is articulated through a sequence of middle and plain style images: the image from painting, or drawing, in the middle style, the images of execution in the plain style. The final example from his own work is a typical plain style illustration of his point. Dryden's prose is full of varied but concise images that advance argument even though the argument is often general. This is the fundamental improvement that he brought to the polite prose styles of literary genres. He reduced the range of prose to exposition and a superficial analysis.

Dekker shows the exuberance of an intensely inventive mind, full of ingenious arguments, none of which have much in common with each other. The impression of disorder this creates we have already seen, but it is the result of a 'logical' view of topic ordering. The prolixity of argument and explanation is entirely in the tradition of logical invention. The writer finds new reasons and arguments in a string of propositions, but he loses sight of the general drift of his thought. There is also little thematic control of argument or discussion in his prose because he is concerned with small topics, often of no great substance. In this example of an incident in *The Gull's Horn-Book*, we can see the way logical invention obscures the actual episode:

> If you smell a watch (and that you may easily do, for commonly they eat onions to keep them in sleeping, which they account a medicine against cold): but if you come within danger of their brown bills, let him that is your candlestick and holds up your torch from dropping (for to march after a link is shoemaker like), let *Ignis Fatuus*, I say, being within the reach of the

Constable's staff, ask aloud, 'Sir Giles' or 'Sir Abr'am, will you turn this way' or 'down that street?' It skills not though there be none dubbed in your bunch, the watch will wink at you only for the love they bear to arms and knighthood. Marry, if the sentinel and his court of guard stand strictly upon his martial law and cry 'Stand!', commanding you to give the word and to show reason why your ghost walks so late, do it in some jest, for that will show you have a desperate wit and perhaps make him and his halberdiers afraid to lay foul hands upon you; or if you read a *mittimus* in the Constable's look, counterfeit to be a Frenchman, a Dutchman or any other nation whose country is in peace with your own, and you may pass the pikes; for being not able to understand you, they cannot by the customs of the City take your examination and so by consequence they have nothing to say to you.   13–31/107

At every possible point in the narrative, Dekker inserts explanation and reasons; the work is a guide-book, and that may account for some of it. But is the passage as clear as Dryden's example? There seems to be too much argued explanation, and the reader is harassed by the writer's inventiveness. Dryden knew how to avoid giving the reader too much to cope with. But here, in this example, diversity of argument is reinforced by diversity of register. There is a continual shift from middle to plain style and back again, as Dekker changes his attitude, at first striking a lofty pose and then arguing in false logic as an adviser and intimate of the gull. The passage begins in plain style, with a jocular metaphor that has to be explained, in false logic as it happens. The inconsequentiality of this beginning sets the reader back somewhat, and he has to be reminded of the main topic, 'If you come within danger of their brown bills . . .'. This middle style politeness is sustained in the periphrasis of 'he that is your candlestick . . .', and contrasted with the plain style insertion, 'for to march after a link is shoemaker like'; again, '*Ignis Fatuus*' is another middle style phrase, with a plain style sarcasm concealed in it, for this pretension of the gull that he is a gentleman is of course ridiculous. Dekker continues in the middle style with direct speech, but quickly shifts again into plain style ('It skills not though there be none dubbed in your bunch . . .'). Then once more he returns to the poetic middle style in the phrase, 'only for the love they bear to arms and knighthood'. The watch would have no respect for that nonsense at all, most likely. However, the fiction must be kept up, and Dekker continues in this middle style vein, 'if the sentinel and his court of guard stand strictly upon his martial law . . . commanding you to give the word and to show reason why your ghost walks so late'. But the actual advice (a nice irony, since it is proper to commonplace remarks) is given in the plain style: 'do it in some jest, for that will show you have a desperate wit'. But it is doubtful whether the watch ('him and his halberdiers' in the middle style periphrasis) would be 'afraid to lay foul hands upon you' (in the plain style figurative mode). Again, the plain style contrasts with the middle in what follows: 'if you read a *mittimus* ('a legal summons') in the Constable's look', plain style, 'counterfeit to be a Frenchman . . . and you may pass the pikes,' middle style. The logical explanations for this are of course spurious, as we have come to expect. But they appear reasonable, as Dekker meant them to be, in an earnest plain style, as though he was giving sound and sensible advice to the gull. There is no clear sustained direction in this kind of prose; the constant variation interrupts the movement of events, and obscures analysis with a cumbersome gloss. It is entertaining but strenuous to read. Dekker's wit consists in repartee, in a plain style, while Dryden's wit shows itself in the variety and reasonableness of his discussion. Both are indebted in their different ways to the traditions of Ramistic logic for the finding out of arguments, even if Dekker may have thought up too many.

Dryden's sense of order in a paragraph is undoubtedly the main feature of his usage; he recognises that metaphor, vague though it may be, can stand development alongside literal statement of the argument. (This aspect of Ramistic invention is more remarkable and dramatic in the analytical middle style imagery of Donne's prose.) In this example, a plain style image is developed alongside literal statement, in a sequence of single contexts:

> I am also bound to tell your Lordship, in my own defence, that, from the beginning of the First Georgic to the end of the last Aeneid, I found the difficulty of translation growing on me in every succeeding book. For Virgil, above all poets, had a stock, which I may call almost inexhaustible, of figurative, elegant, and sounding words. I, who inherit but a small portion of his genius, and write in a language so much inferior to the Latin, have found it very painful to vary phrases, when the same sense returns upon me. Even he himself, whether out of necessity or choice, has often expressed the same thing in the same words, and often repeated

two or three whole verses which he had used before. Words are not so easily coined as money; and yet we see that the credit not only of banks but of exchequers cracks when little comes in and much goes out. Virgil called upon me in every line for some new word: and I paid so long, that I was almost bankrupt; so that the latter end must needs be more burdensome than the beginning or the middle; and, consequently, the Twelfth Aeneid cost me double the time of the first and second. What had become of me, if Virgil had taxed me with another book? I had certainly been reduced to pay the public in hammered money, for want of milled; that is, in the same old words which I had used before: and the receivers must have been forced to have taken anything, where there was so little to be had.   II, 6–29/250

The passage begins in the middle style, with a formal and careful diction. Metaphor in this opening sequence is very conventional and uninteresting: 'I found the difficulty of translation growing on me in every succeeding book', 'inherit but a small portion', 'found it very painful'. These are typical indexical markers of polite middle style. They advance the analysis without any significant effort or pressure on the reader's attention. This is important in modern prose style, especially in good journalistic prose, and we have not seen this aspect of prose style before. Bacon's images are arresting, compact and difficult; Sidney uses many arguments in stern succession; Donne and Andrewes are preoccupied with analysis to the exclusion of easy development of argument. But Dryden is clear and easy to follow, although his ideas are in fact complex; but this is commercial writing, not serious intellectual argument. We should not expect complexity, and we do not find it. For Dryden keeps the complexity under control by these easy metaphors from polite usage in the middle style. The central plain style image in this paragraph is developed to explain the difficulty of finding the right word without using the same words again and again. First Dryden states the proposition in figurative plain style: 'Words are not so easily coined as money', then he develops the image, drawing out from it its associated metaphors of credit and a run on the bank or exchequer. He treats the commonplace metaphor of coining words as though it had a literal and deliberate sense, which can be brought out in what follows. This inventive approach to meaning is a common device of Ramistic logic; we have seen the same method in Donne's poetry, and in Dryden's early verse. Here Dryden presents the reader with an unequal comparison, between money and words, which can then be used to advantage by pursuing the difficulty and dangers of coining money. Dryden controls the images in a thematic way, frequently returning to the primary idea, in literal statements: 'called upon me in every line for some new word', 'in the same old words which I had used before'. But these clauses are woven in with the figurative imagery: 'I paid so long, that I was almost bankrupt', 'cost me double the time', 'taxed me with another book?' (where 'taxed', like 'cost' is a further witty enlargment of the associative meaning in context, for it has the sense, 'collect money from'), 'pay the public in hammered money', 'the receivers must have been forced to have taken anything, where there was so little to be had'. The argument of the passage is not difficult, but it is quite complex; Dryden's gift is for presenting these potentially complex ideas in an easy and fluent fashion. This has been the way of dealing with complex ideas in literary criticism ever since. The division between concepts and things is often unimportant in popular prose writings, and Dryden exploits it to advantage in this example. We all know words are not the same as money, but the obscure processes by which words are invented are expensive of time and effort for anyone, and especially writers. The reader knows this and it gives authenticity to the imagery and to Dryden's development of it. He appeals always to the reasoning powers of his audience, and there is always a close conceptual control over his language. This is precisely why sometimes the imagery he chooses seems insufficiently clear, because the general standard of clarity in his writing is very high. We have to distinguish too between clarity of a general kind, when dealing with complex ideas, and clarity of a spurious kind that appears to give insights, but doesn't. Dryden rarely writes in the second manner.

A final example from Dekker will remind us of the real measure of advance in Dryden's prose. In these panoramic sentences, Dekker shows the exuberance of proposition and the disorder that is typical of his styles:

> But, calling to mind the particular points of his commission, of which a principal one was that he should visit prisons in his progress, into a gaol our infernal catchpole the next morning conveyed himself. And looking to hear there nothing but sighing, lamenting, praying and cryings out of afflicted and forlorn creatures, there was no such matter but only a clamorous noise of

> cursing creditors, drinking healths to their confusion, swaggering, roaring, striking, stabbing one another as if that all desperviews of sixteen armies had been swearing together. Considering the desperate resolutions of some, he wished himself in his own territories, knowing more safety there than in this Hospital of Incurable Madmen, and could not till about dinner-time be persuaded but that the gaol was Hell, every room was so smoky with tobacco, and oaths flying faster about than tapsters could score up their frothy reckonings. But the time of munching being come, all the sport was to see how the prisoners, like sharking soldiers at the rifling of a town, ran up and down to arm themselves against that battle of hunger-some whetting knives that had meat, others scraping trenchers aloud that had no meat, some ambling downstairs for bread and beer meeting another coming upstairs carrying a platter more proudly aloft, full of powder beef and brewis, than an Irishman does his enemy's head on the top of his sword, every chamber showing like a cook's shop where provant was stirring, and those that had not provender in the manger nor hay in the rack walking up and down like starved jades new overridden in Smithfield. This set at maw being played out, all seemed quiet. The water under London Bridge at the turning was not more still.   6–31/253[5]

The passage is clearly plain style; literary diction and formal metaphor is kept out of the context, and the writer delights in broad contrasts of sense and image. He develops the context by contrary arguments ('there was no such matter but only . . .'), or by distribution of logical effects ('some whetting knives . . . others scraping . . . some ambling downstairs . . . etc.). The passage is rich in synonymy and colloquial metaphor, but there is too much variety of image for ease of reading. The writer works through local images from one clause to the next and there is no obvious dominant image; even the imagery of warfare has so many diverse forms that it is scarcely coherent and makes no clear impression on the reader. But this was not Dekker's primary purpose; his plain style is caricature and repartee, and he has no set intentions. He values lexical invention as a device of style as much as logical invention in propositions, and the two combined together in this passage give a wild energy and fluency to his writing. These were the aspects of style which Dryden brought under close control in his new polite essays.

8 Browne and Johnson

Now we must turn from the more popular prose writers of the period to some examples of learned and scientific prose. The growing importance of fact and observation, instead of logical invention, is the chief distinction between the prose of Sir Thomas Browne (1605–82) and that of earlier writers. His example was immensely influential on the writing styles of Samuel Johnson (1709–84). Not only does Johnson refer very frequently to Browne in his *Dictionary* (1755), quoting extensively from his works in the entries,[1] but he seems to have regarded the language of science and philosophy as peculiarly accurate and precise. In the *Preface* to the *Dictionary* he remarks that 'Many of the distinctions which to common readers appear useless and idle, will be found real and important by men versed in the school philosophy, without which no dictionary shall be accurately compiled, or skilfully examined.'[2] Even though this may be a mistaken view of the spurious precision of technical words, it does suggest the confidence Johnson placed in scientific usage, and precise differences of meaning. The middle style of his essays bears out this implicit belief, for much of the irony and subtlety of his analysis depends on exact and controlled distinctions of sense. This belief in the precision of learned usage can be found in Browne's own works; in his remarks *To the Reader* before *Pseudodoxia Epidemica* (1646), he suggests that he might have written the work in Latin rather than English:

> Our first intentions considering the common interest of Truth, resolved to propose it unto the Latine republique and equal Judges of Europe, but owing in the first place this service unto our Country, and therein especially unto its ingenuous Gentry, we have declared our self in a language best conceived. Although I confess the quality of the Subject will sometimes carry us into expressions beyond meer English apprehensions. And indeed, if elegancy still proceedeth, and English Pens maintain that stream we have late observed to flow from many, we shall within a few

years be fain to learn Latine to understand English, and a work
will prove of equal facility in either. Nor have we addressed our
Pen or Stile unto the people (whom Books do not redress, and are
this way incapable of reduction), but unto the knowing and
leading part of Learning. As well understanding (at least
probably hoping) except they be watered from higher regions
and fructifying meteors of Knowledge, these weeds must lose
their alimental sap and wither of themselves. Whose conserving
influence, could our endeavours prevent, we should trust unto the
sythe of Time, and hopefull dominion of Truth.
30/228–10/229[3]

This describes his usage throughout all his works, and is itself a
characteristic middle style passage. The traditional images of the
scythe as an attribute of Time, and Truth as the daughter of Time
are placed beside a far more technical and scientific metaphor from
plants; the 'alimental sap' is the source of the food supply, as the
adjective states. But this learned metaphor for a literary diffidence is
quite novel in this middle style context; yet it is formal and precise,
without the plain style associations of the legal language of
Shakespeare's sonnets. Science is a subject fit for gentlemen, while
the law was more commonplace. Browne delights in the pedantry of
his images because they can be understood only by the learned, not by
the common reader. There is a new politeness and precision about
his usage in plain, middle and high styles. He contrasts markedly
with Dekker, and in the intellectual curiosity he displays he shows
greater range of knowledge than Dryden. Beside Johnson's use of
the three styles he seems less clear, and more inclined to pedantry
and needless complexity. But Johnson undoubtedly learnt much
from him about the precision of meaning in specialised vocabulary,
and Browne may in fact have been the original inspiration for
Johnson's *Dictionary*.

In the plain style there is an increased seriousness of observation
and a more sober record of information in both writers, although
Browne is clearly fascinated by eccentric opinion. In *Pseudodoxia
Epidemica*, an enquiry into 'vulgar and common errors', he remarks
on the superstitions attached to a common species of spider:

There is found in the Summer a kind of Spider called a Tainct,
of a red colour, and so little of body that ten of the largest will
hardly outway a grain; this by Country people is accounted a

deadly poison unto Cows and Horses; who, if they suddenly die, and swell thereon, ascribe their death hereto, and will commonly say, they have licked a Tainct. Now to satisfie the doubts of men we have called this tradition unto experiment; we have given hereof unto Dogs, Chickens, Calves and Horses, and not in the singular number; yet never could find the least disturbance ensue. There must be therefore other causes enquired of the sudden death and swelling of cattle; and perhaps this insect is mistaken, and unjustly accused for some other. For some there are which from elder times have been observed pernicious unto cattle, as the *Buprestis* or Burstcow, the *Pityocampe* or *Eruca Pinuum*, by Dioscorides, Galen and Aetius, the *Staphilinus* described by Aristotle and others, or those red Phalangious Spiders like *Cantharides* mentioned by Muffetus. Now although the animal may be mistaken and the opinion also false, yet in the ground and reason which makes men most to doubt the verity hereof, there may be truth enough, that is, the inconsiderable quantity of this insect. For that a poison cannot destroy in so small a bulk; we have no reason to affirm.   11-32/296

Browne's argument is that the smallness of the insect may well be no reason for doubting that it could contain a deadly poison, even though experiment shows that it is not the cause of death in animals. The passage has no learned English words, though there are a few Latin terms, and one technical term from zoology ('Phalangious' refers to a species of poisonous spiders). The indexical markers of the plain style are already well-known to the reader: the linear syntax, without complex subordination, the familiar diction of common life, the use of colloquial metaphor found in non-literary usage, so distinct from the scientific metaphor of the middle style. For example, 'mistaken, and unjustly accused for some other', or 'satisfie the doubts of men'; such metaphors are not the vehicle of analysis, but simply advance the exposition of the argument. Yet there are also some examples of the new politeness in the plain style: words like 'pernicious', 'observed', 'ensue' (for 'follow'), and 'inconsiderable' are not frequent, but add a note of formality to this exposition. They do not overturn the primary register of the style, for they are not part of a systematic paradigm of middle style elements. They merely indicate the new precision of plain style usage in educated English in the period; they have a learned exactness that Sidney's plain style, for example, cannot achieve.

There is too in this passage the traditional plain style use of examples and authorities to support argument, and in this part of the register Browne shows a strength of scholarship that we might expect from his learned diction. The syntax is also additive, and loose, implying little formality in the writer's attitude to the reader, in spite of the occasional learned term. But again, the use of the first person plural suggests a new formality of stance towards the reader: Browne focuses attention on the subject matter in a direct and neutral way. The personality of the author does not appear in the plain style in Browne any more than it does in Johnson's version of the register. In this example from Johnson's *Life of Pope* we find the same blend of politeness and respect for fact:

> Most of what can be told concerning his petty peculiarities was communicated by a female domestic of the Earl of Oxford, who knew him perhaps after the middle of life. He was then so weak as to stand in perpetual need of female attendance; extremely sensible of cold, so that he wore a kind of fur doublet under a shirt of very coarse warm linen with fine sleeves. When he rose he was invested in boddice made of stiff canvas, being scarce able to hold himself erect till they were laced, and he then put on a flannel waistcoat. One side was contracted. His legs were so slender that he enlarged their bulk with three pairs of stockings, which were drawn on and off by the maid; for he was not able to dress or undress himself, and neither went to bed nor rose without help. His weakness made it very difficult for him to be clean.
>
> His hair had fallen almost all away, and he used to dine sometimes with Lord Oxford, privately, in a velvet cap. His dress of ceremony was black, with a tie-wig and a little sword.
>
> 11–26/435

The formality of diction in this passage gives dignity to the subject, where such a personal account might be in danger of assuming too much, and invading the privacy of an individual. So such terms as 'petty peculiarities', 'female domestic', 'female attendance', 'invested', 'contracted', and 'enlarged' have a deliberate abstraction and formality which avoids caricature and keeps the writer's attitude polite and neutral. So too with the phrase, 'His hair had fallen almost all away' (compare 'he was nearly bald', which today would not seem so impolite). The passage is important as an example of Johnson's fascination with every sort of fact, even the most commonplace and potentially trivial. But nothing can be trivial in the details of a writer's life, and this gives Johnson's account significance. The precision with which detail is ordered and presented is also another feature of his plain style; there is less colloquialism of syntax than in Browne's version of the register. In this passage from Browne's plain style we see a more colloquial syntax than in the first example:

> The first shall be of the Elephant, whereof there generally passeth an opinion it hath no joints; and this absurdity is seconded with another, that being unable to lie down, it sleepeth against a Tree; which the Hunters observing, do saw it almost asunder; whereon the Beast relying, by the fall of the Tree, falls also down itself, and is able to rise no more. Which conceit is not the daughter of later times, but an old and gray-headed error, even in the days of Aristotle, as he delivereth in his Book, *De incessu Animalium*, and stands successively related by several other Authors: by Diodorus Siculus, Strabo, Ambrose, Cassiodore, Solinus, and many more. Now herein methinks men much forget themselves, not well considering the absurdity of such assertions.
>
> For first, they affirm it hath no joints, and yet concede it walks and moves about; whereby they conceive there may be a progression or advancement made in Motion without inflexion of parts. Now all progression or Animals' locomotion being (as Aristotle teacheth) performed *tractu et pulsu*; that is, by drawing on, or impelling forward some part which was before in station, or at quiet; where there are no joints or flexures, neither can there be these actions. And this is true, not onely in Quadrupedes, Volatils, and Fishes, which have distinct and prominent Organs of Motion, Legs, Wings, and Fins; but in such also as perform their progression by the Trunk as Serpents, Worms, and Leeches.   1–25/270

The passage exploits the verbal conciseness of the plain style; clauses are short, and expository, and there is frequent use of loose participle clauses. Intonation serves in place of explicit clause connectors in the sentence, 'Now all progression or Animals' locomotion being (as Aristotle teacheth) performed *tractu et pulsu*; that is, by drawing on, or impelling forward some part which was before in station, or at quiet; where there are no joints or flexures, neither can there be these actions.' Browne does not say 'since . . . therefore', which is the explicit syntax of the middle-style usage. But some words have a formality we would not expect to find in the plain style: 'observing', 'successively', 'related', 'assertions', 'concede', 'inflexion'. These words (and others) mark the new precision of language in this style, making it a fit vehicle for learned discussion, where the reader is assumed to know the Latin sense of such terms. Today many of these words would pass unremarked in educated standard English prose; it is rather the density of usage here which attracts attention. In another example from Johnson we can see how much simpler his plain style can be:

> The only fuel of the Islands is peat. Their wood is all consumed, and coal they have not yet found. Peat is dug out of the marshes, from the depth of one foot to that of six. That is accounted the best which is nearest the surface. It appears to be a mass of black earth held together by vegetable fibres. I know not whether the earth is bituminous, or whether the fibres be not the only combustible part; which by heating the interposed earth red hot, make a burning mass. The heat is not very strong nor lasting. The ashes are yellowish, and in large quantity. When they dig peat, they cut it into square pieces, and pile it up to dry beside the house. In some places it has an offensive smell. It is like wood charked for the smith. The common method of making peat fires, is by heaping it on the hearth; but it burns well in grates, and in the best houses is so used. 25/364–2/365

In this example there are only a few words we should regard as unusually formal in modern English: 'consumed', 'accounted', 'interposed'. The sentences bear no traces of colloquial rhythms of speech; they are however typical of the plain style in their careful additive sequence. Again Johnson's interest in information of an exact and almost scientific kind is strikingly evident. It is clear that certain styles were appropriate, as we have argued all along, to certain subjects; in Browne the whole of *Pseudodoxia Epidemica* is set in the plain style, while Johnson writes the account of his *Journey to the Western Islands of Scotland* (1775) in the register.

The middle style Browne reserves for literary topics or for the polite discussion of religious belief. There is a steady formality of expression in this passage from *Christian Morals* (published after his death):

> Bring candid Eyes unto the perusal of men's works, and let not Zoilism or Detraction blast well-intended labours. He that endureth no faults in men's writings must only read his own, wherein for the most part all appeareth White. Quotation mistakes, inadvertency, expedition, and human Lapses, may make not only Moles but Warts in Learned Authors, who notwithstanding, being judged by the capital matter, admit not of disparagement. I should unwillingly affirm that Cicero was but slightly versed in Homer, because in his Work *De Gloria* he ascribed those verses unto Ajax, which were delivered by Hector. What if Plautus in the account of Hercules mistaketh nativity for conception? Who would have mean thoughts of Apollinaris Sidonius, who seems to mistake the River Tigris for Euphrates; and, though a good Historian and learned Bishop of Auvergne, had the misfortune to be out in the Story of David, making mention of him when the Ark was sent back by the Philistins upon a Cart; which was before his time? Though I have no great opinion of Machiavel's Learning, yet I shall not presently say, that he was but a Novice in Roman History, because he was mistaken in placing Commodus after the Emperour Severus. Capital Truths are to be narrowly eyed, collateral Lapses and circumstantial deliveries not to be too strictly sifted. And if the substantial subject be well forged out, we need not examine the sparks which irregularly fly from it.   5–28/214

We notice the interest in example and illustration of general points, and the arrangement of the passage in a modern way, with the general topic announced first. Browne returns to repeat his general proposition at the end of the passage. This careful formality of presentation adds to the politeness of the middle style. There are traces of irony and an analytical use of metaphor. The passage is quite heavily nominal in mode, as we would expect in the register. There are many devices of analysis in the grammar: antithesis, qualifying phrases ('for the most part', 'notwithstanding', 'unwillingly', 'but slightly' etc), careful use of modals and auxiliary verbs of various kinds ('must', 'may', 'seems', 'need'), deliberate parallelism for contrast and comparison (e.g. 'narrowly eyed' – 'strictly sifted', 'well forged out' – 'irregularly fly'). The middle style has already many of the features which make it a powerful rhetorical weapon in Johnson's writing.

The paradox on which the last passage is based, and the relative truth of it, are exactly the kinds of argument Browne appreciated and made his own. In this example he uses the same techniques of paradox to write of more serious truths:

> Againe, I am confident and fully persuaded, yet dare not take my oath of my salvation; I am as it were sure, and do beleeve, without all doubt, that there is such a city as *Constantinople*; yet for me to take my oath thereon, were a kinde of perjury, because I hold no infallible warrant from my owne sense, to confirme me in the certainty thereof. And truely, though many pretend an absolute certainty of their salvation, yet when an humble soule shall contemplate her owne unworthinesse, she shall meete with many doubts and suddainely finde how much wee stand in need of the precept of Saint *Paul, Worke out your salvation with feare and trembling.* That which is the cause of my election, I hold to be the cause of my salvation, which was the mercy, and beneplacit of God, before I was, or the foundation of the world. *Before Abraham was, I am*, is the saying of Christ; yet is it true in some sense if I say it of my selfe, for I was not onely before my selfe, but *Adam*, that is, in the Idea of God, and the decree of that Synod held from all Eternity. And in this sense, I say, the world was before the Creation, and at an end before it had a beginning; and thus was I dead before I was alive; though my grave be *England*, my dying place was Paradise, and *Eve* miscarried of mee before she conceiv'd of *Cain*   13-34/64

The tentative style of this register, with its careful parallelisms, gives sincerity and clarity to the statement. By avoiding complex examples, Browne manages to give his own beliefs a simple dignity. But we may feel that the imagery of the last sentences owes more to his interest in paradox and medicine than to faith. Browne's control of subject matter in an eccentric and subjective way is one of the most obvious features of his own style, but we cannot easily define what it is. We can say it indicates that he falls into the category of social-philosophical writers, who explore experience rather than reducing it to clear patterns. The search for unexpected truths becomes, in a way, an end in itself; the total picture of Browne's views on any matter is quite difficult to arrive at. He offers a number of insights, and that is all. For him, unlike Johnson, great thoughts were not general, but particular truths discovered in humility by the writer in his own meditation. This subjectivity is the cause of the complex tone of some multiple contexts, in which Browne is at pains to bring out the truthfulness of his thinking. Unless he, the writer, can give authentic form to his meditations, he loses something of their inner truth. Here is an example of middle and plain style variation:

> I thanke God, and with joy I mention it, I was never afraid of Hell, nor ever grew pale at the description of that place; I have so fixed my contemplations on Heaven, that I have almost forgot the Idea of Hell, and am afraid rather to lose the joyes of the one than endure the misery of the other; to be deprived of them is a perfect hell, and needs me thinkes no addition to compleate our afflictions; that terrible terme hath never detained me from sin, nor do I owe any good action to the name thereof: I feare God, yet am not afraid of him, his mercies make me ashamed of my sins, before his judgements afraid thereof: these are the forced and secondary method of his wisedome, and which he useth not but as the last remedy, and upon provocation: a course rather to deterre the wicked, than incite the vertuous to his worship. I can hardly thinke there was ever any scared into Heaven; they goe the surest way to Heaven, who would serve God without a Hell; other Mercenaries that crouch unto him in feare of Hell, though they terme themselves the servants, are indeed but the slaves of the Almighty.   9–26/59

The passage varies from clause to clause, so that intimacy of tone in the plain style is balanced off against the more formal and analytical middle style. These are the plain style elements: 'I thanke God', 'I was never afraid of Hell', 'I have almost forgot the Idea of Hell', 'am afraid rather to lose the joyes . . . ', 'to be deprived of them is a perfect hell', 'yet am not afraid of him', 'before his judgements afraid thereof', 'which he useth not but as the last remedy', 'I can hardly thinke there was ever any scared into Heaven; they goe the surest way to Heaven', 'other Mercenaries that crouch unto him in feare of Hell'. This is an educated plain style, and there is very little colloquial metaphor. The middle style is markedly more formal and Latinate: 'with joy I mention it' (marked word order), 'grew pale at the description of that place', 'I have so fixed my contemplations on

Heaven', 'endure the misery of . . . ', 'needs me thinkes no addition to compleate our afflictions', 'that terrible terme hath never detained me from sin', 'nor do I owe any good action . . . ', 'I feare God', 'his mercies make me ashamed of my sins', 'the forced and secondary method of his wisdom', 'a course rather to deterre the wicked, than incite the vertuous to his worship', 'though they terme themselves the servants, are indeed but the slaves of the Almighty'. Now this variation is quite deliberate and in no way the product of a mechanical analysis by the present writer; Browne is balancing the actual truth of his feelings and memory against the public traditions of Christianity. These are not a matter of his opinions and judgements but a matter of public knowledge and agreed interpretation. They can be expressed neutrally and without any familiarity. But the link between the personal and individual and the public statement is the whole essence of Browne's prose style. He constructed a personality out of the traditional registers.

Sometimes this technique of variation can be used for scholarly wit, as in the early chapters of *Urne-Burial* (1658). A typical example would be these two paragraphs:

> The old *Balearians* had a peculiar mode, for they used great Urnes and much wood, but no fire in their burials, while they bruised the flesh and bones of the dead, crowded them into Urnes, and laid heapes of wood upon them. And the *Chinois* without cremation or urnall interrment of their bodies, make use of trees and much burning, while they plant a Pine-tree by their grave, and burn great numbers of printed draughts of slaves and horses over it, civilly content with their companies in effigie, which barbarous Nations exact unto reality.
>
> Christians abhorred this way of obsequies, and though they stickt not to give their bodies to be burnt in their lives, detested that mode after death; affecting rather a depositure than absumption, and properly submitting unto the sentence of God, to return not unto ashes but into dust againe, conformable unto the practice of the Patriarchs, the interrment of our Saviour, of *Peter*, *Paul*, and the ancient Martyrs. And so farre at last declining promiscuous enterrment with Pagans, that some have suffered Ecclesiastical censures, for making no scruple thereof.   24/122–2/123

The first paragraph has two sentences, the first in plain style, and the second in middle style. In the next paragraph, Browne inserts a quizzical plain style aside ('though they stickt not to give their bodies to be burnt in their lives'), before returning to a learned middle style usage.

In the high style, Browne develops his speculative reasoning to generalise about the transience of all humanity:

> What Song the *Syrens* sang, or what name *Achilles* assumed when he hid himself among women, though puzzling Questions are not beyond all conjecture. What time the persons of these Ossuaries entred the famous Nations of the dead, and slept with Princes and Counsellours, might admit a wide solution. But who were the proprietaries of these bones, or what bodies these ashes made up, were a question above Antiquarism. Not to be resolved by man, nor easily perhaps by spirits, except we consult the Provinciall Guardians, or tutellary Observators. Had they made as good provision for their names, as they have done for their Reliques, they had not so grosly erred in the art of perpetuation. But to subsist in bones, and be but Pyramidally extant, is a fallacy in duration. Vain ashes, which in the oblivion of names, persons, times, and sexes, have found unto themselves a fruitlesse continuation, and only arise unto late posterity, as Emblemes of mortall vanities; Antidotes against pride, vain-glory, and madding vices. Pagan vain-glories which thought the world might last for ever, had encouragement for ambition, and finding no *Atropos* unto the immortality of their Names, were never dampt with the necessity of oblivion. Even old ambitions had the advantage of ours, in the attempts of their vain-glories, who acting early, and before the probable Meridian of time, have by this time found great accomplishment of their designes, whereby the ancient *Heroes* have already out-lasted their Monuments, and Mechanicall preservations. But in this latter Scene of time we cannot expect such Mummies unto our memories, when ambition may fear the Prophecy of *Elias*, and *Charles* the fifth can never hope to live within two *Methusela's* of *Hector*.

And therefore restlesse inquietude for the diuturnity of our memories unto present considerations seems a vanity almost out of date, and superanuated peece of folly. We cannot hope to live so long in our names as some have done in their persons, one face of *Janus* holds no proportion unto the other. 'Tis too late to be ambitious. The great mutations of the world are acted, our time may be too short for our designes. To extend our memories by Monuments, whose death we dayly pray for, and whose duration we cannot hope, without injury to our expectations in the advent of the last day, were a contradiction to our beliefs. We whose generations are ordained in this setting part of time, are providentially taken off from such imaginations. And being necessitated to eye the remaining particle of futurity, are naturally constituted unto thoughts of the next world, and cannot excusably decline the consideration of that duration, which maketh Pyramids pillars of snow, and all that's past a moment.   23/149–12/150

The meditative and leisurely pace of this text should not disguise the high style formality of the thought and language. Browne favours complex Latinate noun phrases, often linked together in a sequence of prepositional phrases: 'restlesse inquietude for the diuturnity of our memories unto present considerations'. We have to translate this into verbal style, into clauses, to get at the meaning: 'if we agree that time is now running out, we should not need to worry too much about how long we are remembered after death'. Somehow the meaning does not come over so easily in the Latin form, which only goes to show that Browne was wrong to assume that Latin influence would increase after his time. For these nominal sequences are very much Latin in their syntax, and quite unusual in English even in his own day. This is not a sustained style of writing, and Browne often slips into plain style to focus his emphasis: 'never *dampt* with the necessity of oblivion', 'live within two *Methusela's* of *Hector*', 'a vanity almost out of date' (in two senses: 'at the wrong time', 'old fashioned vanity'), 'peece of folly', ''Tis too late . . . ', 'and all that's past a moment'. In some instances, where he finds a number of examples, the plain style is more obvious, because proper to separate items of information:

> But the iniquity of oblivion blindely scattereth her poppy, and deals with the memory of men without distinction to merit of perpetuity. Who can but pity the founder of the Pyramids? *Herostratus* lives that burnt the Temple of *Diana*, he is almost lost that built it; Time hath spared the Epitaph of *Adrians* horse, confounded that of himself. In vain we compute our felicities by the advantage of our good names, since bad have equall durations; and *Thersites* is like to live as long as *Agamemnon*. Who

knows whether the best of men be known? or whether there be not more remarkable persons forgot, than any that stand remembered in the known account of time? Without the favour of the everlasting Register the first man had been as unknown as the last, and *Methuselahs* long life had been his only Chronicle.
15–28/151

The first sentence is perhaps the most famous Browne wrote; but it is followed by a plain style sequence of ironic single truths, each sustaining the argument of the dramatic metaphor in the high style. He returns to high style mannered writing in the first part of the fourth sentence: 'In vain we compute our felicities by the advantage of our good names, since bad have equall durations', but shifts again into plain style to focus the point: 'and *Thersites* is like to live as long as *Agamemnon*'. The rest of this passage is plain style; Browne's modern turn of mind questions the very basis of our knowledge of history. The text ends on a characteristic paradox; Methuselah himself would have been the only 'chronicle' of his own long life but for the 'everlasting Register' of the Book of Life itself. It is not difficult to detect in such a remark the influence of Ramistic logic with its fusion of abstract and concrete, concepts and things. But the general methods of this logic are far too mechanical for such a speculative mind as Browne's, and there is little evidence of its influence elsewhere in his work. We may conclude that the high style occurs where he has a large general theme to work on, as in the last chapter of *Urne-Burial*, or in that extraordinary and wide-ranging work, *The Garden of Cyrus* (1658). The influence of this style level cannot be found in Johnson, but the middle style provided a norm for the essay genre which was so popular in the eighteenth century.

To this genre we must now turn. The consistency and orderliness of the middle style is very much apparent in Johnson's essays. Here is a typical example, where the analysis is advanced through careful use of word form and intricate parallelism in syntax:

> Every man is prompted by the love of himself to imagine, that he possesses some qualities, superior, either in kind or in degree, to those which he sees allotted to the rest of the world; and, whatever apparent disadvantages he may suffer in the comparison with others, he has some invisible distinctions, some latent reserve of excellence, which he throws into the balance, and by which he generally fancies that it is turned in his favour.

> The studious and speculative part of mankind always seem to consider their fraternity as placed in a state of opposition to those who are engaged in the tumult of public business; and have pleased themselves, from age to age, with celebrating the felicity of their own condition, and with recounting the perplexity of politics, the dangers of greatness, the anxieties of ambition, and the miseries of riches.
> Among the numerous topics of declamation, that their industry has discovered on this subject, there is none which they press with greater efforts, or on which they have more copiously laid out their reason and their imagination, than the instability of high stations, and the uncertainty with which the profits and honours are possessed, that must be acquired with so much hazard, vigilance, and labour.
> This they appear to consider as an irrefragable argument against the choice of the statesman and the warrior; and swell with confidence of victory, thus furnished by the muses with the arms which never can be blunted, and which no art or strength of their adversaries can elude or resist. 1–24/159

The discrimination of sense which operates at phrase and clause level gives a spurious precision to the analysis. It sounds better than it is, for after all it is only the merest commonplace. But that is the whole point of the genre; the essay dealt with widely held opinions, and showed often that they were mistaken. The subjective belief in the insecurity of public life and a military career must be balanced, as Johnson goes on to show, against the equal though distinctive uncertainties and pitfalls in a writer's career. The idea of the essay is to balance views off against each other, while rejecting no particular view. Johnson's use of parallelism and balanced clauses enacts this assumption of balance and reason in the grammar of the text. It is a classifying and moderating genre where we would not expect to find the emphatic tones of the high style. Each sentence has a carefully ordered syntax which allows a finished pattern. In the first sentence, a pair of prepositional phrases appears in an adjectival phrase: 'either in kind or in degree'; towards the end of the sentence, a pair of noun phrases, each with its qualifying adjective, occurs, 'some invisible distinctions, some latent reserve of excellence'. This pair of noun phrases has the same syntax, determiner plus adjective plus noun, and balances the parallelism of preposition plus noun in the first pair. But there is also variation, for 'some qualities, superior, either in kind or in degree' is a heavily post-modified phrase. We have already seen the parallelism in the adjectival phrase; there is also the parallelism of syntax between those prepositional phrases and the one in the second pair. The parallelism of clause in the first sentence is also noticeable, especially at the end, where two relative clauses sustain the pattern of the noun phrases. Again, they are variations at clause level, for they are both non-restrictive, additive clauses, and contrast with the single restrictive relative clause, 'those which he sees . . . '. Lastly, the noun clause as object in the main clause, 'that he possesses some qualities . . . ' is balanced by the second object clause, 'and (that) he has some invisible distinctions . . . '. The concessive clause is deviant from this pattern of syntax and is therefore all the more significant structurally. It marks the scepticism of the writer, for he will go on to argue that these disadvantages are in fact real and far from apparent. The reader is made to notice this clause because of its isolation, and there is a measure of syntactic focus, however abstract. This kind of analysis is exhausting, and so we will not continue further, although it is worth pointing out that Johnson regularly works like this in his middle style. The rest of the example is closely similar with consistent parallelism at clause and phrase levels.

In diction, Johnson uses a carefully graded range of senses that advances the analysis of the essay theme. His technique is to get the reader to concede something which later he finds to his cost is unreasonable and uncertain. To do this, Johnson presents his arguments in a careful mixture of severe formality and relative informality, pressing the reader to accept his authority and then relaxing ever so slightly to allow him to agree with relief at the change of tone. As readers, we are alerted at once to the fact that we must be on our guard against irrational self-esteem, even if every man suffers from it. The first half of this sentence is formal, authoritative, and admits of no uncertainty. We wince at the irony and condescension of 'some invisible distinctions, some latent reserve of excellence', and we nod in agreement when Johnson uses relative informality to suggest self-delusion in the phrase, 'throws into the balance', or in the sarcasm of 'generally fancies'. We assume, wrongly, that we ourselves are free from these weaknesses, and have no need of such reminders. But Johnson wanted us to think that, and brings about a complete reversal of established opinion in the rest of the essay. For the apparent disadvantages of military and political careers turn out to be no more oppressive than the concealed dangers of a writer's trade. We readily agree with the conventional wisdom he offers us, only to find that 'distinctions' may prove all too 'invisible', while 'apparent disadvantages' turn out to be exactly that, and no more. Johnson exploits exact meanings and plays them off against looser common usage. He also uses the morphology of words to reinforce parallelism of syntax at phrase level. We can note the following pairings: 'prompted'–'allotted', 'qualities'–'disadvantages'–'distinctions', 'throws'–'fancies', 'felicity'–'perplexity', 'anxieties'–'miseries', 'instability'–'uncertainty', 'possessed'–'acquired'. As we might expect in the middle style, we find comparative constructions of an evaluating and aesthetic kind: 'with greater efforts'–'more copiously'.

Johnson takes further the tendency in Browne to employ scientific analogies and natural metaphors from polite usage. None of these images carries much conviction today. They represent however a new development in the middle style; the older tradition of the middle style with its imagery of love and true feeling has been replaced by more accurate observation of the real world of nature. We expect new insights and originality in metaphor nowadays, and since the 'natural logic' of the Ramists allowed something of this, we are prepared to tolerate and even admire some of their invention. But with Johnson we take a different view; few people find his metaphors of any interest. By and large they are dismissed as unimportant aspects of his work, yet they combine that accuracy and care of observation that makes his literary criticism so valuable. 'The work of a correct and regular writer is a garden accurately formed and diligently planted, varied with shades, and scented with flowers; the composition of Shakespeare is a forest, in which oaks extend their branches, and pines tower in the air, interspersed sometimes with weeds and brambles, and sometimes giving shelter to myrtles and roses; filling the eye with awful pomp, and gratifying the mind with endless diversity.' (12–18/281) We cannot imagine the myrtles and roses, which is a traditional detail, nor does the 'awful pomp' strike the modern reader as acceptable language. But the rest of this metaphor is quite realistic; only in those details does Johnson show his reliance on middle style poetic tradition. This is an echo of Browne's more poetic metaphor; in the realism of the contrast we can see a genuine observation, translated into the formality of the middle style without too much difficulty. Here too we have an example of Johnson's observation at work: 'Dryden's page is a natural field, rising into inequalities, and diversified by the varied exuberance of abundant vegetation; Pope's is a velvet lawn, shaven by the scythe, and levelled by the roller.' (4–7/449) It tells us something of the general difference between the two writers; like Dryden himself, Johnson rarely descends to specific points of analysis in his criticism. One major area of development in Johnson is his use of scientific metaphor. His interest in science was considerable, as his *Dictionary* entries show.[4] This too is a tradition in which Browne took great interest, like many late seventeenth-century writers. But Johnson went beyond Browne in using direct analogies with the language of science. Here he describes why Shakespeare's comic scenes survive in spite of their date:

> The force of his comic scenes has suffered little diminution from the changes made by a century and a half, in manners or in words. As his personages act upon principles arising from genuine passion, very little modified by particular forms, their pleasures and vexations are communicable to all times and all places; they are natural, and therefore durable; the adventitious peculiarities of personal habits, are only superficial dies, bright and pleasing for a little while, yet soon fading to a dim tinct, without any remains of former lustre; but the discriminations of true passion are the colours of nature; they pervade the whole mass, and can only perish with the body that exhibits them. The accidental compositions of heterogeneous modes are dissolved by the chance which combined them; but the uniform simplicity of primitive qualities neither admits increase, nor suffers decay. The sand heaped by one flood is scattered by another, but the rock always continues in its place. The stream of time, which is continually washing the dissoluble fabrics of other poets, passes without injury by the adamant of Shakespeare.   8–24/269

The analogy with dyes and with natural colour is analytical and revealing, even if rather obvious. Johnson assumes that Shakespeare is a 'natural genius' whose qualities are 'primitive' like those of natural objects. There is a profoundly mechanistic view of the universe behind such phrases as 'the force of his comic scenes', 'the accidental compositions of heterogeneous modes', 'the chance which combined them'; but this is what we would expect in an eighteenth-century writer, if he were to use scientific analogies. The conventional middle style metaphor that concludes this passage is of course a marker of the more traditional features of this register. Again, we should note the natural imagery Johnson uses; it is precise and based on accurate observation, even though conventional enough. Elsewhere, Johnson uses the same metaphor of a scientific kind to describe the similarities in all human experience; here too we notice the mechanical analogy that underlies the whole analysis:

> I have often thought that there has rarely passed a life of which a judicious and faithful narrative would not be useful. For, not only every man has, in the mighty mass of the world, great numbers in the same condition with himself, to whom his mistakes and miscarriages, escapes and expedients, would be of immediate and apparent use; but there is such an uniformity in the state of man, considered apart from adventitious and separable decorations and disguises, that there is scarcely any possibility of good or ill, but is common to human kind. A great part of the time of those who are placed at the greatest distance by fortune, or by temper, must unavoidably pass in the same manner; and though, when the claims of nature are satisfied, caprice, and vanity, and accident, begin to produce discriminations and peculiarities, yet the eye is not very heedful or quick, which cannot discover the same causes still terminating their influence in the same effects, though sometimes accelerated, sometimes retarded, or perplexed by multiplied combinations. 12–29/169

Occasionally, we find multiple contexts in which Johnson uses all three styles to create a complex synthesis of meaning. This is perhaps one of the most modern examples in Johnson, although the high style is too conventional as metaphor for the modern reader:

> On the next day we began our journey southwards. The weather was tempestuous. For half the day the ground was rough, and our horses were still small. Had they required much restraint, we might have been reduced to difficulties; for I think we had amongst us but one bridle. We fed the poor animals liberally, and they performed their journey well. In the latter part of the day, we came to a firm and smooth road, made by the soldiers, on which we travelled with great security, busied with contemplating the scene about us. The night came on while we had yet a great part of the way to go, though not so dark, but that we could

discern the cataracts which poured down the hills, on one side, and fell into one general channel that ran with great violence on the other. The wind was loud, the rain was heavy, and the whistling of the blast, the fall of the shower, the rush of the cataracts, and the roar of the torrent, made a nobler chorus of the rough music of nature than it had ever been my chance to hear before. The streams, which ran across the way from the hills to the main current, were so frequent, that after a while I began to count them; and, in ten miles, reckoned fifty-five, probably missing some, and having let some pass before they forced themselves upon my notice. At last we came to Inverary, where we found an inn, not only commodious, but magnificent.

The difficulties of peregrination were now at an end.

5–26/402

The passage begins in the plain style, with little or no subordination, simple vocabulary, and a good deal of fact. The central metaphor is high style, with marked formality in a sequence of noun phrases which build up to it: 'the whistling of the blast', 'the fall of the shower', 'the rush of the cataracts', etc. Johnson soon abandons this emphatic and poetic vein for the factual plain style that he generally uses in his *Journey*. At the end of this text he returns to a middle and high style to express his own sense of relief after the exhausting day's travel: the inn was 'not only commodious' (middle style), but 'magnificent' (high style). The first adjective is evaluating and formal, implying the discriminating traveller; the second is emphatic and poetic, without any claim to realism. The last sentence is a careful middle style summary; the syntax is formal and literary (note the placing of 'now' in a marked position), and the diction is abstract. The choice of 'peregrination' would have won Browne's approval.

Conclusion

The concept of 'style' in common use is a primitive and complex term. It suggests a direct access to the actual personality and usage of the writer in a mystical and intuitive way. Rather than attempt to use such a clumsy term, we have tried to limit the area of discussion to what we can reasonably expect to know of a writer's language and intentions. The purpose of this book is to suggest that there is a well-founded relation between theories of language use and the particular features of literary language. We have taken the traditional and often repeated ideas of plain, middle and high styles, and given them a more specific framework in the grammar and semantics of the text. We have tried to avoid the pursuit of peripheral detail such as the imagery of the text, or its vocabulary as significant features in themselves. They are part of a larger complex of features which represent the register or style area of the text. This complex of features is in fact the 'norm' or controlling strategy that the writer exploits in his usage. It is a very broad and variable range of features, and can be realised in many forms. There are dense and delicate versions of the same traditional register, and the frequency of indexical markers varies according to the writer's choice. But there are limits to the range of choice; these limits are imposed by the principle of contradiction which is fundamental to all meaning. For stylistics, as we should call this study of style, is not to be separated from semantics, without making the whole discipline impoverished and arid. The structure of a work is part of its meaning and its meaning is part of its structure. The distinction made between form and content is an arbitrary one, and does not convey the reader's experience of the text, nor the writer's. The value of a registerial approach to style is that it relates subject matter, or content, to certain choices of style level. This can of course only apply to the period covered by this book, or perhaps a little later in the history of English literature. The doctrine of the three styles did not survive for very long into the late eighteenth century, and the writers of the Romantic period were in large part motivated by a new approach to literary language. In the period before Chaucer there may well be examples of rhetorical variation of the traditional kind, but the oral traditions of much medieval literature make it difficult to find examples of fully realised styles.

We can divide our conclusions into two parts: those conclusions which have a synchronic basis and describe the period as a whole, and those conclusions which have a diachronic aspect and describe the sequence of changes as we have observed them. First, from a synchronic viewpoint, we can say that the three styles have a range of common properties throughout the period. Writers clearly understood that they were creating a traditional range of style levels in their work, and that these styles were recognised by everyone else, both readers and other writers. This puts the concept of style on a public basis, as something people consciously interpreted; it is not a private and intuitive activity that by accident produces a particular effect. Nor is it therefore a mechanical and contrived activity: the writer's choices are still his own even if he works within a public tradition. In fact the writer creates the tradition himself, every time he writes successfully (we are only concerned with the finished work, not working drafts). We gain a sense of the variety and uniqueness of a writer's style from a knowledge of the traditional doctrine as it is realised in other writers. But uniqueness is an unscientific concept, and not susceptible of analysis or discussion. We should note that a great deal of literary criticism is related to the ideas and philosophy of a writer, or his life, as much as to his work. Even in literary criticism, the writer's work is rarely considered on its own without any external reference. Tacitly, literary critics agree that the text must be placed in a general cultural context of some kind (even the writer's life partly represents this idea) if it is to have meaning. An utterly unique work could not be understood.

Secondly, we can see that the tradition of the three styles operates across the genres of poetry and prose, and that there is no clear distinction between these forms of discourse in rhetorical tradition. We can of course find distinctions: in the technical matter of rhythm and metrics generally, which is more marked in poetry than prose, or in the formal features of rhyme which do not occur in prose. But literary language in the period nevertheless seems to have been remarkably homogeneous, and the close study of any one author should give access to the others. It is largely because this common tradition of literary language has disappeared that modern readers have the trouble they do with texts from this period. It is rather uninteresting to read works of literature solely for their ideas or philosophy; these are only aspects (and sometimes quite minor aspects) of art. Now if a literary critic were to claim that his chief interest in style is to identify period styles or individual styles, we can answer that our approach does in fact provide the basis for such evaluations. But the analysis throws into relief the fact that such generalisations are bought at a high cost. For what is completely unique cannot be satisfactorily identified, and what is common to all writers in a period may be very trivial. The literary critic is mistaken to demand such a function from stylistics, but the demand is understandable since it reflects the methodology of literary criticism. It is still very much a study of historical periods with the conventional assumptions of historical chronology and of the uniqueness of separate events. But the whole tenor of the analysis in this book has been that we should not overvalue uniqueness. Art is not a matter of unique achievement, but a controlled exploitation of tradition by the individual talent.

Thirdly, we can give new meaning to the idea of a rhetorical tradition of literary language. We no longer need to consult rhetorical handbooks to identify particular tropes or schemes of rhetoric, and imagine that this is what historical stylistics is all about. We can rely on our own knowledge of language variation and see how local contexts condition and alter the function of different rhetorical figures. These figures are no more than perfectly recognisable variations in syntax and meaning in the text; their value is not to test whether we know the contemporary label for them, but how they function as markers of style, and what their role is in the local context. To know these things we need to be able to recognise style level, and to know about the tradition of style described above. While there is an area of indeterminacy in vocabulary, so that common diction can occur at any style level, there is almost never any doubt about the style of a particular text or passage. Literary language is non-casual, and there must be some indexical marker at some point in the text, if we take a large enough context. We no longer need to raise the question of those texts that have 'nothing remarkable' stylistically about them, for we can see that most texts do not show excessive deviation from the way we use natural language. The literary text in this period is a selection from natural language use in a particular order and in a particular range of topics. This does not necessarily imply deviation of an explicit kind.

Conclusion

Lastly, from a synchronic point of view, we can see a consistent difference between general contexts. Those writers who show in their general context a moral or political tendency are on the whole more preoccupied with formal variations of style than writers in the social and philosophical group. Andrewes, for example, did not enlarge his work with new topics from common life, like Donne; instead, he found a new technique, based on the use of conciseness for emphasis in speech, and adapted this principle to the various styles of his work. Shakespeare made minor variations in the form of the sonnet, but most people would not regard those variations of form as a striking or important aspect of his originality. On the other hand, Milton's formal variations in *Lycidas* (in his adaptation of an Italian rhyme scheme), and his powerful rhythms in *Paradise Lost*, show the need for order and structure which are essential to his imagination. The reader's impression of the writer's interest in the formal structure of his work can usually be relied on. Milton may be sceptical of the traditional middle style in *Lycidas*, but the reason is that he knows it to be untruthful and a betrayal of simple fact, whereas Shakespeare finds the middle style inadequate as a means of analysing the truth, which is far from simple. Again, there seems little doubt that Skelton, Spenser and Dryden are also moral-political writers in their usage, while Chaucer, Donne and Pope place less emphasis on formal devices. The reader's attention in the latter is always on their lexical meaning, and there is less attention required by the formal patterning of syntax. Of the prose writers, Bacon, Dekker and Browne have an organic richness of meaning in their styles which is always more difficult to analyse than the formal ordering of Sidney, Dryden or Johnson. The lexical set, or associated groupings of vocabulary, is a prime feature of the social-philosophical type of writer. Each kind of writer, in poetry and prose, offers a different approach to the problem of meaning, as we have suggested above in the *Introduction*.

At a diachronic level, we can conclude that throughout the period the writer's intention (the 'situation' of use) gradually becomes more and more important. This is very clear in the example of Pope, and in the ingenuity and complexity of his multiple contexts, especially with the high and plain styles. We could almost postulate a stylistic law that as a register becomes more atrophied and impervious to the writer's meanings, he must make more strenuous efforts and show greater daring in his invention of contexts for its use, if he is to keep the tradition alive, albeit in a moribund form. This is rather similar to the facetious use of outmoded slang in natural language; the next stage is for the expression to become entirely obsolete, and unintelligible. The comparison is of course crude compared to the subtlety and wit of Pope's usage, but the general principle applies. However, in the example of Browne it is much more difficult to say where the element of facetiousness ends and the serious usage of traditional styles begins. Both elements seem present at all times, and his style has a bizarre effect, which may often be accidental. In the example of Skelton we can see what strenuous attempts a moral-political type of writer may make to reanimate the traditional doctrine. Skelton's weakness is his lack of variety in argument and logical invention, and his consequent reliance on fluency in place of content. His satire is often facetious and serious at almost one and the same time, because his traditional material is not quite viable for the issues he wants to raise. Literary language in the period is kept alive by constant enlargement and renewal of topics, although there are writers who can only repeat the formulas, without new content. The development of styles in this period is towards a new politeness and urbanity, and there is a gradual but steady elimination of colloquial expressions of a more vulgar kind from writers' usage. The homely metaphors of Chaucer, Skelton, or Sidney, and the coarse language of Dryden's plain style, are not to be found in Browne and Johnson. There is a spread of middle style vocabulary into the plain style usage, and the doctrine of the three styles can be seen to be in decline. The growth of interest in fact and observation (not a strong feature of the traditional styles which were poetic in their most influential form) may also be seen as contributing to that decline. The final effect of Ramistic theories of meaning was to undermine the traditional images of poetry, especially in the middle and high styles, and prepare the way for a more limited realism in prose and verse.

Notes

NOTES TO THE INTRODUCTION

1. Cicero, *Orator*, xxiii, 76 ff., in the translation of D. A. Russell and M. Winterbottom, *Ancient Literary Criticism*, Oxford, 1972.
2. See further E. Auerbach, *Literary Language and its Public*, London, 1965, translation by R. Manheim, pp. 37–8.
3. *Orator*, xxvi, 91 ff.
4. Ibid, xxviii, 97.
5. I am indebted to the discussion of register set out in the following articles: M. Gregory, 'Aspects of varieties differentiation', *Journal of Linguistics*, III (1967), pp. 177–98; R. Hasan, 'Code, Register and Social Dialect', chapter 10 of *Class, Codes and Control*, vol. II, *Applied Studies towards a Sociology of Language*, (ed.) B. Bernstein, London, 1973, pp. 271 ff.; D. E. Ager, 'Register', *Nottingham Linguistic Circular*, V (1976), pp. 7–19.
6. St. Augustine, *On Christian Doctrine*, IV, 37.

NOTES TO CHAPTER 1

1. *The Knight's Tale*, ll. 1005–19. All references are to *The Works of Geoffrey Chaucer*, (ed.) F. N. Robinson, 2nd. ed., London, 1957.
2. See the note to ll. 2155–86 in Robinson, op. cit.
3. *Upon the Dolorous Death . . . of the most Honourable Earl of Northumberland*, 1–7/4. All references are to *The Complete Poems of John Skelton*, (ed.) P. Henderson, 2nd. ed., London, 1948, with occasional emendations as found in *John Skelton: Poems*, (ed.) R. S. Kinsman, Oxford, 1969.

NOTES TO CHAPTER 2

1. For a recent discussion of the subject, see J. Shearman, *Mannerism*, Harmondsworth, 1967, repr. 1973.
2. Shearman, op. cit., pp. 15–48.
3. Cf. M. Levey, *High Renaissance*, Harmondsworth, 1975, pp. 44 ff.
4. All references are to *The Works of Edmund Spenser*, (ed.) R. Morris, London, 1909.
5. Cf. E. Wind, *Pagan Mysteries in the Renaissance*, 2nd. ed., London, 1968, pp. 86–96.
6. All references are to *Shakespeare's Sonnets*, (eds.) W. G. Ingram and T. Redpath, London, 1967.

NOTES TO CHAPTER 3

1. Pierre de la Ramée, *Dialectique* (1555), (ed.) M. Dassonville, Genève, 1964. The standard discussion of Ramistic logic is to be found in W. S. Howell, *Logic and Rhetoric in England, 1500–1700*, New York, 1961; W. J. Ong, *Ramus, Method and the Decay of Dialogue*, Cambridge, Mass., 1958 sets Ramism in its European traditions. N. E. Nelson, 'Peter Ramus and the confusion of logic, rhetoric, and poetry', *Contributions in Modern Philology*, II, 1947, Ann Arbor, University of Michigan, is a more detailed discussion of Ramism and its intellectual pretensions. I have not found the case against the influence of Ramism persuasive; the two main articles are A. J. Smith, 'An Examination of some claims for Ramism', *Review of English Studies*, VII (1956), pp. 348–59; G. Watson, 'Ramus, Miss Tuve, and the new Petromachia', *Modern Philology* LV (1958), pp. 259–62.
2. I am indebted to the approach taken by J. P. Thorne, 'A Ramistical commentary on Sidney's *An Apologie for Poetrie*', *Modern Philology* LIV (1957), pp. 158–64.
3. This point is explained more fully by M. McCanles, 'Paradox in Donne', *Studies in the Renaissance* XIII (1966), pp. 266–87.
4. All references are to *The Poems of John Donne*, (ed.) H. Grierson, London, 1933, repr. 1960.
5. All references are to *The Poems and Fables of John Dryden*, (ed.) J. Kinsley, London, 1958, repr. 1962.

NOTES TO CHAPTER 4

1. See R. Daniells, *Milton, Mannerism, and Baroque*, Toronto, 1963, and W. Sypher, *Four Stages of Renaissance Style*, New York, 1955. The view of mannerism advanced in these works is not the one I have adopted in chapter 2 above.
2. All references are to *Milton's Poems*, (ed.) B. A. Wright, London, 1956.
3. All references are to *Pope: Poetical Works*, (ed.) H. Davis, London, 1966, repr. 1974.
4. *Of Reformation in England*, p. 23 of *Milton's Prose Writings*, (Introd. by) K. M. Burton, London, rev. ed. 1958, repr. 1970.
5. Ibid. p. 57.
6. See F. T. Prince, *The Italian Element in Milton's Verse*, Oxford, 1954.

NOTES TO CHAPTER 5

1. See further P. A. Duhamel, 'Sidney's *Arcadia* and Elizabethan Rhetoric', *Studies in Philology*, XLV (1948), pp. 134–50.
2. See Sir Philip Sidney, *An Apology for Poetry*, (ed.) G. Shepherd, Manchester, 1973, pp. 1–4.
3. See G. W. Hallam, 'Sidney's Supposed Ramism', *Renaissance Papers*, (Durham, N.C.) 1963, pp. 11–20.

4. See the discussion in the Introduction to Sir Philip Sidney, *The Countess of Pembroke's Arcadia*, (ed.) M. Evans, Harmondsworth, 1977, pp. 19–27.
5. All references are to Evans, op. cit.
6. See *An Apology for Poetry*, op. cit., pp. 100–1.
7. Ibid., pp. 53–5.
8. Temple's work is analysed in J. P. Thorne, art. cit.
9. *Apology*, op. cit., 38–9, 123.
10. Ibid., 30–5, 112.
11. Ibid., p. 61.
12. All references are to Bacon, *The Advancement of Learning*, (ed.) W. A. Wright, fifth edition, Oxford, repr. 1963.
13. See further, in the example of Sidney, F. G. Robinson, *The Shape of Things Known: Sidney's Apology and its Philosophical Tradition*, Harvard, 1972.
14. All references are to Francis Bacon, *Essays*, (Introd. by) O. Smeaton, London, 1906, repr. 1946.
15. All references are to the cited edition of the *Apology*.

NOTES TO CHAPTER 6

1. See *The Works of Aurelius Augustine, Bishop of Hippo*, (ed.) M. Dods, Edinburgh, 1871–3, vol. IX.
2. All references are to *Lancelot Andrewes: Sermons*, (ed.) G. M. Story, Oxford, 1967.
3. All references are to *John Donne: Selected Prose*, (eds.) E. Simpson, H. Gardner, T. Healy, Oxford, 1967.
4. The reading 'he' in the *Selected Prose*, op. cit., does not seem good sense; I have emended the reading to 'be' from the Scolar Press facsimile, John Donne, *Death's Duel*, (1632) Menston, 1969.
5. For example, *Selected Prose*, op. cit.

NOTES TO CHAPTER 7

1. For example, Sidney attacks the Euphuists in his *Apology for Poetry* (op. cit., 6/139 ff. and see Notes).
2. All references are to *Thomas Dekker: Selected Prose Writings*, (ed.) E. D. Pendry, London, 1967.
3. All references are to *John Dryden: Of Dramatic Poesy and other Critical Essays*, two vols., (ed.) G. Watson, London, 1962, repr. 1964. The Latin, from Virgil, means 'as cypresses often do among bending osiers'.
4. In his *Life of Dryden*.
5. Some words in this passage are part of the colloquial usage of the day and strange to the modern reader: 'desperviews', 'desperadoes, or poor beggars'; 'brewis', 'bread and gravy'; 'powder beef', 'salted beef'; 'provant', 'rations'. I am indebted to Pendry's *Glossary* for these references.

NOTES TO CHAPTER 8

1. The influence of Browne on Johnson is documented in W. K. Wimsatt, *Philosophic Words*, New Haven, 1948.
2. *Samuel Johnson: Selected Writings*, (ed.) P. Cruttwell, Harmondsworth, 1968, pp. 236–7. All quotations from Johnson are from this edition.
3. All quotations are from *Sir Thomas Browne: Selected Writings*, (ed.) Sir G. Keynes, London, 1970.
4. See Wimsatt, op. cit.

Index

Amplification, 18, 43, 55, 56
Andrewes, Lancelot, 20, 190, 215
  high style, 155, 156–7, 160–1, 167–8
  middle style, 155, 163–5, 167, 168–9
  plain style, 155, 172–3
Argument, 32, 33, 36, 42, 44, 48, 49, 50, 51, 85, 91, 97, 98, 102, 104
Aristotle, 89–92, 138
Augustine, St, 13, 155, 173
Authorship, 22

Bacon, Francis, 16, 161, 190, 215
  Advancement of Learning, 135, 140–4, 154
  Essays, 13, 17, 19, 135, 141, 143, 144, 148, 154, *Of Truth*, 148–51
  high style, 139–44
  middle style, 150
  plain style, 149–51
Baroque, 25, 99, 110
Boethius, 12, 39, 40, 41
Browne, Sir Thomas, 193, 211, 215, 216
  Christian Morals, 199
  Garden of Cyrus, 205
  Pseudodoxia Epidemica, 193, 194, 198
  Urne Burial, 202, 205
  high style, 194, 203–4, 205
  middle style, 193–4, 201–2, 202, 203
  plain style, 194, 194–6, 197–8, 198–200, 201, 202, 203, 204–5

Chaucer, Geoffrey, 5, 6, 10–11, 12, 15, 21, 213, 215, 216
  Book of the Duchess, 45–6, 56
  Clerk's Tale, 14
  Franklin's Tale, 21, 36
  General Prologue, 7, 17, 56–62

  Knight's Tale, 12, 14, 29–42, 43
  Man of Law's Tale, 14
  Miller's Tale, 14, 15, 36, 52–3
  Reeve's Tale, 14, 15
  Wife of Bath's Prologue, 14
  high style, 29–30, 33–5, 41, 56
  middle style, 31–3, 35–7, 40, 41, 45–6, 56–8, 59, 60, 62
  plain style, 30–1, 32–3, 37–9, 40–1, 42, 52–3, 56, 58–9, 60, 61–2
Chaucerian diction, 64–5, 111, 112
Cicero, 7, 8, 11, 64
Ciceronian, 141, 145, 154
Classical rhetoricians, 6–7, 18
Cognitive usage, 70
Conceptual imitation, 138–9
Context, contrastive, 9, 70, 71, 74, 103, 105, 109, 121; *see also* Register and Style
  determination of contexts, 2–3, 66, 78
  general context, 21, 23, 73, 173, 215
  local context, 9, 21, 46, 57, 63, 66, 173, 214
  multiple context, 9, 52, 60, 71, 80, 81, 83–5, 99, 104–5, 106–7, 108–9, 119, 120–1, 127, 130, 175, 182, 188–9, 201, 210, 215
  normative context, 22
  single context, 9, 52, 85–6, 107, 111, 114, 175, 179
Contradiction, 9, 102, 104, 136, 138, 142, 153, 154, 212
Copiousness, 44, 48
  copious, 8, 44, 50

Dekker, Thomas, 13, 17, 174–6, 194, 215

Dekker, Thomas, (Contd.)
  Gull's Horn-Book, 183, 185, 187
  high style, 176–7, 182–3
  middle style, 182–3, 184–5, 188, 189
  plain style, 176–7, 182–3, 184, 185, 188, 189, 191–2
Dialect, 54
Dichotomies, 93, 103, 107, 140, 152, 167, 169, 170, 174, 177
Donne, John, 17, 18, 19, 20, 97, 113, 141, 174, 175, 189, 190, 215
  Apparition, 105–7
  Good Morrow, 93–6
  Holy Sonnets, 99, 108–9
  Lovers Infinitenesse, 99–102
  Satyres, 110
  high style, 108, 157–60, 167–8
  middle style, 92–3, 94, 95, 99, 100, 101, 102, 105, 106–7, 161–3, 165–7, 169–70, 171
  plain style, 92, 94, 95, 99, 100, 101, 102, 105, 106–7, 108, 158, 170–2
Dryden, John, 13, 174–6, 194, 215, 216
  Absalom and Achitophel, 96
  Death of Lord Hastings, 96
  Dedication to Fables, 110
  A Discourse concerning Satire, 186
  Killigrew, Anne, Mrs, 110
  MacFlecknoe, 109, 121
  Medal, 110
  Religio Laici, 110
  high style, 99, 103, 109, 178, 179, 180, 181
  middle style, 97, 98, 99, 180, 182, 186–7, 190
  plain style, 97, 98, 103, 107–8, 109, 110, 179, 180, 181, 182, 186–7, 189, 190–1

Epic, 11, 12, 15, 16, 135
Equative clauses, 34
Evaluation, 4

Fabliaux, 14, 15
Familiarity, 32, 35, 48, 61, 77, 87, 182, 202
Fathers of the Church, 12

Formality, 30, 32, 35, 36, 38, 46, 47, 48, 56, 60, 67, 70, 76, 86, 111, 115, 122, 123, 126, 160, 165, 182, 183, 185–6, 194, 195, 196, 198, 199, 201, 204, 207, 208

Generalisation, 22, 214

High style, 8, 11–12, 13, 14, 15, 16, 17, 18, 216, see authors cited

Idealism, 138
Indexical marker, 10, 72, 81, 161, 168, 171, 172, 179, 190, 195, 212, 214
Invention, lexical, 192
  logical invention, 26, 91, 108, 113, 129, 131, 174, 177, 184, 187, 192, 215, 216
  Ramistic invention, 110, 116, 117, 121, 138, 189
  rhetorical invention, 26, 91

Johnson, Samuel, 6, 193, 194, 205, 215, 216
  Dictionary, 193, 194, 209
  Journey to the Western Islands, 198, 211
  Life of Pope, 196
  high style, 210–11
  middle style, 205–10, 211
  plain style, 196–7, 198, 211

Kirke, Edward, 63–5

Language, diachronic study of, 25, 213, 215–16
  idiolectal language, 3
  literary language, 6, 10, 213, 214, 216
  synchronic study of language, 25, 213–14
la Ramee, Pierre de, 26, 89, 90, 91, 135, 141, 156
Legal terms, 74, 75, 77–8, 82, 84, 101, 102, 171

Index

Literary technique, 36
Logic, 89–92
  'natural logic', 26, 93, 96, 99, 102, 107, 135, 154, 174, 208
  Ramism, 99, 121, 139
  Ramist, 98, 208
  Ramistic logic, 90–2, 94, 96, 98, 100, 104, 107, 111, 125, 135, 136, 139, 141, 147, 166, 173, 174, 181, 189, 190, 205
  Ramistic logical treatise, 107–8
  Ramistic method, 91, 92–3, 94, 96, 108, 109, 135, 139, 140, 147
  Ramistic table, 108, 181
Logical division, 104
Logical invention, *see* Invention
Low style, *see* Plain style
Lyly, John, 135, 174

Machiavelli, Niccolo, 13
Mannerism, mannerist, 25, 63, 65, 66, 73, 81
Medium of discourse, 10, 19–21, 30, 34, 37, 53
Method, *see* Logic
Middle style, 8, 12, 13, 14–15, 16–17, 216, *see* authors cited
Milton, John, 9, 10, 11, 12, 14, 15, 16, 18, 20, 215
  Comus, 121–2
  Lycidas, 111–14
  On the Morning of Christ's Nativity, 118–19
  Paradise Lost, 121, 122–6
  high style, 118, 119, 122–3, 125
  middle style, 111, 112, 113, 114, 122, 123, 124, 125–6
  plain style, 111, 112, 113, 118, 119, 122, 123, 124–5, 126
Mimesis, 138
Mode of discourse, 10, 18–19, 30–2, 73, 99, 164, 179
Montaigne, Michel Eyquem de, 135
Moral-political writers, *see* Style
'Moving', *see* Persuasion

'Natural logic', *see* Logic
Natural rhetoric, *see* Rhetoric

Naturalism, 42, 46, 48
Nominal style, Nominality, *see* Style
Non-literary texts, 155

Paradox, 61, 81, 85, 88, 92, 98, 99, 100, 102, 104, 116, 124, 146, 147, 148, 154, 167, 173, 179, 200
Parallelism, 18, 29, 31, 50, 51, 88, 94–5, 96, 100, 115, 128, 140, 141, 145, 156, 157, 159, 166, 167, 200, 205, 206, 207
Parameters, 10, 118
Periphrasis, 30, 60, 67, 84, 86, 87, 99, 123, 145, 152, 165
Personification, 32, 35, 38
Persuasion, 139
Petrarch, Petrarchan diction, 13, 76, 78
Philologist, 2
Plainness, 31, 157
Plain style, 7, 8, 12, 13, 14, 15, 16, 17, 113, 216, *see* authors cited
  archaic plain style, 66, 112
  sacred plain style, 13, 14, 17, 50, 56, 57–8, 59, 61–2, 113
Plutarch, 180–1
Pope, Alexander, 18, 215, 216
  Dunciad, 121, 130
  Elegy, 111, 114–18
  Eloisa to Abelard, 119–20, 127
  Epistle to a Lady, 126–7
  Essay on Man, 120–1
  Rape of the Lock, 121, 127–8, 130
  Windsor Forest, 120
  high style, 115–16, 117, 119, 120, 121, 127, 128, 130
  middle style, 114, 115, 116, 117–18, 119, 121, 126–7, 128, 131
  plain style, 116–17, 120, 121, 128–9, 130, 131
Proverbial images, 7, 13, 19, 38, 41, 50, 51, 58–9

Quintilian, 89

Ramism, *see* Logic
Ramist, *see* Logic
Ramistic dialectic, *see* Logic, Ramistic logic

224 Index

Ramistic invention, *see* Invention
Ramistic logic, *see* Logic
Ramistic method, *see* Logic
Ramistic table, *see* Logic
Reader, 2–3, 5–6, 10
Realism, 216
  conventional realism, 54, 61
  fully representational realism, 54, 55–6
Register, 3, 9, 100, 212
  archaic register, 4
  neutral register, 10
  registerial variation, 10, 22, 78, 103
  stereotyped register, 21–2
Rhetoric, 91
  natural rhetoric, 2, 6, 50
  rhetoric of text, 22
  rhetorical figures, 1, 2, 214
Rhetorical invention, *see* Invention
Roles, 10, 16–17, 86, *see* Familiarity, Formality

Sermon, 12, 13, 14, 15, 17, 61, 155–73
  Shakespeare, William, 11, 13, 17, 89, 91, 194, 215
  Sonnets: 2, 87; 7, 78; *12*, 83–4; *21*, 78–9; *35*, 76–8; *60*, 85–6; *63*, 81; *70*, 81; *71*, 86–7; *73*,81; *74*, 86; *81*, 86; *94*, 81–3; *107*, 74–6; *121*, 87–8; *130*, 79–81
  high style, 75, 76, 78–9, 80, 81, 84, 85
  middle style, 74, 75, 76, 77, 78, 81–2, 83, 84, 85, 86, 87
  plain style, 74, 76, 77, 78, 79, 80, 81, 82, 83, 84, 85, 86, 87
Sidney, Sir Philip, 10, 16, 19, 20, 82, 161, 174, 190, 195, 215, 216
  Apology for Poetry, 135, 139, 151–3
  Arcadia, 135–6, 144, 153–4
  high style, 136–7, 137–8, 145
  middle style, 136, 144–8, 152, 154
  plain style, 136, 151–2, 153–4
Situation, 10, 14–16, 47, 83–6, 215
Skelton, John, 9, 14, 15, 42, 44, 215, 216
  Bouge of Court, 46–8, 51, 53
  Colin Clout, 15
  Elegy, 43
  Garland of Laurel, 45, 49

Magnificence, 50
Philip Sparrow, 44, 48, 51, 55–6
Speak, Parrot, 15, 51
Tunning of Elinour Rumming, 15, 51, 54–5
  view of Chaucer, 44
  high style, 43–4, 45
  middle style, 45, 46–9, 55
  plain style, 15, 49, 50–2, 53–6
Social-philosophical writers, *see* Style
Spenser, Edmund, 15, 89, 91, 215
  Epithalamion, 111
  Faerie Queene, 65–74
  Shepheardes Calender, 63–5, 73, 111–12, 113
  high style, 67, 68–9, 72, 73
  middle style, 67, 68, 70, 71, 73, 74
  plain style, 69–70, 71, 72
Style, traditional approach to, 1–2, 4–5
  general style, 22
  group styles, 24
  idiolectal styles, 3
  linear style, 157
  moral-political writers, 22–5, 43, 47, 52, 73–4, 102, 104–5, 110, 154, 173, 215, 216
  nominality, 139
  nominal style, 18, 30, 32, 37, 38, 45, 137, 142, 168, 204
  social-philosophical writers, 22–5, 43, 74, 102, 104–5, 154, 173, 185, 200, 215
  style area, 212
  style as unique choice, 21, 213, 214
  style level, 10, 161, 179, 212, 214
  three styles, 7–8, 161, 194, 212, 213, 216
  verbal style, 19, 32, 38, 46, 48, 204
Subject-matter, 10, 11–14
Syllogism, 91, 108
Syntax, 1, 3, 4, 5, 155, *see* Mode, Medium and authors cited

Temple, William, 139
Trichotomies, 93, 95, 169

Verbal style, *see* Style
Vocabulary, 4–5, 6, *see* authors cited

PENSACOLA JUNIOR COLLEGE LIBRARY
PR83 .G5 1979
Gilbert, A. J. cn   000
Literary language from Ch 210101

3 5101 00065253 2

81-3469

PR   Gilbert, A. J.
83
.G5   Literary language
1979   from Chaucer to
          Johnson

DATE			
APR 2 1 1982			
MAY 1 '82			
OCT 0 5 1982			
OCT 1 3 1982			

81-3469

PENSACOLA JR. COLLEGE LRC

WITHDRAWN

© THE BAKER & TAYLOR CO.